D1154525

ALSO BY
CHARLES LEERHSEN

Ty Cobb:
A Terrible Beauty

Blood and Smoke:
A True Tale of Mystery, Mayhem,
and the Birth of the Indy 500

Crazy Good:
The Story of Dan Patch,
the Most Famous Horse in America

THE
TRUE STORY
OF AN
AMERICAN
OUTLAW

BUTCH CASSIDY

CASSIDY

Charles Leerhsen

SIMON & SCHUSTER
New York   London   Toronto   Sydney   New Delhi

Simon & Schuster
1230 Avenue of the Americas
New York, NY 10020

Copyright © 2020 by Charles Leerhsen

All rights reserved, including the right to reproduce this book
or portions thereof in any form whatsoever. For information,
address Simon & Schuster Subsidiary Rights Department,
1230 Avenue of the Americas, New York, NY 10020.

First Simon & Schuster hardcover edition July 2020

SIMON & SCHUSTER and colophon are registered trademarks
of Simon & Schuster, Inc.

For information about special discounts for bulk purchases,
please contact Simon & Schuster Special Sales at 1-866-506-1949
or business@simonandschuster.com.

The Simon & Schuster Speakers Bureau can bring authors to
your live event. For more information or to book an event,
contact the Simon & Schuster Speakers Bureau at 1-866-248-3049
or visit our website at www.simonspeakers.com.

Interior design by Lewelin Polanco

Manufactured in the United States of America

10 9 8 7 6 5 4 3 2 1

Library of Congress Cataloging-in-Publication Data
Names: Leerhsen, Charles, author.
Title: Butch Cassidy: The True Story of an American Outlaw / Charles Leerhsen.
Other titles: True story of an American outlaw
Description: First Simon & Schuster hardcover edition. | New York : Simon &
Schuster, 2020. | Includes bibliographical references and index. | Summary: "For
a century Butch Cassidy has been the subject of legends about his life and death,
spawning a small industry of mythmakers and a major Hollywood film. Charles
Leerhsen sorts out fact from fiction to find the real Butch Cassidy, who is far
more complicated and fascinating than legend has it" -- Provided by publisher.
Identifiers: LCCN 2019 034980 | ISBN 9781501117480 (hardcover) |
  ISBN 9781501117497 (trade paperback) | ISBN 9781501117503 (ebook)
Subjects: LCSH: Cassidy, Butch, 1866- | Outlaws -- West (U.S.) -- Biography. |
  Gangs--West (U.S.)--History--19th century. | Frontier and pioneer life--West
  (U.S.) | West (U.S.)--Biography.
Classification: LCC F595.C362 L44 2020 | DCC 364.15/52092 [B]--dc23
LC record available at https://lccn.loc.gov/2019034980

ISBN 978-1-5011-1748-0
ISBN 978-1-5011-1750-3 (ebook)

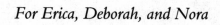

For Erica, Deborah, and Nora

There are few subjects that interest us more generally than the adventures of robbers and bandits.

—SCOTTISH WRITER CHARLES MACFARLANE,
CA. 1830

CONTENTS

≡ PART 2

≡ PART 3

1

1

THE THORNY ROSE

Start at the end, they say.

The last member of Butch Cassidy's gang, the Wild Bunch, went into the ground in December 1961. Which means that someone who held the horses during an old-school Western train robbery, or had been otherwise involved with the kind of men who crouched behind boulders with six-guns in their hands and bandannas tied around their sunburnt faces, might have voted for John F. Kennedy (or Richard Nixon), seen the movie *West Side Story* or heard Del Shannon sing run-run-run-run-run-away—that is, if she hadn't been rendered deaf years earlier during the blasting open of a Union Pacific express car safe. Her outlaw buddies were always a little heavy-handed with the dynamite.

Yes—she. The Wild Bunch, which some writers have called the biggest and most structurally complex criminal organization of the late nineteenth century, came down, in the end, to one little old lady sitting in a small, dark apartment in Memphis. Laura Bullion died in obscurity eight years before the movie *Butch Cassidy and the Sundance Kid*, starring Paul Newman and Robert Redford, revitalized the almost-forgotten semilegend in which she had played a minor but authentic part. Her obituary did not make the newspapers. If anyone saw the cryptic hint of a previous life on her headstone—"The Thorny Rose," the inscription says—he didn't question it publicly. Yet for a time, in a different world, a world where outlaws needed their horses held and their ashes hauled, Laura was in several ways a wanted woman. Reporters and Pinkerton detectives knew her name and sought her out for interviews.

Laura Bullion had been a gun moll before the term existed—not one of the all-time greats, perhaps, owing to her natural reticence and plain face. She stands, for example, eternally in the shadow of Ethel Place, Sundance's mysterious inamorata (usually referred to, mistakenly, as Etta), who was every bit as beautiful as Katharine Ross, the actress who played her on the screen, and whom Cassidy once called "an excellent housekeeper with the heart of a whore." Yet in terms of curriculum vitae, at least, Laura was a classic "Molly." She had danced, as she put it euphemistically in Texas gambling halls, taken on a bewildering number of aliases—including Della Rose, a name she used while working in Fanny Porter's famous sporting house on Delarosa Street in San Antonio—and traveled with the kind of bad boys who had pistols in their pockets *and* were happy to see her.

Laura's first love, chronologically, was the dapper Will Carver, given the nickname "News" in the movie because he liked to see his name in the frontier dailies. She met him when she was fourteen and he was married to her Aunt Viana; they all lived together in a small house in West Texas, and Laura said she and her uncle "got brushed up a heap agin each other" in the tight quarters, which eventually caused romantic sparks. It was around then that Carver transformed himself from an honest ranch hand who worked for the standard dollar a day to an associate of outlaws like Tom "Black Jack" Ketchum and Butch Cassidy. Though inevitably cast in a supporting role by his crew leaders, Carver became over time almost a caricature of an old-time criminal, dressing "like a

Texas gambler," according to one lawman; affecting a haughty, R. Crumb-ish way of striding out in which his feet preceded the rest of his body; and talking like a dime-novel desperado. When he was confronted in a Sonora, Texas, bakery (where he had gone to buy grain for his horse) by a sheriff who wanted to speak to him about the very badass-sounding crime of killing a man in Concho County, Carver whipped out his six-gun—like other Wild Bunchers, including Cassidy himself, he was known as a superior marksman—but the barrel got tangled in his fancy suspenders, and the sheriff just shrugged and shot him in the chest. Carver's last words were supposedly, "Die game, boys!"

Laura took the news with mixed emotions. In her diary she wrote: "W. R. Carver, killed Tuesday, April 2, 1901. He has fled. I wish him dead, he that wrought my ruin. O, the flattery and the craft, which were my undoing." (She herself was no stranger to dime novels.) Before long, though, seeking consolation, she moved on to another member of the gang, Ben Kilpatrick. Laura and "the Tall Texan," as he was known in those nickname-crazed days, made an odd-looking couple: he was in the vicinity of six feet; she, four foot eleven. But they became soulmates—and in a poetic sense, cellmates, who served long, more-or-less simultaneous sentences in far-distant penitentiaries after they were arrested in Saint Louis in 1901 with $8,500 in stolen banknotes. They stayed in touch while incarcerated. "I received the little lead pencil you sent and it just could not be prettier," she wrote to Ben. "I think it is too sweet to be used and would not take anything for it"—and briefly reunited years later, following his release. They might have grown old together if Kilpatrick had grown old. Instead, while robbing the safe on a train full of oysters near Sanderson, Texas, in 1912, he had his skull fatally fractured by a railroad messenger wielding an ice mallet. Excited townsfolk prepared Kilpatrick's body for the trophy photo that was practically de rigueur in those days after you'd assassinated a well-known outlaw, but rather than keeping him horizontal, they propped him up on his feet so the local shutterbug could get a better angle. (You can see the picture in the photo insert of this book.) He and his deceased accomplice, known as Ole Beck, look like a couple of high-end scarecrows.

Not every cowboy bandit came to such a calamitous and entertaining end, of course. Many were dim-witted, depressing, murderous men—"human donkeys," to borrow a phrase from Mark Twain's Western travelogue *Roughing It*—who simply disappeared from history. Or they went straight, settling for quotidian jobs like bartender or, in more than a couple of cases, lawman. I will not concern myself overly much with such ordinary criminals but will focus instead on the more evolved class of outlaws who embodied the populist spirt of the late nineteenth century and showed enough self-awareness and style to give the newspapers and other mythmakers something to work with. A few of that sort wound up serving as consultants on early Hollywood Westerns. The handsome and witty Elzy Lay, a likely ancestor of the potato chip magnate and Butch's best friend in the years before he moved to South America with the Sundance Kid (ne Harry Alonzo Longabaugh), is buried in Los Angeles's Forest Lawn cemetery among the movie stars he is said to have coached occasionally. He was sixty-five when he died in 1934—exceedingly old for an outlaw, though Bat Masterson and Wyatt Earp lived to sixty-seven and eighty, respectively. Laura Bullion survived until age eighty-five, having supported herself in later life as a department store seamstress. Even in her final days, spent in a charity ward of Tennessee's Shelby County Hospital, "she remained mentally alert and retained a sense of humor," one relative said.

Butch Cassidy also had a well-honed wit—but the ones who left others laughing were the exceptions. Most Western outlaws, be they dashing or dull, wound up demonstrating the dreary dictum that crime does not pay—and, on the contrary, tends to extract a heavy toll on the perpetrator. So many died young after being pursued and shot at and penned up like animals until the morning they were led through a sea of gawkers to the gallows. None of them, as far we know, died rich. Yet—and this is what I think makes at least some of them worthy of our extended consideration—even though they knew just how awful the terms were, they persisted in making the bargain. Riding with the gang was all that mattered—if only because when you were doing that, you weren't herding cattle or mending fences or shoveling horse manure amidst relentlessly picturesque scenery while the idiot wind howled. That cowboy crap gets old fast. The much-romanticized Western way of life was in practice often boring and nerve wracking at the same time. (Yes, you slept out under the stars, but the cowboy code said that you always woke up a colleague by voice, never by touch, because if you prodded or shook him, he might come to with a start, grab his gun, and kill you.) "I have worked six years in cow outfits and am fed up on cow punching so I am quitting," wrote Reuben B. Mullins in his memoir, *Pulling Leather*, published in 1988, more than fifty years after his death. "Any young man who will punch cows for an extended number of years isn't normal."

As Caroline Fraser, the biographer of Laura Ingalls Wilder, author of *Little House on the Prairie*, has noted, you can romanticize it all you want, but the life made possible by the Homestead Act of 1862 destroyed more people than it helped.

A new day was soon coming when many rural Americans, wanting something better for themselves and seeing how the little man was getting squeezed out of farming and cattle raising, would sell their homesteads and migrate to big cities, work only fifty hours a week, drive cars, and make enough money to go to ball games and photoplays (and develop all kinds of emotional and digestive disorders that their ancestors never knew existed). But that day wasn't coming fast enough for the more restless members of the post–Civil War generation born out beyond the 100th meridian, the line that separated arable from arid soil on the great American grid.

Those young men and women thirsted for a dose of excitement and a shot at wealth, and as fate would have it, the chance to try your luck at the game of "throw 'em up" (outlaws actually said this more often than "stick 'em up," it seems) was as close as the nearest train or bank.

The nice thing about gang life, at least in the Wild Bunch, was that everyone seemed to understand his role. Ringleader was not a position many aspired to—for the most part, it was like being the alpha steer in a cattle herd; either you were or you weren't, for reasons that are best ascribed to "nature" and left at that. As masterminds of a sort, Cassidy and Sundance probably took a bigger cut of the booty than their cohorts did, but by the time the money was divvied up and then squandered in the stupid but obligatory post-heist spree, not enough remained for anyone to get excited about. Especially in the early years of their careers, the Wild Bunch were like struggling actors who have to support themselves as waiters or dog-walkers; between gigs, everyone was equally in need of legit work. This kept them humble and meant that when the gang reconvened to pull a heist, the roles had been already assigned; office politics—or, rather, campfire, politics—were usually not an issue, and no one got stabbed in the back. At least not figuratively. Laura, Will, Ben, Elzy, Sundance, Ethel—all of them and a raucous gaggle of others were content to be mere ripples so long as Butch Cassidy was the stone.

2

RULES OF THE GAME

Decades *after his initial encounter* with Butch Cassidy, when he was a retiree doing an interview on the radio about the bygone days of the Wild West, Christian Heiden, a kid who drove the stagecoach on Wyoming's Greybull River Road in the early 1890s, remembered the moment vividly—as well he might, since Cassidy that day rode right up to him dragging an angry mountain lion on the end of a rope. They made quite a picture: the smiling, bright-eyed cowboy and the snarling, spitting cat. Heiden, newly arrived from Mecklenburg, Germany, and all of fifteen at the time, fell instantly in love.

It was easy to be smitten by Cassidy, who was then about twenty-five years old and, with only one bank robbery and a smattering of small-time cattle rustling to his credit, really still an outlaw in training. He wasn't yet known much outside the sparsely populated Big Horn Basin—he would never be as famous as his predecessors Jesse James and Billy the Kid, at least not until Hollywood made a movie about him and the Sundance Kid—but he moved with grace, dressed with flair, and displayed a fine if sometimes overly raucous wit.

He also possessed the complete cowboy skill set, no small thing at a time when Westerners turned out in force to see their culture celebrated in Buffalo Bill's traveling extravaganzas. After deftly lassoing the mountain lion earlier that day, Cassidy had thought it might be amusing to take it to the saloon in the nearby hamlet of Embar—outside of which young Heiden happened to be standing. Game animals were going the way of the buffalo in those parts, and the predators who depended on them were venturing closer to civilization, arousing curiosity. Cassidy knew that a 150-pound kitten tied to a hitching post in the middle of town could be counted on to draw appreciative cusses.

These were the innocent times. Butch at this point was still more interested in battling the crushing monotony of daily existence in the intermountain West than in robbing banks and railroads. He liked to ride and bet on horses in races at the local carnivals; go to Friday-night dances; play poker, faro, and the harmonica; shoot at targets, sip a little Old Crow; chat up the ladies; fool with the children—all while presenting himself to the world as a carefree cowpoke named George Cassidy who had made his way out to those parts from New York City. In fact, he was Robert LeRoy Parker, born poor in Beaver, Utah—but cloaking himself in a colorful persona somehow added to the fun.

Cassidy's life just then was on the verge of change. Within a year or so, a harsh—and, he sincerely felt, unjust—punishment would jolt him out of his prolonged adolescence and dim the brightness in his sea-blue (at times verging on gray) eyes. While he may not have ever actually *said*, "If you're going to treat me like a criminal, I might as well act like one," that effectively became his credo as he segued over the course of his initial, two-year prison stay into a complicated, sometimes contradictory adult. From the moment he had decided to turn outlaw, he wondered if the life was worth it. Butch in flush times might be so weighed down with gold pieces that his horse hated the very sight of him, and he suffered at least once from what may be the ultimate mixed blessing: money-belt sores. Meanwhile, he could no longer sleep soundly or sit for a meal with his back to the door. (In 1876 Wild Bill Hickok had been fatally shot during a card game while sitting with his back to the door.) He had no peace. After he got out of prison, and promptly resumed his life of crime, he saw the world through an even darker lens. His sense of humor became braided with cynicism; his once lighthearted playacting took on a new and more serious purpose: confounding the people who sought to kill him or take away his freedom. To put it in poker terms, he was all in at that point, a man on the lam, guilty as charged—and yet always observing a strict moral code.

He would never have called it that, of course. Butch read a lot of books for a poor Mormon farm boy, and his letters show that he could turn a phrase nicely, but he was never one to get highfalutin or preachy. He exhibited no vestiges of the religious beliefs that had brought his grandparents from England to Utah; from (he could not have helped noticing ruefully) one unspeakably horrible situation to another, with an awful lot of anguish in between. He may not have been driven by ethical considerations at all; he may have simply come over time to believe, as some practical-minded Mafia dons did later, that gratuitous violence only made one's work life more difficult. Blood, after all, is slippery stuff. Still, it is tempting to admire him because all of his rules, such as they were—meaning unwritten and quite likely unspoken as well—were about doing what he thought was right, even if that was relatively difficult.

For one thing, he did not kill people, and neither did the men (and, on rare occasion, women) who rode with him in a loosely organized gang that local folks and newspapers liked to call the Wild Bunch. Not that they were milquetoasts or pacifists, those Civil War babies gone bad; virtually all, in fact, were violent criminals before and after their time with Butch—and even he did not hesitate to conk a railroad conductor with the barrel of his big, wooden-handled Colt .45 if the man took too long to open a strongbox. The difference was that Cassidy's outbursts were always strategic. In a criminal operation, the *appearance* of ruthlessness was key to a smooth, safe operation, he knew—just as being freshly bathed and well dressed sent a signal that he and his cohorts were serious professionals not to be trifled with. "Our greatest defense was our reputation as being bad men," said one gang member. "It was a game of draw and bluff."

They played the game with panache—and admirable restraint. Triggers were squeezed mostly in celebration as the gang galloped off into the sunset (yes, just like in the movies), or in self-defense to discourage a pursuing posse. With one late-career exception, which we will discuss ahead, no one ever died as a result of one of Cassidy's carefully planned heists. Indeed, ordinary folks were not even hurt financially by Butch and his boys, who drew a bright line between banks and railroads and the people who patronized them. "Put that away!" they would say when nervous bystanders and train passengers proffered pocket watches and purses. "We don't want *yours*, we want *theirs*"—meaning the loot about to be liberated, sometimes with the help of lavish amounts of dynamite (cowboys will be boys), from some company-owned safe. What the academics call "social bandits" have always cast themselves as friends of the little man, but it's usually a specious, self-aggrandizing claim. Cassidy and company, however, were actually willing to limit the return on their risk based on their populist principles.

And make no mistake, the risk they assumed was considerable. Railroad robbery was then a capital crime in several Western states. One of Cassidy's coevals, Tom Ketchum, received a death sentence for "felonious assault on a train," even though no one was killed during his transgression. When they hanged him in Clayton, New Mexico, on April 26, 1901, his head got yanked off because he had put on so much weight during the appeals process—but that is a story for another campfire.

Cassidy's style of leadership was as ineffable as his sense of right and wrong. So subtle were his methods, in fact, that some Old West researchers question whether he was the leader at all, noting that the occasional gang member Harvey Logan, aka Kid Curry, the shame of Richland, Iowa, was a more notorious outlaw than Cassidy for a while and had a thicker file at the Chicago headquarters of the Pinkerton Detective Agency, often hired by railroads and other companies to combat robberies in those days before the FBI.

It is only logical to think Logan would dominate Cassidy in the hierarchy of an outlaw clique. The former was a fierce and pitiless man, small and sinewy with, said one writer, "dark, blowtorch eyes," not to mention several dozen notches on his gun butt. "He would shoot a man just to see him quiver," said an agent for the Union Pacific. Butch, never judgmental about the company he kept, effusively praised Logan's temperament and marksmanship as well as his loyalty and overall competence in the clutch. And because Logan had already established himself as a master thief (he once managed to steal the pack of bloodhounds that was pursuing him) and a varmint supreme (he didn't just kill people, he killed people named Pike Landusky, in places like One-Legged Jew Jake's Saloon), it seemed likely that he could make others kowtow to his orders.

On top of that, Logan had done things a cowboy who dreams of executive-level outlawry was supposed to do: he'd acquired a newspaper-friendly nickname, Kid Curry; he'd plucked a trophy (if common-law) wife out of Madam Fannie Porter's sporting house, in San Antonio, one of the finest names in whoredom; and he'd cultivated a seriously bushy moustache, which theoretically added to his air of authority. (In fact, it made him look like the silent-movie comic Ben Turpin.) Butch, on the other hand, was clean shaven and quick witted, a wannabe New Yorker, and a blue-eyed, handsome heartbreaker so culturally attuned and conversationally nimble that some outlaw historians have wondered about his sexual orientation. By all rights, he should have been muscled to the side by the hellish Harvey.

Yet that's not what happened. Instead, from the beginning it was Butch who silently set the tone and Logan and all the others—a bevy of curs and Gun Mollies including Sundance's stunning paramour Ethel Place—who fell in line and copied his example. Yes, it probably helped that he could put a pistol shot through the center of a playing card at fifty paces and leap a bank counter in a single bound. But something more powerful than professional admiration defined the group dynamic: the legendary Cassidy charisma. "In many ways, Butch was the wisest of all the outlaws I knew," said one gang member who had fallen under his thrall, "and you could depend on his hunches."

Whether that was entirely true was less important than the fact that so many, in and out of the Wild Bunch, believed that he was a special person; the best bad man they had ever encountered. "I wouldn't have wanted to be in a teller's cage when he came through the door of a bank," said a Wyoming codger interviewed by the Cassidy biographer Richard Patterson, "but if I ever met him in a saloon, I sure would have bought him a drink." Children flocked to Butch, who always had some rock candy in his saddlebag, and was willing to hoist them onto his horse and give them a ride. Women got into knock-down-drag-outs over him, even as he moved on to fresh pastures. More than one Western governor took an extraordinary interest in his welfare and tried to persuade Butch to use his powers for good. A Wyoming judge who sent him to prison, only to have a change of heart, wrote a letter to the governor in which he pleaded for Cassidy to be pardoned, calling him "a brave, daring fellow well calculated to be a leader." The author Charles Kelly, who tracked down several Cassidy contemporaries for his groundbreaking 1938 book *Outlaw Trail*, wrote that "All old-timers interviewed for this biography, including officers who hunted him, were unanimous in saying 'Butch Cassidy was one of the finest men I ever knew.'"

To some extent, Cassidy's appeal is explainable. Over and over, he proved to be a man of his word. If he assured a sheriff that he did not need to be shackled on a long journey to the hoosegow, he did not run away, even if his chaperone dozed off. Asked why once, he shrugged and said, "Honor among thieves, I guess." He also seemed to have taken pity at times on the hardworking lawmen who risked their lives for $50 a month.

Clearly, Bob Parker was born to play the role of Butch Cassidy. He was five foot nine or so, the perfect size for a long rider (burly six-foot-something types being hard on the average horse). He was square jawed and sandy haired, good-looking yet not so beautiful as to incite ridicule or jealousy. He also seemed to possess from birth a set of standards below which he believed a gentleman should never sink. Served a meal of jackrabbit at a backcountry inn one evening, he quietly rose from the table, rode a short way off, and shot a cow, so that everyone in the place could have steak.

Generosity was his strong suit, even if he was not really the Robin Hood figure his adoring fans have sometimes made him out to be. People liked to tell the story of how he once paid off a poor widow's mortgage, then the next day robbed back those funds and more from the same bank. While that has the whiff of a conventional outlaw legend—the sort of folk yarn that might have been spun just as easily about Jesse James or Giuseppe Musolino, the legendary Italian bandit king; or Sandor Rozsa, the highwayman of the great Hungarian plain; or the Australian bushranger Ned Kelly—it is true that Cassidy displayed the profligate spending habits of a heavyweight champ, and that the money that ran so quickly through his fingers often found its way into the households of the needy (as well as the cash boxes of saloons and the garter belts of dance hall girls). So, no, the second coming of the seraph of Sherwood Forest he was not. But if you tugged at his sleeve (or his heartstrings) as he passed through town, he might well flip you a $10 gold piece or slip you a stack of dynamite-singed bills, along with his sincere good wishes. "Butch took care of more people than FDR, and with no red tape," is how one of his ex-girlfriends later put it.

Charisma, though, is never just the sum of someone's sterling attributes. Nor is it always the same mysterious thing, as the diverse cases of Joan of Arc, Willie Mays, and Steve Jobs demonstrate. Butch's particular power to impress people was rooted in his convivial personality; he was a man, like the sixteenth-century French essayist Michel de Montaigne, "born for company and friendship." Source after source mention his openness, his quick smile, his genuine zest for ordinary conversation with regular folk, especially in contrast to the often aloof and sometimes surly Harry Longabaugh (Sundance). "In Argentina, we have the slang word *extrador* for someone like Butch," Carlos Dante Ferrari, a retired judge from Patagonia, who has spent decades studying the outlaw, especially his late-career South American sojourn, told me. "It literally means 'incoming.' Butch was more than just an outgoing man. He was also *extrador*—the sort who could somehow seduce you, pierce your exterior, and get inside you."

The sexual entendre is apt. When you engage with an inveterate mingler like Cassidy, you gaze into a very forgiving mirror, the magical kind that comes complete with airbrushing and back lighting. In his smiling eyes, you see your own best self, leading you to instantly relax and slip into something more comfortable in terms of mood. For the effect to work, the seducer must be sincere—and yet how can a man be truly taken with virtually everyone he encounters on the long receiving line of life?

What Cassidy seemed to delight in consistently was society itself—the admittedly artificial and byzantine ways that homo sapiens, when they come together in circumscribed groups and defined spaces, agree to behave, as a way of tempering chaos, making things pleasanter, or avoiding existential angst. Unlike his pal Longabaugh, who had grown up in a bustling Pennsylvania canal town and came west in search of the vast empty spaces he had read about in dime novels, Butch dreamt of dwelling in the civilized world as he slept beneath the stars and behind the familiar rock formations that provided sanctuary along the Outlaw Trail, a loose network of hideouts stretching from Montana to Mexico. Because he'd been born into the Western country, he didn't romanticize it; rather, his life became in part a reaction to its well-known powers to numb the mind, heart, and soul. He was, at bottom, a dude in desperado's clothing, yearning ever eastward and toward the twentieth century.

Sometimes, though, he was a dude in dude's clothing. Cassidy loved Tiffany watches, patent leather shoes, derby hats—and the new ragtime. He died in a suit of yellow cashmere. Not surprisingly, given his proclivities, he studied manners and carefully minded his own. An ex-boss at one of his occasional legit jobs called him "an exceptionally pleasant and even cultured and charming man. He used good language and was never vulgar." So it was even when he entered a railroad express car, waving a gun and wearing a bandanna around his face: the mask of the bandit concealed the mask of the man in the workplace, behind which was the boy from Beaver eager to play his role to the hilt. "Pardon us," he once said while flashing his smile at a rider transporting a hefty mine payroll, "but we know you have a lot of money, and we have a great need."

Doesn't that sound like a line from a movie? It has been a long time since most people saw *Butch Cassidy and the Sundance Kid*, but if, as I describe the historical Butch, the image of Paul Newman, playing a charming and witty character of the same name, comes gradually into focus, be assured you are in good company. Many of those who have spent their lives and life savings researching the outlaw have concluded that William Goldman, who wrote the screenplay for the 1969 film, got it right in some fundamental way, especially about the outlaw born Robert LeRoy Parker. "Goldman may have invented the dialogue, but he captured the spirit of the real Cassidy," the historian Daniel Buck says in an intriguing book about the Cassidy obsession called *Digging Up Butch and Sundance*, written by his once equally obsessed but now admirably patient wife, Anne Meadows.

Butch's much younger sibling, Lula Betenson, who was still alive (and kicking about not getting any money) when the movie came out, even said that Newman had "a certain 'family' look," especially as it pertained to those blue eyes. Normally, of course, accuracy is of little concern in the world of feature films. The composer Antonio Salieri did not attempt to poison Mozart, as the movie *Amadeus* would have us believe; in *Braveheart*, Scottish rebels wear kilts three centuries too soon; Krakatoa is west of Java everywhere but in *Krakatoa, East of Java*. And so on. Westerns, by now, are almost by sacred tradition wildly off base—sanitized, usually—so that we can cheer for Wyatt Earp (Henry Fonda, Burt Lancaster, Kevin Costner), Wild Bill Hickok (Gary Cooper, Guy Madison, Jeff Bridges, Josh Brolin), and Calamity Jane (Jane Russell, Yvonne De Carlo, Doris Day, Catherine O'Hara) without troubling over their having been, respectively, a shameless self-promoter, a convicted pimp, and a drunken, disease-ridden prostitute.

That *Butch Cassidy and the Sundance Kid* managed to capture a much more elusive figure than any of the above may look at first like a rare confluence of entertainment and scholarship, but, in fact, it was only an accident. Though the movie begins famously with the epigraph "Most of what follows is true," most of it patently isn't because Goldman did only sporadic and superficial research over the eight-year period he kicked around the idea (he said he didn't want to be "constricted by the facts"), and Newman, in keeping with his laid-back approach to his craft, apparently did none whatsoever. It just so happened that the real Butch Cassidy had molded himself, avant la lettre, into a figure with a high cinematic sheen. *"Pardon us, but we know you have a lot of money, and we have a great need."* Almost any cunning and debonair Western movie hero, quick on the draw and tall in the saddle, is bound to resemble him at least a little.

———

It's the Cassidy-and-Sundance *story* that refused to follow the Western movie rulebook. One inconvenient truth for someone trying to fashion a feel-good big-studio film in the late 1960s was that Cassidy's career owed much to the failing promise of the supposedly golden West. Frontier life in the 1880s and '90s, the historian Bernard DeVoto tells us, was not marked by a rousing spirit of adventure and an appealing rough justice, as Hollywood would have us believe, but rather by "loneliness, hardship, and social deterioration" on a scale that was nothing short of shameful. Mark Twain set out to dig for gold in the hills of Nevada, not to practice agriculture and raise a family—still, the moral of his memoir *Roughing It*, as the writer Christopher Knowlton has noted, could also apply to the majority of those who went west in the late nineteenth century, fleeing the financial panics and bank failures that occurred every decade back east. "So vanished my dream. So melted my wealth away. So toppled my airy castle to the earth and left me stricken and forlorn."

Despite what people had been told by politicians, bankers, and railroad magnates trying to encourage settlement beyond the 100th meridian—and what they'd been told, the courageous myth busting geologist and explorer John Wesley Powell (1834–1902) reminds us, was that "agriculture was effortless; no forests needed clearing, manual tillage was not required, even the use of the plow was not essential, so eager were seeds to germinate in this Paradise"—the conditions were, in fact, far too dry to support commercial farming. Most of the trusting, optimistic souls who followed the false advertising out west after the Civil War, willing to work hard and hoping for a new start or at least a fair shake, struggled to feed even their own families.

As a way of compensating for the arid soil and the corresponding low crop yields, the federal government tried giving away much
larger plots of land than were doled out under the original Homestead Act of 1862: in some cases 4 square miles, or 2,560 acres, as
opposed to the once-standard 160-acre parcel. But that didn't solve
the basic problem because, oddly enough, the skies did not accom-
modate themselves to the activity of the pioneers below, as the pro-
moters of the West had with a straight face assured the settlers they
would. ("Don't worry," the land speculator Charles Dana Wilber
said, "the rain will follow the plow!") Rather, the main effect of
the larger land parcels was to leave the homesteaders in a state of
what DeVoto called "fearful isolation" from one another, especially
during the lengthy winters. More than a few committed suicide,
while others slouched back east, broken in sundry ways. Still others
stayed and survived, barely, as small-time cattle and sheep raisers, at
least until the big corporate ranchers—by bribing local officials or,
in some cases, by simply murdering the homesteaders—finally got
hold of their grazing land.

Here and there, the little guys fought back, in the courts and
with guns, but what we saw on *Little House on the Prairie* and a score
of other TV shows and movies was basically one large lie; the system—if you can call unfettered capitalism a system—was designed
to defeat the hardworking farmer. Men in suits proved far more
dangerous than the increasingly prevalent gray wolves. Western
banks, then virtually unregulated, preyed on the little man's naivete
and desperation; the railroads charged punishing rates, as monop-
olies will, to ship their scrawny animals to market and bring in expensive supplies.

Men wearing badges weren't any better. They were often con-
veniently absent, or sometimes appallingly present, when "detectives" working for the cattle barons broke into a home, dragged out
the breadwinner, and took him somewhere to be shot, poisoned,
or hanged. "The cattlemen . . . were always arrogant and always

deluded," wrote Bernard DeVoto. "They thought themselves the freest men who ever lived, but even more than other Westerners, they were peons of their Eastern bankers and of the railroads."

One short-term solution was alcohol. Many settlers drank themselves into a stupor as often as possible, further fueling their depression. Society was crumbling, and because law enforcement was so thinly spread and so erratic, citizens had no real recourse. Wyoming, in particular, had an end-of-days feel, never more so than in October 1893, when Governor John Eugene Osborne danced at his inaugural ball in shoes made from the skin of convicted murderer George "Big Nose" Parrott, who had gone to the gallows a dozen years earlier.

Such dystopian conditions no doubt fostered the rise and ensured the popularity of a dashing, corporation-bedeviling bandit like Butch Cassidy. But William Goldman, a practical man with finely tuned commercial instincts, realized that he could not in the late 1960s sell a script about a broken American dream. The country was still in denial about the nervous breakdown it was going through with the slow-motion failure of the Vietnam War and the assassinations of John F. Kennedy, Robert F. Kennedy, and Dr. Martin Luther King Jr. Goldman had to keep things simple and light and true to the patriotic myths, which decreed that rugged individualism was always rewarded and the Old West had offered unlimited promise to all. Which was fine with him because no one, he knew, would object to handsome, funny outlaws strutting around up there on the screen. Such characters, the historian Eric Hobsbawm has noted, are "considered by their people as heroes, as champions, avengers, fighters for justice, perhaps even leaders of liberation, and in any case as men to be admired, helped, and supported." When it comes to box office receipts, bad boys will always trump good history.

On another crucial point, though—the fact that Butch, Sundance, and Ethel had in 1901 suddenly up and left for South

America—Goldman and the studio powers butted heads. He thought that the trio's decision to "run away," as he put it, was what made the story unusual in a good way, elevating it to something beyond your average horse opera. "Butch and Sundance did what Gatsby only dreamed of doing," Goldman wrote in his memoir *Adventures in the Screen Trade.* "They repeated the past. As famous as they were in the States, they were bigger legends in South America: *bandidos Yanquis.* We all wish for it; they made it happen."

But by Hollywood's lights, the strangeness of what the protagonists accomplished was precisely the problem: studio executives in those days were trained to pounce on any aberration, to instantly reweave any fraying of the formula, and the main characters' flight from American soil was something they thought would confuse the mainstream audience. "The first time the script was shown, only one studio showed the least interest," Goldman wrote. "And I remember an executive of that studio saying to me that South America had to go—that Butch and Sundance, in order for the movie to work, had to stand and fight the Superposse [that the railroad magnate E. H. Harriman had created to hunt them down]. Right here. In the Old West. I tried explaining that they really did go to South America, that what was so moving to me was these two guys repeating the past, then dying alone in a strange land. He replied, 'I don't give a shit about that—all I know is one thing: *John Wayne* didn't run away.'"

Goldman eventually won this argument—sort of. Instead of spending time in Argentina, Chile, and Bolivia, as the outlaws actually did, the movie characters go only to the latter country, where they meet an ambiguous fate. Whatever you might think about the compromises made along the way in the creation of *Butch Cassidy and the Sundance Kid* (including the last-minute title change from *The Sundance Kid and Butch Cassidy,* and the insertion of a cringe-inducing, three-minute musical interlude during which Newman and Ross ride a bicycle to the tune of "Raindrops Keep Fallin' on

My Head"), the movie, after surviving some early mixed reviews, worked in all the ways that matter to the industry—which is to say it made a lot of money and won a lot of prizes, including four Oscars. Paul Newman affirmed his already lofty status, and Robert Redford, who went into the picture a promising newcomer, came out of it a top-tier star. "It forever changed the way I lived my life," he said. For Goldman, too, it was a career turning point: he won his first Academy Award and demonstrated to the industry that he had the ability to create a story line from scratch.

Still, it's what the film *didn't* do that made it truly special: namely, it didn't fade quickly from memory like the frothy, fizzy "action-comedy" that it may at first have seemed to be. Relatively few people had heard of the two main characters before the movie premiered in September 1969, but by the time it had worked its way through the distribution system, they were household names, and at least a few hundred people were studying them and their cohorts with varying degrees of academic rigor. Newly minted buffs started turning up at conventions of Western historians to sit on panels and deliver papers with titles such as "When Did Butch and Sundance Meet?" "The Possible Identities of Etta Place" (she is still called Etta by most American researchers), and "Did Butch and Sundance Come Back from South America?" A good number of those people, along with many of their less bookish brethren, also started spending their summer vacations in godforsaken parts of Wyoming, Montana, and Colorado, where the outlaws had committed robberies, served time, or drunk whiskey, at least according to the local tourist boards. The Cassidy charisma, it seemed, had woken from a long hibernation and was working its magic again. "The way things usually happened is that people got interested because of the movie and then stayed interested because both guys were just so decent and nice when they didn't have to be," says Bill Betenson, a grand-nephew of Butch's who himself got swept up in the tide of interest postfilm and published a book called

Butch Cassidy, My Uncle. (His great-grandmother Lula Betenson also wrote her own book, *Butch Cassidy, My Brother.*)

Not even the stars of the film were immune to their characters' magnetic pull. Newman never did become a serious student of the outlaw; but for the rest of his life, the actor haunted rare book and manuscript shops wherever he happened to find himself, searching for what he told one dealer was "the only thing I want that I don't have: Butch Cassidy's autograph." Three years after the film's release, Redford, saying he was more intrigued than ever by the story of the pair, took a long and arduous horseback trek with a group of friends, historians, and photographers through the chain of picturesque hideouts along the Outlaw Trail, and wrote a sumptuous coffee-table book about the experience for the National Geographic Society. At around the same time, the actor bought a ski resort near Provo, Utah, and rechristened it Sundance, after both his character and the town, about a dozen miles distant, where Harry Longabaugh once escaped from jail and gained a euphonic nickname. Obviously enthralled with the word, Redford used it multiple times over the years, for a film festival, a TV channel, an institute that supports screenwriters and playwrights, a merchandise catalog, and a chain of movie theaters.

Goldman's attempts to explain his own fascination with the Butch and Sundance story were not unromantic, but they were crepuscular, in a writerly sort of way. "Two people sharing life and death who really don't know each other at all," he scribbled at the bottom of the second page of his working copy of his script. And elsewhere: "Being chased is what keeps them alive."

Redford, in contrast, had a more earnest, less nuanced take on the boys. "I have become increasingly intrigued by the many outlaws who had demonstrated wit and brains unmatched by any but the most brilliant in legitimate society," he wrote in *The Outlaw Trail: A Journey Through Time.* "We have an abiding impression of the outlaw as a low-life renegade, a violent fool who lived off luck and the gun. We view him as one of society's misbegotten who had to be hunted down like an animal by morally superior men in white hats. But it was not so. In truth, the line between the 'good guy' and the 'bad guy' in the West was often blurred, and many of the outlaws, in spite of their errant and often violent natures, were men of extraordinary skill and cunning, who by comparison made the lawmen look pathetic."

While that may be true, it is precisely the kind of remark that makes the scholars wince. In the half century since the movie came out, the cult of Cassidy has shrunk and hardened. Its elite members now tend to play the role of party poopers, wagging their fingers and reminding the occasional wide-eyed newbie that nobody should make too much those glamorous grifters. Yes, Cassidy could be charismatic, not unlike Paul Newman, they concede, but so what? He did not free slaves or bust trusts; he did not create art or develop anything beyond a few innovations—such as a system of planting fresh mounts along his escape route as a way of easily outrunning his pursuers—that could be of benefit only to criminals. Rather, he took things that did not belong to him, and sometimes frightened innocent people in the process. "Cassidy is not worth studying," I was told by a woman who has studied him for more than forty years. "It's a slippery slope you're on with this guy, so turn back while you still can."

Butch Cassidy was "nothing but a lowlife!" Dan Buck, America's leading authority on the subject, and his English counterpart, Mike Bell, informed me, virtually in unison, one winter evening as the three of us sat around Buck's dining room table at his cozy house in Washington, DC. Their crankiness is understandable—even commendable—considering the high standards it connotes. Paging through moldering Montana hotel registers, searching in Mormon archives, or digging for bodies in some obscure Bolivian boneyard (as Buck and Anne Meadows did in the early 1990s) is a grinding, low-percentage business, even by the normally frustrating standards of historical research. All those aliases (if a guy had one, he probably had a half dozen; even perfectly innocent people had aliases in the Old West, and no one seemed to spell his name the same way twice) and all that unreliable Wild West journalism (Butch Cassidy—or Cassady, or Cassidey—was reported dead more times than can be counted) can make your Stetson spin. Many of the foundational texts are filled with errors. Cassidy's first biographer, Charles Kelly, got his subject's real name wrong, calling him George Parker instead of Robert throughout his book. Oops. Butch no doubt would have enjoyed that—and those who insist that he was still very much alive and clomping around Nevada (or Wyoming or Utah) when Kelly's *Outlaw Trail: A History of Butch Cassidy and His Wild Bunch* came out in 1938, will tell you that he most definitely did take it all with a wry laugh.

You are always on marshy ground when dealing with professional obfuscators, scrambling in pursuit like a panting Pinkerton—and the Cassidy-Sundance game only gets more frustrating as time passes and fresh clues get harder and harder to come by.

As in a long marriage, familiarity has bred a kind of mock contempt among the researchers, some days less mock than others—yet never entirely real. The woman who said that Cassidy is not worth studying searches for him daily, still. The evening Buck denounced Butch in my presence, he was pouring a quite decent Mendoza Malbec in tribute, he admitted, to the bandits' Argentinian adventures, his particular area of specialty. In vino veritas. Behold the strange and enduring power of Maxi and Annie Parker's peculiar little baby boy.

3

PROMISED LAND

*L*atter-Day Saints are not always *so saintly.*

   No one understood that better in 1866 than the Indians around Circleville, Utah, who, by then, had been
dealing with Mormon settlers for nearly two decades. So when a
gaggle of white men, wearing their best poker faces, rode into a
community of about twenty impoverished Paiutes on the morning of April 23 and announced that the local bishop wanted the
residents to come to town to hear a letter he had written to them,
the adults in the camp reacted warily. Was this an order or an
invitation? Were they out of favor with the Mormon holy man,
who had already shown his disdain for Indians? The Paiutes had
seen more than once how easily these pale newcomers could turn
purple with rage.

   To go or not to go? Even in that dry and crushingly desolate
environment—historian and novelist Wallace Stegner would later
describe the southern Utah landscape as "the geography of de-
spair"—listening to a sermon, or whatever it was, did not seem
to the Paiutes like an agreeable way to spend an evening. Clearly,
the prudent choice would be to stay at home in their tumbledown

wickiups, eat a bit of lizard or deer, and fall asleep as usual. But still they were torn.

The Paiutes, after all, were the "good Indians," known for doing what they were told. They liked to emphasize to the white men, who sometimes didn't seem to grasp the distinctions between tribes, that they were not the more prosperous but also more warlike Utes, who kept the Saints in a constant state of anxiety. The Utes liked to ride out of the hills without notice, screaming and swinging blankets, to drive off the settlers' cattle. They also had a knack for materializing six or so inches outside the windows of the white people's cabins, painted for battle and staring fiercely.

The Paiutes, in contrast, came to town smiling and bearing fresh antelope meat to trade for the Mormon ladies' breads and cakes. They, too, endured raids by the Utes, who kidnapped their women and children and sold them into slavery in Mexico; in another world, they might have bonded with the settlers over their common enemy. But the Paiutes sensed that the white men tended to see all Indians as trouble—the only good one was a dead one, some of the Saints liked to say—especially when they were angry about something, and they were angry about something now. One week before, at nearby Fort Sanford, a Mormon militia base, two settlers had argued with two Utes about some matter now lost to history, and one of the settlers had wound up injured and one of the Indians had wound up dead. Even though the white men had come out better in the clash, their exasperation was palpable. They seemed sick to death of the fear they lived with constantly on account of their conflicts with the Utes.

Despite the sour mood that hung over the valley, four or five Paiutes decided to heed the summons to Circleville and walked the several miles into town (they were too poor to own horses), arriving in midafternoon. The Mormons weren't satisfied with a partial turnout, though, and so they rode back and rounded up the rest—except for one Paiute man who panicked and bolted into the brush and was shot dead in his tracks. Not a good omen.

———

Life was difficult in Utah's Circle Valley—whether you were an Indian, a Mormon, a flower, or an antelope—but just then it was a lot harder than it had to be because of the white men's failure to get along with the red.

Poor treatment of Indians was not supposed to be the Mormon way. Joseph Smith, who'd founded the religion in upstate New York some forty years earlier, taught, incorrectly but ardently, that the Indians were a people set apart—Israelites who had come to North America by boat around 600 BC. Converting the "Lamanites," as he called them, to Christianity was the number one priority of the Angel Moroni, provider of the mystical golden plates that Smith claimed were the source material for the foundational Book of Mormon.

But no such missionary work was then in progress. While Brigham Young and other Mormon leaders advised their followers to respect the area's tribes, and to remember that they had preceded them to Utah and had first rights to the land, rank-and-file Saints treated Indians with the same callous disregard as the gentiles, or non-Mormons, did.

In the mid-nineteenth century, Mormons were aggrieved aliens. R. Laurence Moore, in his *Religious Outsiders and the Making of Americans*, wrote: "Mormons followed a lesson, already by their time well established in American experience, that one way of becoming American was to invent oneself out of a sense of opposition." Although they could be strikingly cheerful at times when interacting with one another, the early Saints made no pretense of being a gentle, settled sect. "The whole nation will soon be at the feet of the Mormons," one LDS settler wrote in 1850, "suing for mercy and protection!" Their colony, which they called Deseret, was supposed to be the staging ground for a holy but likely bloody revolution that would upend the government in Washington and replace it with a Mormon theocracy in time for Christ's return in 1890 or, at the latest, 1891.

Brigham Young, who became the second LDS president in 1844, after Joseph Smith and his brother Hyrum were murdered by a mob in Carthage, Illinois, wanted a place, Stegner tells us, where his followers could live "without interference from politicians, mobocrats, and all that the United States stood for in the Mormon mind." When he arrived in the Salt Lake Valley in 1847 and saw a land where "distances were terrifying, cloudbursts catastrophic, heat withering, and beauty flamboyant and bizarre and allied with death"—a land, in other words, where very few settlers in their right mind would put down stakes—he stopped his wagon and said, "This is the place!" A few years later, when he needed people to stock his off-putting paradise, a stream of Saints began to pour in from Iowa and Missouri, pushing and pulling rickety wooden handcarts, a method that Young thought would spare them (and his Church) the hassles associated with horses, even if that meant the faithful had to walk as much as 1,400 miles, often in extreme weather, to reach their promised land.

Maps of North America looked considerably different in those days. What we now call Utah was part of Mexico, a country then at war with the United States. Several months after the fighting ceased and the Treaty of Guadalupe Hidalgo reconfigured the continent in a way that we would recognize today, Mormons started settling there. The Saints, without having to pack so much as a bindle, found themselves back within the borders of the nation they were trying to escape.

It was a wrenching nonjourney: for a community of polygamists and insurgents, being inside America meant being outside the law. But rather than trying to fit in with the majority, the Mormons in 1849 cheekily asked the federal government to create a bespoke state, Deseret, where they could plant their signature Lombardy trees, plan and build their standardized towns, plot their revolution, and define marriage however they pleased. Congress responded by signing off instead on a conventional secular territory to be called Utah. This was no cold bureaucratic rebuff: by affixing a name redolent of the Mormon-hating Utes, the government was showing the Saints a Washington Monument–size middle finger.

Ultimately, though, the squabbling didn't really matter; no declaration from DC would have kept the Mormons isolated, not when their New Jerusalem sat squarely in the path of western migration. Oregon-bound gentiles were already traipsing through, and, as one historian has written, "shiny material reflected in the wash of California's American River in January 1848 soon made Great Salt Lake City an indispensable way station for those westering 'with golden visions bright before them.'"

The Saints profited from the gold rush by selling supplies to "the Americans," as they called the travelers, at exorbitant prices, but, in the process, they gave travelers a peek at their controversial ways. What the LDS Church called "plural marriage" titillated and frightened mainstream Americans to a degree that's hard to fathom if you've seen the photographic saltpeter that is the Saints' old bonnet- and beard-heavy family portraiture. The Republican Party, in its defining first platform of 1854, singled out Mormon polygamy and Southern slavery as "twin relics of barbarism," and three years later, President James Buchanan sent 2,500 army troops into the territory to enforce monogamy laws. It was an odd job for soldiers, arresting men for "cohabitation" with two or more wives. The year-long Utah War turned out to be an almost bloodless affair in which the Saints pushed back against the federals in an indirect, possibly Indian-inspired way—by stealing their rations and stampeding their mules. According to the *New York Times*, they also "ridiculed the effeminacy and credulity of President Buchanan." But we shouldn't infer from their tactics in this instance that the Saints of those days always stopped short of killing. In September of that same year, at a place in the southern part of the territory called Mountain Meadows, the Mormon militia—provoked, it seems, by a wave of radical local leaders who exhorted them to gain "blood vengeance" for the humiliations they had suffered in the East and the Midwest—tried to goad Indians into attacking a wagon train on its way from Arkansas to California. When that didn't work out, they did the dirty work themselves and slaughtered about 120 gentile men, women, and children who they felt had insulted them by scoffing at their overt religiosity.

———————

What would happen in Circleville was different from the Mountain Meadows Massacre—smaller in scale, not so extensively covered in the press or in history books, and a crime against Indians instead of white men—but it is no less instructive about the Mormon mindset as it existed in those days on the Western frontier. By the time the settlers returned with the remainder of the Paiute Indians, all pretenses of friendliness had vanished. The ten or so captive men who were herded into the meeting room in Circleville with their hands tied behind their backs, probably were not surprised to discover that no "bishop's letter" existed—or that the Saints, while nervous and perhaps still undecided about their endgame, were eager to punish Indians of any tribe.

The denouement was both swift and pathetic. As anxiety mounted in the meeting room, the Paiutes started slipping out of their ropes. They must have signaled or whispered in their language, because, for a time, they stayed in place, hoping to make one big concerted rush and overwhelm their captors. But the gambit fell short. When the moment came and they surged desperately toward the doors and windows, none made it out. The militiamen shot every one of them at close range.

As the men lay on the floor dead or dying, the Mormons went

into the basement of the house, where they had locked the Paiute women and children. One by one, those panicky people were taken upstairs and led outside, where a militiaman slit their throats. Only a few infants who could not serve as witnesses were spared.

The Saints by then had about twenty bodies to dispose of. The militiamen brought them to another house nearby, where they buried them in the basement. Then for several hours, the town stood still in a kind of shocked silence.

As night fell in Circleville, a lone traveler arrived. He was carrying a message from the regimental commander of the Mormon militia, in Salt Lake City. It said, "Be sure to see that your prisoners are treated kindly."

———————

It was into this welter of hatred, violence, fear, and stupidity that the outlaw known to history as Butch Cassidy was born. Robert LeRoy Parker arrived exactly ten days before the Circleville Massacre, on Friday the thirteenth of April 1866, and about twenty-five miles to the west.

Little is known about the circumstances of his birth, starting with its precise location within the town of Beaver, Utah. Was it the modest and still-occupied house built of pink granite and red brick on what today is forlorn, semirural South 200 West Street? (When I visited the site in 2016, a pickup truck rolled slowly by, leading a bedraggled horse. Then nothing happened for quite a while.) That is the conventional wisdom among those historians who have addressed the subject, even though, as the researcher Bob Goodwin has shown, the building didn't exist until 1870. Census records indicate that little Bobby Parker did indeed live in the house between the ages of four and ten, however, so it's possible he was born somewhere else on the property, in a structure no longer standing—or in North Creek, a sort of suburb just outside the town proper, in a house owned by his paternal grandfather, Robert, or at an unknown location elsewhere in town, in a house owned by his maternal grandmother, Jane Sinclair Gillies, as some say. Does it matter? Not to the tourist trade, which, in Beaver's case, comes down to a trickle of Patagonia-clad trekkers who justify the town's bumper sticker boast: "Gateway to the Tushar Mountains!" For forty-something dollars a night, you *can* stay at Beaver's Butch Cassidy Inn, but don't expect to find any pamphlets in the reception area directing you to a museum or even a statue erected in memory of the town's most famous native. The sole statue in Beaver honors the inventor Philo T. Farnsworth, who was born nearby in a log cabin in 1906 and who for his work with electronic imaging technology has become known, somewhat misleadingly, as "the Father of Television." The receptionist at my (different) motel had never heard of Butch Cassidy.

What we can say with some certainty about the future outlaw's entrance into the world is that it came amidst relative peace and quiet. His parents, Maximilian and Ann Parker, married nine months and one day earlier, did not have other children yet, nor did they practice polygamy, so their household, in contrast with those of many nearby Saints, would not have been crowded with crying babies and redundant wives trying to outdo one another in the hierarchy.

Probably not even the new father was present. Maxi, as he was called, then twenty-two, had enlisted in the Mormon militia a few weeks earlier, and its records indicate he was stationed elsewhere on that day and for about three months thereafter. It was his second hitch in the semiofficial army of Saints, not because he was so devout—he wasn't—but because service in the militia was a paying job he needed badly: for his four-month 1866 tour of duty and the use of his horse, he received $85.50. Maxi does not appear to have participated in either the Mountain Meadows or Circleville Massacres, but he said in an affidavit filed forty-four years after Robert's birth that he was involved in a battle with Indians on April 22, 1866, which was almost certainly the scuffle at Fort Sanford.

What voices Bob Parker did hear in his first few years would have tended to be tinged with the accents of working-class Britain. Nearly 20 percent of the people in Utah at that time had been born in England, and plenty of Irish-, Scots- and Welshmen were also digging irrigation ditches, attending dances at the ward house, and doing all the communal things that good Saints did. Their robust presence in the American West was a testament to both the persuasive powers of Mormon missionaries and the extreme difficulty of life in the polluted factory towns back home.

Butch Cassidy's paternal grandfather, Robert, was baptized into the LDS church on November 7, 1840, the same day, by no coincidence, that his Church of England parents threw him out of their house in Lancashire County, England. The Mormons saw leadership potential in the well-built, bright-eyed Lanky though, and in exchange for his singing at their street-corner revivals, they let him live at their mission house. On May 25, 1843, he married Ann Hartley, a pretty Lancashire girl who worked in the same textile mill, and soon the newlyweds moved from Burnley to Accrington. It was there, in 1844, that Maxi, the future father of a famous cowboy outlaw, was born.

Accrington provided a front-row seat for the changes then roiling European society. A year before the Parkers arrived, protests against low pay and dangerous conditions in the mills turned violent. Despite this, the family did manage to eke out a living, with Ann fitting her six-in-the-morning-to-seven-at-night shifts around the birth of five additional children, two of whom died in their first year.

If the Parkers' life sounds Dickensian, it almost literally was: no sooner had they relocated to bustling Preston in 1853, than Charles Dickens himself came through town doing research for his novel-in-progress *Hard Times*. Karl Marx also paid a visit to observe the English version of the class struggle. If the philosopher had peeked inside the Parkers' cottage, he might have seen nine-year-old Maxi striking a blow for the proletariat by refusing to polish the boots of visiting Mormon missionaries, as his father had requested.

Maxi was clearly a headstrong lad, as his firstborn son would be. When his father apprenticed him to the mill a short time later, he ran away, then refused to go back even after Robert found him and administered a beating. Rather than continue to whip his son, though, the elder Parker experienced an epiphany: not only would he not send Maxi back there, but also he and Ann wouldn't return, either. Instead, the Parker family would go . . . well, if not to America, exactly, then to the Mormon colony deep within it: to Deseret. In her memoir *Butch Cassidy, My Brother*, Lula Betenson says her grandfather sold his cottage, cow, and furniture at a loss and joined a band of 534 Mormons on a seventy-four-foot clipper ship called the *Enoch Train*. They sailed from Liverpool on March 23, 1856.

The crossing took five weeks and was followed by a seriously bumpy eleven-day train trip to Iowa City. After a month spent hammering out handcarts, the five Parkers and about 220 other newly minted Mormons set out for their long walk west, with Robert pulling and twelve-year old Maxi pushing their crude vehicle. The carts, crafted from unseasoned wood by amateurs, did not have rubber tires, just leather strips around the wheels, and the axles had no lubrication; breakdowns came early and often. In terms of provisions, the Parkers had only cornbread and salt pork. By the time they'd reached Fort Laramie, Wyoming, they'd run out of that and had to sell their wedding silver to buy more food.

After that they had to contend with broiling heat as well as migrating buffalo herds that occasionally overwhelmed their ranks and swept away their few scraggily heads of cattle. At some point, Robert suffered a foot infection, and Ann had to pull the handcart. After she collapsed a week or so later, the family was taken the final fifty miles to Salt Lake City in the buckboard of a kindly gentile stranger, arriving on September 27, 1856.

The new life may have been vastly different from the old, but it was no easier. In early 1852, Robert was "called" by the church to Beaver, where the Mormons had built a mill to process wool. With cold weather moving in and no time to build a house, the Parkers spent their first Deseret winter in a dugout—essentially a cave with a wooden door and poles holding up a ceiling of pounded earth. "Be thankful we have a roof over our head!" Robert supposedly announced one rainy evening, just before a large slab of mud came crashing down on his family and everything they owned.

Despite the hardships in Deseret, the Mormons kept coming. Ann Campbell Gillies, Maxi's future wife, was part of a group of about 850 converts who made the Liverpool-to-Boston trip on a ship called the *Horizon* two months after the Parkers. She was a native of Newcastle upon Tyne and the daughter of a cabinetmaker named Robert Gillies and his wife, Jane, "a peppery little Scotswoman" known for her sense of humor, Lula Betenson tells us.

The Civil War had little effect on life in Utah. Sheer distance from the battlefields was one reason, but as the historian John Gary Maxwell writes, Mormon leaders, and the newspapers that reflected their thinking, went out of their way to ignore the conflict. The reelection of President Abraham Lincoln and the treaty signing at Appomattox ending the war in 1865 received no acknowledgment from the pulpit or in the Mormon press. Joseph Smith had predicted in 1832 that a great war would begin in South Carolina and that the two sides would annihilate each other, creating a vacuum that would be filled by the LDS theocracy. While the Saints waited for this prophecy to play out, they stayed on the sidelines, privately leaning toward the Confederacy (which they felt would be easier for them to beat when the time for the revolution came) but mostly living their prewar lives, oblivious to the nation's existential crisis.

Maxi and Ann met in Beaver in 1864 while performing together in a church-sponsored theater group that routinely presented light musical entertainment. Maxi was said to be a natural comedian; Ann, a good singer. As such, they were in the right religion. The

Saints loved wholesome playacting and felt they could pursue their personal interests while the Americans did the spadework for the coming revolution by slaughtering one another over the issue of slavery.

For all his love of tuneful Mormon theatricals, though, Maxi Parker wasn't exactly fully committed to his faith. Although he and Ann had a church wedding in 1865, and he liked the idea of his father blessing the newborn they'd decided to call Robert in honor of both his and Ann fathers, he was known to be among the nonobservant. This was no small thing in southern Utah, and his absence from the pew did not go unnoticed, or unpunished. Some years later, when he was on a trip to Saint Louis, where he went to sell his services as a guide for newcomers to Deseret, a slick-talking saloon keeper swindled Ann out of fifty acres of land. Upon Maxi's return, he sought justice from the local "church court" that settled such disputes—but the bishop found for the gentile, favoring him over a "Jack Mormon" who never attended services. Although Maxi was normally an even-tempered sort, the decision was said to have left him seething and cursing the Church. By then, though, he had more immediate family worries: in the form of a firstborn son who was eager to explore the wider world but seemed almost from the outset to have difficulty playing by its rules.

4

BOY INTERRUPTED

Bob Parker's parents would always be ashamed of his career path—there are relatives in Utah who are ashamed still—but they could not have been entirely surprised by it. Because of their poverty, Maxi, and sometimes Ann as well, had to hire themselves out to more prosperous ranchers, who were usually, given the isolating distances between rural dwellings in those days, too far away to reach by daily commute. That meant that one or the other or, after a certain point, both, could be gone for days, weeks, or even months at a time, connected to their family only via the postal service, if that. The kids never went hungry, it seems, but even by the flexible parenting standards of that era, supervision was lacking.

Maxi's absences during Bob's formative years were especially pronounced as he grabbed at seemingly every job he could get to support his growing family: guiding wagon trains full of Mormon settlers from the Missouri River to Utah; delivering the mail to Panguitch, on the other side of the Tushars from the Parkers' Circleville-adjacent home; hauling lava stone for the construction of Fort Cameron; cutting railroad ties at a mining town called

Frisco, which lay forty-five miles to the northwest; transporting timber for the Silver Reef Mine in Pershing County, Nevada, a hundred miles away from his home—all in addition to serving here and there around Utah in the Mormon militia and tending to the crops and cattle, as best he could, at his own out-of-the-way place.

Considering the frequency and length of Maxi's hiatuses from the hearth, not to mention his and Ann's constant exhaustion, it's a wonder that the family continued to grow—Bob Parker would eventually have a dozen siblings—and hold together as well as it did. In her 1975 memoir, Lula (born in 1884, and so reporting things she was apparently told by her family but hadn't seen for herself) depicts her eldest brother as intensely devoted to his mother. "Bring the crown, Ma's the queen!" Bob would say "in moments of euphoria," waltzing Ann around their little living area, then lifting her up and setting her on the table that was supposed to be her throne.

Lula's accounts of life in the Parker household tend toward the idyllic. She doesn't mention the endless days when, after chores were done, there was nothing better for the kids to do than hand drill holes in a large rock that sits to this day not far from the cabin door, a monument to the numbing ennui that, like the weather, was a major but largely unspoken factor in many Western lives. Nor does she bring up the harassment of her grandfather by local authorities, another sure source of familial anxiety.

From most angles, the elder Robert Parker appeared to have become a solid citizen by any definition of the term. Having finally escaped the cotton mills, he ran a general store in Washington, Utah, served as postmaster, and was twice appointed an election judge in his district. His family understandably saw him as the archetypical Mormon patriarch. To the soldiers and sheriffs, though, he was a wanted man, especially when they were in the mood to crack down on federal laws against "cohabitation." As polygamists go, Grandpa Parker, who had taken one additional wife since arriving in Utah, was barely in the game; many of his fellow Saints married four or five times and were still cruising the weekly dances. (Brigham Young had at least fifty-five wives, some of whom were still legally married to their gentile husbands.) Yet to avoid arrest, Robert often had to lay low (he returned to England at least once) and defend himself against trumped-up charges of postal fraud, a sententious term for stealing a few stamps. As far as can be told, he never served time, but his neighbors took to calling him "Cockleberry Jim" because of the burrs and thistles that clung to his beard and clothing after he'd hide in the bushes to avoid the US marshals. Young Bob had little in common with his pious, foreign-born grandfather, but he probably was appalled by all the effort expended to hunt down a man he considered a harmless old codger just trying to get by.

Rather than dwell on the hardships and harassment, though, Lula chose to remember a cozy, happy way of life. When her parents were both at home on an evening, she wrote, everyone present sang popular songs of the day such as "Oh, Shenandoah," Maxi and Ann told stories about their early years in England, and Bob played his harmonica. They seemed, despite their centrifugal circumstances, to have had a strong sense of themselves as a family and felt secure enough in their web of relationship to tease one another with sarcastic nicknames. Lula, the doted-on baby of the bunch, was "Cute" when she was being horrible and "Hag" when being sweet. Dan, the second eldest and a self-consciously skinny lad, especially when compared with the stocky, square-jawed Bob, was mocked, gently, as "Snip." Bob, whom Dan revered, was "Le-Roy" when being admonished for misbehavior—such as like stealing away to smoke in the barn or teaching his caged magpie to say something salty—and "Sallie" on other occasions. That curious nickname has helped fuel speculation that the young Bob may have shown signs of being "girlish"—though, of course, the name might also have been applied ironically.

Yet no matter how rosy a picture Lula (and in his 2012 memoir, her grand-nephew Bill Betenson) paint of the early Parker household, the reality of Bob's early years always bleeds through. Not that he withered, as a result, into the lonely, fearful latchkey child of today's psychology textbooks; rather, he reveled in his freedom and used it to perpetrate the kind of homespun, Huck-Finnish hijinks that no doubt would have been discouraged if Daddy were on the scene more consistently. (He may have even been inspired by Huck, who made his debut, in *Tom Sawyer*, in 1876, by which time young Bob was already a constant reader.) Bob stole wine from a gentile neighbor, put it out in pans for the chickens to drink, then delighted in watching his siblings and mother laugh as the birds staggered around the barnyard. He organized kiddie rodeos using the calves, goats, and other small animals on the ranch; he built a raft and offered free rides to neighbors on a nearby pond. Instead of being surreptitious, his mischief making seemed always to be plotted for public consumption. A natural-born ham, he often cast himself as the master of ceremonies—but acted mostly as an impresario who conceived and staged crowd-pleasing events, a regular little Buffalo Bobby. His greatest, or at least his most often-recollected, moment of frontier showmanship came when he supposedly tied strings to katydids—Mormon crickets, they were called—and staged races for the pests, shrinking the sport of kings down to cabin-floor scale, in the manner of the then-popular flea circuses.

I have stood on that cabin floor, in the modest house made of hand-squared logs and hand-cut nails, three miles south of Circleville, where the family moved in 1878. The structure, built by its previous residents, bore no plaque or other marker when I visited in 2016, prior to an extensive restoration effort, and had no lock on the door. It had been stripped bare by vandals over the years; when I mentioned this to an antiques dealer I met later in Provo, he reached under his desk and proudly pulled out what he said was the original wooden threshold. But even when the Parkers first lived there, it was quite primitive: essentially three tiny rooms with a loft at one end for the boys to sleep in and a lean-to kitchen outside. Ann tried to dress up the place by hanging sheets of the unbleached muslin that Mormons called "factory" on the ceiling to hide the rough beams and by covering the walls with cheap paper. She put stiffly starched white lace curtains on the windows, wove a colorful wool carpet for the planked floor, and padded it with straw. (All traces of those soft items have long since vanished, probably into Mormon crickets.) She also planted sapling trees and lilac bushes in the front yard to provide natural beauty and shade; two towering cottonwoods stand there still, monuments to the maternal instincts of a woman born in early Victorian England and now long since gone to dust.

As hard as she tried, though, Ann's loving cosmetic touches could not give Bob and his siblings what they needed most: a decent amount of space to turn around in, especially when the number of occupants swelled, in the early 1880s, to a dozen. Maxi and Ann must have wondered at times if their life was any better on balance than it had been back in the old country. Given that in England the Parkers had closer neighbors, no Indians to worry about, and a more comfortable cottage, the answer is probably no. Maxi had shrugged off the chains of the factory worker and the yoke of religion, but he remained a prisoner to poverty.

Why did the Parkers have so much less than even their hard-pressed neighbors? The reason, it seems, is simply that Maxi, perhaps because he learned the agricultural arts from someone who grew up in a sooty English factory town, was not, at least at that point in his life, a very good farmer. He certainly wasn't a lucky one. The Parkers' first winter on their Circle Valley ranch, Lula wrote, "was perhaps the most severe ever recorded. The extreme cold wiped out the herd of cattle except for two cows named Hutch and Sal." That spring, fierce winds blew the seed Maxi had planted—by hand, with a homely little grubbing hoe, but not deeply enough—right out of the arid soil. He bought more seed and hurriedly replanted it, but the same thing happened again. The third time he sowed his fields, the seeds sprouted, but by then he'd lost too much of the growing season to harvest a decent crop. Said Lula: "The family didn't recover financially from this setback for years."

To linger even briefly in that crude little cabin is to see why Bob would have wanted something different and better for himself; something that as a first-generation American, he probably defined as his natural right. But if he was determined not to replicate his father's life, he could have become a storekeeper or a traveling salesman or moved to Chicago, where his options would have been myriad. Why did he instead choose a path down which he would be relentlessly pursued by posses and Pinkertons eager to take away his freedom, if not his very life? The obvious answer is the possibility of big money—not just taking a step up but living large. But was it really all about that?

There are conflicting theories about how and why Bob turned outlaw. In his massive 2010 book *Butch Cassidy: The Untold Story*, the veteran researcher Kerry Ross Boren says that the boy was led astray initially by (of all people) Maxi, who was not just an absentee father but also a bandit himself, sometimes working in concert with an obscure desperado named Idaho Bill. When Bob was fourteen, Boren writes, Maxi enlisted him to rob a stagecoach in Pioche, Nevada. The heist went so well, according to Boren, that it wound up getting the boy permanently addicted to the exciting and highly rewarding life on the wrong side of the law.

This is nonsense, but nonsense worth noting because of who its perpetrator is. Kerry Ross Boren deserves a place in our story right alongside the Tall Texan, the Thorny Rose, and all the other colorful secondary characters; call him the Heavyset Historian. No one is more steeped in Butchiana than this native of Manilla, Utah, who has spent most of his nearly eighty years ransacking archives, tracking the movements of the principals, and, in his earlier days, interviewing people who allegedly rode with the Wild Bunch or who knew someone who did. The dedication page of his 680-page magnum opus says, "To Butch: My boyhood companion, my life's pursuit, may you ever play the game!"

Back in the day when Butch and Sundance were hotter commodities, Boren was the go-to guy for information on the outlaws, his name nestled in many a ritzy Rolodex. He served as a consultant to screenwriter Goldman on the 1969 movie, advised Bruce Chatwin on the Cassidy-and-Sundance portion of his classic 1977 travelogue *In Patagonia*, and rode with Robert Redford on the trek chronicled in *The Outlaw Trail*. Redford was impressed by his seemingly limitless passion. Listening to Boren, he wrote, "was like listening to a waterfall—names tumbling out of him like a hasty confession." Forty years on, he's still that way. I had dinner with him and his third wife, Lisa (who met him when he was in prison, serving eight years for the killing of his second wife), at a Salt Lake City steakhouse, and I didn't even try to take notes. Yet somewhere along the way, Boren's obsession got the better of him, and he veered out of the nonfiction lane. He is hardly the most out-there of the out-there aficionados—that would probably be the late Art Davidson, who posited a theory of five Cassidy clones roaming the landscape and wreaking mayhem—but he is the angel who has fallen the farthest. His specialty these days is startling claims that arrive evidence free and lacking all credibility: Butch fought alongside Pancho Villa in the Mexican Revolution; Sundance taught Lawrence of Arabia how to derail trains; Ethel Place was a Scottish princess; Sundance and Ethel went to Paris, where they stole radium from Marie Curie; Maxi was an outlaw, and so on. It's hard to tell whether Butch Cassidy is keeping him sane or driving him crazy. (For the record, Boren told me he got his exclusive information from "family sources" that he declines to name.) But we should—and will—cross paths with him again as our story progresses because we can learn something about the power of Maxi and Ann's peculiar little baby boy from the weirdly Butch-smacked life of Kerry Ross Boren.

As any Butch Cassidy researcher who has spent even a few hours dozing in the library of the University of Utah or smoking outside the Wyoming State Archives knows, in the conventional literature it is not Maxi but an obscure, small-time outlaw named Mike Cassidy who is usually said to have led Bob Parker astray. There is at least one big problem with this notion, though. While Mike Cassidy (obviously) had considerable influence on our subject, he came along when Bob was seventeen or so, and the main fork in his career path was already five years behind him. That is when Bob rode into Beaver, Utah, to buy a pair of overalls (or as the cowboys tended to call them, "overhauls") and wound up embroiled in a dilemma that taught him a good deal about the sort of person he was destined to be. Or maybe that's the wrong way to put it because he didn't seem a "sort" at all; he seemed quite sui generis. In any case, some people gain self-knowledge while fighting in a war or running a marathon; he did it while shopping for pants.

The problems started when Bob, arriving in town late in the afternoon, discovered that the general store, which sold the overalls, was closed for the day. Definitely a disappointment—but instead of coming back another time, like a normal person, Bob broke into the establishment, took what he wanted, left a signed IOU on the counter, and calmly rode away.

Bob would later insist that this was a creative and even commendable way for a twelve-year-old to deal with an imperfect situation; he lived, after all, quite a few miles from town. But the store owner had a different take on the matter. The next morning, when he discovered what had happened, he swore out a complaint against Bob, which resulted in the sheriff calling on Maxi Parker to collect the price of the clothing and to ask him to talk to his son. This Maxi did, and it was definitely one of those Lee-*Roy* moments. But Bob, though never known as a fresh boy, appeared highly indignant. What had he done, he wanted to know, except come up with a plan that was convenient for him and would, eventually, leave the store-keeper with a profit? Had he not given his dad-blamed *signature* to seal the deal? And shouldn't that beef-headed sheriff have anything better to do than to ride all over the countryside to serve some silly "complaint"? What a yack!

Here we see already in full blossom an attitude that would never fade (as well as the cowboy term for *moron*). For a person of such obvious intelligence, Bob would all his life have a peculiar and (of course) rather adorable little blind spot about his relationship to authority, seeming not to understand why he wasn't allowed to do what he pleased, even when that was clearly a crime. Although he sometimes empathized with individual peace officers who were hot on his trail, he always seem baffled and annoyed by their pre-occupation with him. They couldn't track a bed-wagon through a bog hole, so just let him go about his business (we might reasonably imagine him saying, in cowboyese) and life would go smoother, wouldn't it? Well, for him, yes, things would be simpler and better. But for the banks, railroads, and cattle barons whose loot he was lifting? Maybe not so much.

Rather than push Bob toward a life of crime, as Boren suggests, Maxi tried his best to keep a closer eye on his boy as Bob reached adolescence and his proclivities became more pronounced. In 1879 or so, when Maxi took a job at the ranch of a well-to-do horse breeder and mine speculator named Pat Ryan, eighty-five miles away in Milford, Utah, he brought Bob with him. By the standards of the day, it should be noted, working for wages was an admission of failure, something akin to going on the welfare rolls. (Abraham Lincoln said that the willingness to work for wages indicated "either a dependent nature which prefers it, or improvidence, folly, or sin-gular misfortune.") But the Parkers couldn't afford to worry about the social stigma that might be involved in them and their children being on someone's payroll. They needed the cash and Bob the oversight. For them, the arrangement worked.

Bob was fascinated by the Ryan spread. Its adventurous owner had come down from Canada to participate in the silver rush then happening in southern Utah, an event that was attracting all kinds of exotic outsiders and making the area much less stringently Mormon. Ryan also bred racehorses, which got Bob dreaming about riding at the tracks around Salt Lake City. (Out west in those days, jockeys came in all sizes.) A decade later, by which time Bob had changed names and become famous, Ryan would tell the *Salt Lake Tribune* that Butch Cassidy had been a hell of a ranch hand, able to do the chores of a full-grown man at the age of thirteen or so—but that, alas, he was a trifle sticky fingered, too. When Bob finally left his employment, Ryan said, he noticed he was missing a saddle and a pistol.

Two years later, in 1881, Bob went off to work with his mother, this time at a horse and cattle operation run by the brothers James and Joseph Marshall about twenty-five miles due south of the Parker homestead, in Panguitch. Ann spent her days there in the dairy barn, milking cows and churning butter, with her son usually just down the way apiece in the horse stables. Perhaps the Parkers had no choice in the matter, but if they were worried about keeping their oldest boy out of trouble, they had picked a strange place for him to work. No ranch in the area had a worse reputation. James Marshall especially was known as a rustler, and not just the common, casual kind who might blithely bring home some unbranded calves that he'd happened to find wandering on the open range. That sort of thing was rustling in quotation marks—not outright stealing so much as simply going with the untidy ebb and flow of Western life in the days when cattle often grazed beyond their owner's deeded acres, on land not yet homesteaded and so still classified as public. *Today I'll filch a few of your mavericks, tomorrow you'll peel off a passel of mine* was the unwritten rule that most everyone grumblingly followed. "They had those cows plum wore out stealing them from each other," said one old-timer. But the "hatchet-faced and foxy-eyed" James Marshall, according to one neighbor, ranked as a more egregious sort of thief. He, his brother, and their hired hands actively hunted for other people's animals, then branded or rebranded them as their own. James Marshall especially behaved like a thug, even in the more legitimate aspects of the brothers' business. If you were a little too slow to pay for livestock he'd sold you, he might pull a gun on you or rough you up. "The worst outlaw in the area," one lawman called him.

Bob had been at the Marshalls' for a year or more, rustling cattle and maybe stealing horses, too (a different and more serious crime), when Mike Cassidy turned up one day seeking work and looking every inch the cool, cocky gunslinger. Men like him, once rare in Mormon country, had become a part of the scene since silver had been discovered in the mountains near Circleville. A town that had been probably 90 percent Saints when Parker was born there in 1866 had become, by the early 1880s, crowded with saloons, hotels, whorehouses, a racetrack, and their attendant temptations. The general store, which once carried only the basics, now had coffee, tea, tobacco, Old Crow whiskey, and other products proscribed by the Mormons. Bob, whose only exposure to the wider world had once come through books, now mingled with dusty miners, silk-hatted speculators, and rowdy soldiers stationed at nearby Fort Cameron. He also read sketchier books: sensational novels about characters named Ragged Dick and Dead-Eye Dick that presented a funhouse mirror view of the West. Mike Cassidy was in some ways just another example of the secular world that was seeping into the sealed-off colony that Brigham Young had tried to create. But he was also precisely the kind of American construct—the smartly dressed, smooth-talking, well-mounted, quick-drawing man of the world—that Bob Parker at that impressionable stage of his life most admired.

But who was Mike Cassidy? After all these decades and a lot of digging by enthusiasts, he remains mostly a mystery. What we think we know about him comes not from any official records but from old stories, told by long-gone Utah folks, that portray him as an attractive fellow, blond and blue eyed, well built and well spoken, prone to laughter, adept with a rope, generous in a saloon setting, and at peace with his reputation as bad boy. Although he was only nineteen or so when they met—a year older than Bob—Bob seemed to look upon him as a mentor, as well as living proof that you didn't have to be a mean, ugly bully like Jim Marshall to be a successful bandit. To Bob, Mike Cassidy was most likely an amalgam of the big brother he never had and the father who was only sporadically present.

He may also have thought of him as a lover. The two seemed inseparable, and Ann, while making butter and cheese in the Marshalls' dairy barn, is said to have heard noises that caused her to wonder, she once said, apparently with one raised eyebrow, "what [Mike and Bob] were doing down by the corral." If that is a reference to possible sexual activity—and a number of outlaw scholars feel certain that it is—it reflected the attitude of the day, which was less judgmental and more matter-of-fact than modern-day folks might imagine. As the historian Richard White tells us, "Sexual contact between men did not in the nineteenth century mark them as homosexual. It might be a sin, but it did not yet signify that men who indulged in it occupied a distinct sexual category." Apart from that, Ann, Bob, and Mike Cassidy were all living in the West, where the ratio of men to women in some areas was about 30 to 1, and folks recognized that stuff happened out there on the range and under the low-hanging stars. According to an 1882 article in the *Texas Live Stock and Farm Journal*, "If the inner history of friendships among the rough and perhaps untutored cowboys could be written, it would be quite as unselfish and romantic as that of Damon and Pythias." The cowboys even had a term for it: "mutual solace," as many familiar with the movie *Brokeback Mountain* know. In his landmark 1948 study of male sexuality, the biologist Alfred Kinsey noted that "there is a fair amount of sexual contact among the older males in Western rural areas . . . a type of homosexuality that was probably common among pioneers and outdoor men in general. Today it is found among ranchmen, cattle men, prospectors, lumbermen, and farming groups in general, among groups that are virile, physically active. These are men who have faced the rigors of nature in the wild. They live on realities and on a minimum of theory. Such a background breeds the attitude that sex is sex, irrespective of the nature of the partner." Homosexual behavior, he added, "rarely conflicts with their heterosexual relations," and the men involved had "a minimum of personal disturbance or social conflict" about it.

To the surprise of probably no one at the Marshall place, when Mike Cassidy quit and pulled out of Panguitch just a few months after he'd pulled in, Bob went with him. They headed west with a small herd of stolen cattle Mike had kept in reserve for himself, to a spot in the remote Henry Mountains. There they met up with a grizzled old varmint named Cap Brown. A frequent guest of the Marshall brothers, Brown was a veteran Utah rustler who supplied rebranded and unbranded horses to mining camps in Colorado. He dwelt in a shack in the shadows of Robbers Roost, an outlaw refuge on the Dirty Devil River, where the gypsum-laced water, if taken too freely, could turn your innards into plaster of Paris. Mike sold his cattle to Brown, then moved on again—but this time without Bob. "You're too good for where I'm going, kid," he was said to have told him, probably using a line he'd used before.

Bob went back to Circleville briefly before leaving home for good in April, a few days before his eighteenth birthday, with friends Heber Wiley and Eli Elder. As long-distance travelers with no set plans beyond starting over, they were part of a pronounced trend. America was on the move in those days, with many Easterners abandoning their first attempt at agriculture to try again out West—and many in the intermountain West giving up and heading to Oregon, California, or returning to the East. Utah was one of several states that had more emigrants than immigrants in the latter half of the nineteenth century, as people came to believe that life there was harder than it needed to be.

Bob was never going to stay put, in any case. Given his constant reading and his curiosity about life, he was a prime candidate to "go see the elephant," as people said in those days when they meant venturing from home to discover the wider world and all its wonders. Still, he didn't so much leave home as flee. When his mother, shaken by the news of his departure, asked him to wait just one more day until his father returned from his latest trip, Bob declined, saying he had to get going the next morning, and the earlier the better. As dawn broke, Ann, choking back tears, packed him cheese, raisins, bread, and a jar of bullberry preserves for the trail.

Several explanations have been offered for his hasty exit. One is that Bob's traveling companion Elder had recently escaped from the Circleville jail, where, according to Charles Kelly, author of *Outlaw Trail*, he was awaiting trial for "chewing off a man's ear in a fight."

But Bob may have been eager to hit the road for other reasons. One oft-told story has it that two other men named Fred and Charlie had recently asked him to sign a false bill of sale for some animals as part of a rustling scheme—and the sheriff may have wanted to question Bob about the suspicious transaction. Since he had no good answers, he might have thought it best to vamoose.

It was also said that Bob had stolen horses from a nearby rancher named Jim Kittleman. Lula, in her book, dismisses this claim, saying that Kittleman was a harmless old drunk and a longtime neighbor (it was his wine that Bob fed to the chickens) whom her brother would never have preyed upon. "One of Bob's most outstanding virtues," she wrote, "was his loyalty to friends and family."

That may have been so—and yet Charles Kelly found a source who told him that a sheriff and his deputy discovered Bob in the mountains that morning with "a small bunch" of Kittleman's horses. Bob, it was said, gave the lawmen a cheerful greeting and offered no resistance as they "slapped on a pair of handcuffs" and "started for the county seat," herding the horses as they went. When they stopped for lunch, though, and the deputy bent over to gather kindling, Bob shoved him to the ground with his boot and grabbed his gun. "In less than a minute," Kelly says, "he had both men's guns and was free from his shackles." He then rode off, "taking the stolen horses and the officers' mounts."

The story, which does not account for the presence of his friends Elder and Wiley, may well be apocryphal, but it does contain a typical Butch Cassidy twist.

Bob had gone only a short way, it was said, before he noticed that the lawmen's canteens were still tied to their horses' saddles. Knowing that they faced a thirty-mile walk back to Circleville, and water was scarce along the way, he took pity on them, went back, and gave them their canteens. At least they wouldn't die of thirst on their long hike.

Then, with a happy little whoop, he turned his herd of horses east toward Colorado and the future.

5

TO-HELL-YOU-RIDE

When *Robert LeRoy Parker abruptly* ended his childhood and lit out from home in the spring of 1884, he was what you might call a semi-outlaw, a man with one foot in sunlight and the other in shadow—but then, so were a lot of other Americans in those days, even presidents. It was, after all, the Golden Age of Boodle, a time when the haves and the have-nots were sorting themselves out amidst the great capitalist surge. Ulysses S. Grant, who served from 1869 to 1877, had set the tone for the times by accepting houses and "business opportunities" from magnates who sought to sway him or thank him for his efforts on their behalf, all the while continuing to go about his proper presidential business. Congress was the same. Corruption wasn't anything new, of course, but the openness and pervasiveness of it throughout the United States were peculiar to the late nineteenth century, when, as the historian Jill Lepore has written, "everything seemed, suddenly, bigger than before, more crowded, and more anonymous, looming, and teeming." From the White House right down to the local level, the growing government Grant presided over had its gears greased by bribes and illegal "fees" that needed to be paid if citizens actually wanted their packages delivered, their complaints acted upon, and their deeds recorded. Reformers railed against the system now and then, but usually nobody got fired, arrested, or fined as long as the recipient of the boodle kicked back a portion to his party boss. "The political and commercial morals of the United States are not merely food for laughter, they are an entire banquet," Mark Twain said.

No one would have called President Grant or any of his cronies an "outlaw," semi- or otherwise, though, no matter how far from the righteous path they strayed. Elected and appointed officials were usually too Eastern establishment, as well as, in many cases, out of scale with the term; the subsidies and tariffs they supported created megafortunes for men such as Andrew Carnegie and Jay Gould. "Outlaw" somehow seems to work best out past the 100th meridian, where one can savor its distinctly Western tang. True semi-outlawry needs the proper conditions to flourish, and in the vast spaces where law enforcement was thin on the ground, life monotonous, and the post–Civil War economy playing out in particularly brutal fashion, it came in myriad permutations.

We've already noted how a certain amount of rustling often figured into an otherwise honest rancher's life and how large cattle corporations barbarically big-footed the little men whose land they coveted, sometimes killing those they could not coerce into handing over land or water rights. Beef men of all magnitudes, meanwhile, harassed sheep herders because their wooly little beasts ravaged the grasslands, vacuuming up vegetation while rendering the ground unnavigable for bovines. Rather than seek redress through the courts, however, the cattle raisers preferred to act extralegally— by shooting the occasional shepherd and/or stampeding herds of frantically mewling Merinos over the nearest bluff. Frontier justice was faster and more cathartic than the proper thing, and sometimes more fun, too.

Bob Parker was yet another kind of semi-outlaw when he arrived in Colorado in May 1884, riding a mare named Babe and leading an unbroken colt he called Cornish—he was Butch Cassidy in larval form. He had some rustling and rebranding on his resume, and he was, if we choose to believe a certain version of events, technically still under arrest for stealing horses, but he wasn't yet the stuff of which wanted posters are made. To anyone who noticed him on the streets and in the saloons of Telluride, Colorado, the archetypical wide-open Western boomtown where he wound up for a while, he probably seemed like just another example of that colorful new kind of American failure: the tramp.

Tramps—later alternately known as hobos, and later still represented as sad-sack clowns like Emmett Kelly's Weary Willie and Red Skelton's Freddy the Freeloader—were a by-product of the boom-and-bust postwar times. They were also a symptom of an age in which Americans seemingly couldn't stay put—with most of the restless following false promises westward, in what one historian has called "one of the greatest social and environmental miscalculations in American history." While there have always been mendicants who huddled along the margins of society, either by choice or by necessity, tramps were suddenly everywhere in the 1880s, scavenging, begging, pilfering pies from windowsills of flustered widows, and unapologetically seeking wage work. The abrupt appearance of tramps alarmed poet Walt Whitman, who saw the "vast crops of poor, desperate, dissatisfied, nomadic, miserably-waged" men, wandering far from home, as proof that "our republican experiment, notwithstanding all its surface successes, is at heart an unhealthy failure."

Whitman may have been overreacting, as poets often must do to make a living. If Bob Parker was any indication, there was at least one rather benign strain of tramp. After escaping from those two overmatched lawmen in Utah, he supported himself and stayed out of trouble for almost three years. He was on the move, but not particularly on the bum.

You couldn't be lazy *and* a traveler in those days. Even drifters didn't really *drift*—not in the West, where the yawning spaces between you and your destination were often the work of weeks and weather conditions were mercurial, to say the least. Some fine mornings you could see for sixty or seventy miles in any direction; the next day, when the wind kicked up and the grit swirled, your horse's head might not be visible from your seat in the saddle. As Robert Redford noted in his book *The Outlaw Trail: A Journey Through Time*, when he rode with a cadre of pals through the same country as Bob did, a hundred years later, the ceaseless sandblast of the open range "felt like a hundred pinpricks on our skin."

Whatever didn't kill the future Butch Cassidy made him stronger, at least in the eyes of his first biographer. Charles Kelly wrote that Bob, "hardened by constant riding on the open range, grew into a stocky young man, 5 feet 9 inches in height, weighing 155 pounds, strong as a bull, tireless, and fearless." If Kelly was in this case correct—and other sources suggest that he was—that meant that Bob was on the tall side at a time when America was shrinking. We think of humans as going in only one direction sizewise as nutrition improves, but for reasons still unknown, the average height of native-born American males actually *decreased* by more than 3 percent in the latter half of the nineteenth century, from 68.3 inches to 66.6 inches, a significant difference. It was "a generation of midgets," the historical economist Robert J. Gordon has exaggeratedly said. Life expectancy dipped, too, just as mysteriously.

Bob's itinerary during this time can't be closely tracked, but we know that in the spring of 1884 he and his two childhood friends made their way through the maze of mesas, canyons, and flatlands known as Robbers Roost as they briefly headed east toward their not-terribly-well-thought-out futures. Their trip was typically slow and arduous. The light from an inn probably beckoned at eventide now and then, but mostly they would have slept in caves, weather-ruined and mouse-infested old trappers' cabins, and the homes of kindly ranchers when they could find such shelter. Many nights they no doubt laid out in the open on their bedrolls. If they didn't actually dream about water, they probably fell asleep wondering about the distance to the next source. It is so dry in those parts, the naturalist and writer Edward Abbey tells us, that you can sometimes see "blue curtains of rain" in the air, dangling out of reach, every drop destined to evaporate before it touches the ground. To avoid ending the day with an empty canteen and a swollen tongue, one had to plot a course between dependable (meaning nonsulfurous or poisonous) springs, waterholes, and streams—"secret places," Abbey called them, "deep in the canyons, known only to the deer and the coyotes and the dragonflies and a few others."

Crossing into Colorado, the three friends visited a ranch on the San Miguel River, where Bob arranged to leave his extra horse Cornish for pasturing, then headed north into Telluride, which was essentially one big, raucous mining camp rolling in dough. "The Town Without a Bellyache," its residents called it. ("Ouray [another town in Colorado] has four churches and fourteen saloons," noted the local paper, the *Solid Muldoon*. "Telluride has ten saloons and plans for a church.") There Bob bade adieu to his buddies and quickly secured a job as a muleteer helping to transport silver ore out of the nearby La Sal Mountains. He would always be drawn to animals, and they to him.

Telluride, though still just a toddler of a town, was in those days a magnet for many a wide-eyed, wanderlusty Mormon lad eager for an antidote to Utah (its other nickname was "To-Hell-U-Ride"). You might have thought that a young buck like Bob would have lingered there awhile, wallowing in the whiskey and the women. But no. Whiskey and women would never much interest him, while his curiosity about what was around the next bend or butte was always unquenchable.

One big thing happening in the West just then was something that modern-day historians call the cattle bubble. Thanks to the burgeoning population of the United States, a growing taste for beef (although pork remained America's favorite meat until World War I) and the rapid spread of railroad lines that effectively brought the major markets closer, Western ranches had become enormously attractive investments. Future US president Theodore Roosevelt owned an especially sprawling one, as did the German aristocrat Walter von Richthofen, uncle of the future World War I flying ace known as the Red Baron. But you didn't need to become a gentleman rancher like Roosevelt with a bespoke buckskin suit and a bowie knife made of fine Tiffany silver to participate in the boom. Britain's Marquess of Tweeddale backed the humongous XIT Ranch in Texas from a safe distance, as did thousands of others who bought shares in operations they had only read about, often not knowing—or caring—exactly how many acres or animals their money was procuring. How could anyone with a speculative bent and a romantic view of the West pass up the chance to earn a profit estimated by experts at between 33 percent and 67 percent annually?

And experts were as common as Mormon crickets, demonstrating what would prove to be their breathtaking lack of expertise. One Colorado rancher wrote in the weekly *Spirit of the Times*, "I do not hesitate to say that this is the grandest opportunity for investment that can be offered. There are no uncertain risks attached to the business to eat up profits, as the losses are almost nothing and the profits many times those afforded by other investments." Von Richthofen, who claimed that beef producers could expect a profit of 156 percent over a five-year period, said in his 1885 treatise *Cattle-Raising on the Plains of North America*, "There is not the slightest element of uncertainty" in the business. "No live-stock company has ever failed to pay large dividends. . . . On the contrary, it is a known fact that many persons have made princely fortunes from this business." The idea of investing in cattle was gathering mass appeal. Among the best-selling general-interest books of 1881 was James Brisbin's *The Beef Bonanza; or, How to Get Rich on the Plains.*

Bob Parker was not opposed to getting rich on the plains, but after watching his father and so many others "face each season's dryness with anguished surprise" (pace the American writer Elizabeth Hardwick), he wanted to see why people were suddenly insisting it was so easy. One thing he discovered was that some ranches had grown larger than anything that he, or anyone else, had ever imagined. For example, the aforementioned XIT spread was said to encompass three million acres. Despite their size, though, many were still operating basically the same as they always had. Economies of scale, if they existed, were not being put to good use; bigger was assumed to be better, for reasons that had never been fully worked through. Bob also might have noticed that wishful thinking had replaced stoicism, or in some cases plain common sense, just as faraway boards of directors were replacing the traditional weathered ranch owner who ruminated on a toothpick as he sat in his front-porch rocker. What might have interested Bob most of all was that, despite what seemed like wild growth and wooly thinking, many cattle operations were, for the time being, much more valuable than they used to be—at least on paper.

The first stop Bob made after leaving Telluride was the remote and now nonexistent hamlet of Burnt Fork, Wyoming, where he may have worked on the Embar Ranch and met Elzy Lay and Harry Longabaugh, future close friends (of his, though not of each other) whose physical characteristics and personality traits would be combined by screenwriter William Goldman to form the character of the Sundance Kid. By the following spring, though, he'd moved along, on his own, to the Coad Brothers Cattle Ranch along the North Platte River in western Nebraska, where he saw the changes in the cattle business writ large. The Irish-born Coads were then in the process of selling their spread to a Boston-based company for $750,000, a staggering sum considering that the buyers were getting just 527 acres of land, albeit along with a bunch of horses and cattle. What's more, the Coads' was a classic fixer-upper: the dilapidated ranch house, its floors strewn with bits of bacon and biscuit dropped by careless cowboys, had an active skunk's nest in the kitchen.

Bob, known to be a fastidious fellow, couldn't have abided that for long, and didn't. By fall, he had moved along to Chugwater, Wyoming, home of the Swan Land and Cattle Company, where, as usual, he hired on without any trouble. The Two Bar, as cowboys called the Swan because of its inverted-U brand, was better known and much bigger than the Coads' ranch—Alexander Swan, a tall, imposing figure said to be "always surrounded by buzzing sycophants," grazed 160,000 head on a spread nearly the size of Connecticut. What had until recently been a privately owned family business was by then a highly leveraged public company, capitalized at $3 million, according to a stock offering floated in Scotland. As the corporate structure got more complicated, and pressure to show ever-greater profit increased, traditional values faded—and cows got double counted. "In our business," Swan would later explain, "we are often compelled to do certain things which, to the inexperienced, seem a little crooked." (So much for Thomas Jefferson's romantic notion that men who worked the land were beyond corruption.)

Still, if the cattle bubble was trembling in the summer of 1885— as production kept rising, and beef prices kept sinking, and Stetson-wearing accountants kept cooking the books—it had not burst quite yet. Outwardly, all seemed fine at the Two Bar upon Bob's arrival. He liked the terms there, as who wouldn't? Standard pay for "punchers" was said to be $45 a month (nearly 50 percent more than the going rate) and, according to one historian, "the promise of a rice and raisin pudding for dessert." He also liked the other Swan Company cowboys, especially a slim seventeen-year-old Illinois native named George Streeter, whom the twenty-year-old Bob called "my kid."

In a pamphlet Streeter composed in 1939 for the Federal Writers Project, he recalled how he and Bob met cute on a fine spring day just before the calf roundup when the hands were loading the chuck and bed wagons. "When I tried to put my roundup bed on the wagon, I found it too heavy, so I let it slip back on the ground," he wrote. "A big, husky fellow who had been watching me stepped up and said, 'Let me do that, kid.'" Before he could answer, Bob had "grabbed it with one hand and thrown it up with the greatest of ease. Then he turned to me and said, 'Let's put our beds together'— meaning in one roll—'and I will always do the loading.' He was a clean-looking fellow, so I said, 'All right, where is yours?'" When Bob replied that he didn't have one, Streeter laughed at the joke and said, "All right, you can sleep with me—which he did all that summer and most of the next."

Streeter liked to boast about how close he was to Bob in any number of ways. He told the bedroll story again in the 1930s to Charles Kelly for *Outlaw Trail*, and no doubt to others over a tin cup of Arbuckle coffee (canned in a factory beneath the Brooklyn Bridge but the cowboys' perennial favorite) or a shot of Old Crow. Nor was he the only man who wanted the world to know that he'd laid beside his "big," "husky," and "clean" friend of an evening. A Wyoming farmer who supplied Bob with hay for a ranch that he ran for a spell in the early 1890s, when he was experimenting with the idea of going semilegit, proudly told another writer, "I slept with Butch Cassidy!"

Of course, as noted in the previous chapter, the Cowboy code gets a bit vague when it comes to bunkmates. Friends and coworkers often shared a bed or bedroll simply for convenience or warmth. Still, it is obvious that Streeter and the hay man were enthralled with Bob and thought of him as something more than just a heat source. "I have never met a more congenial companion or a better friend," Streeter wrote: "If I got into an altercation with anyone, he would step up and say, 'I have no objection to you whipping the kid, but you'll have to whip me first.' That always settled it in my favor, for no one dared to tackle him in a rough-and-tumble fight, and I never saw his equal with a six-shooter." In a passage that might have piqued the interest of a certain Viennese medical student just then on the verge of worldwide renown, Streeter also described Bob "riding his horse at full speed around a tree while firing all six bullets in the same hole in the tree."

———

The Two Bar was fun while it lasted, which seems to have been roughly a year and a half. One day in the autumn of 1886, or thereabouts, a wrangler on a ranch in Forsythe, Montana, by the name of John F. Kelly stepped out the front door of the bunkhouse and saw Bob smiling at him from the saddle of an especially handsome horse. The two had worked together at a couple of "cow outfits," as Kelly called them, but they hadn't been in touch for a good many weeks. In the interim, Bob had apparently made some plans. "He asked me for a loan of twenty-five dollars to get to Butte, Montana," Kelly told a writer in the 1940s. Butte was a center of the copper mining industry, which was then benefitting from the demand for electrical wire, a new product suddenly being ordered by the mile back east, where cities had started to switch over from gaslight. If Bob was checking out all the changes the West was going through, as he indeed seemed to be, Butte was a logical destination, and Kelly, as thoroughly charmed by him as almost everyone else, was an easy mark for the money.

It turned out to be a good investment. A year later, Kelly got an envelope from Bob containing a $100 bill and a letter saying, "If you don't know how I got this, you will learn someday."

Kelly never did receive the promised clarification, but the flashy C-note and the mysterious message suggest something about Bob's circumstances in mid-1886: namely, that he had somehow come into plenty of money and was in a playful mood.

Maybe that's why in the fall of 1886 he decided to abandon his tour of far-flung Western cattle ranches and return to the Town

Without a Bellyache. But whatever the reason, he picked one hell of a winter to make the trip.

———

As a cause of death, hypothermia in those parts ranked right behind dehydration. For five months of the year, temperatures could easily plummet to thirty below. The winter of 1886–87 was particularly tough: the Big Die-Up, they would come to call it, because of all the cattle it claimed.

Initial signs of trouble—Canada geese heading south six weeks early, beavers frantically shoring up their lodges—came during the weirdly hot autumn of '86. In his book *We Pointed Them North: Recollections of a Cowpuncher*, E. C. "Teddy Blue" Abbott tells about seeing snowy owls sitting in trees and on rooftops for the first time in sixteen years. When he asked his Indian pals what they thought the birds signified, they found his ignorance amusing—and no doubt laughed again a month or so later when they saw Teddy Blue waddling around in, by his own count, twenty-one separate articles of woolen, rawhide, and sealskin clothing while complaining that he was still freezing.

Snowy owls, it turned out, meant snow. One blizzard hit Montana in early November 1886 and didn't quit, it was said, for about six weeks. We don't know where Bob was during this whiteout, but Abbott, stopping every now and then to dig out his horse, managed to reach a friend's house for Christmas dinner (deer meat and a cowboy-style plum pudding called son-of-a-gun-in-a-sack). Then it rained. Then the temperature dropped to fifty below, followed by another extended snowfall starting in January. At times the weather seemed more like a cruel burlesque of winter than the real thing. Cattle were walking off cliffs into ninety-foot drifts. On January 2, 1887, in Miles City, Montana, snowflakes came down as big as frying pans; one was measured at fifteen inches in diameter, still a world record. The spring thaw that year turned stomachs and broke hearts. Down in the gullies, cowboys found a putrid parfait of rotting cattle and stained snow. The Montana ranch where Abbott worked lost more than three-quarters of its livestock, as did Teddy Roosevelt's place in the Dakota Territory. When the storm subsided, Roosevelt rode his property for three days without seeing a live animal apart from his own horse. He wrote to his sister Anna that he was "bluer than indigo about the cattle" and called the financial setback "crippling." Throughout the West, more than a million head were killed by the cold. The Big Die-Up is what finally made the cattle bubble burst. It was also, ultimately, the reason Bob Parker went to prison. But let's not get ahead of ourselves.

The West is big. Butte, Montana, and Telluride, Colorado, sound to many easterners like basically the same place, but the distance between them is 780 miles. If Bob had a story about traveling that far that winter, we don't know it. We do know, though, that when the thaw finally came, he was already living in Telluride—and that the outlaw-memoirist Matt Warner spotted him one spring night in "the most high-toned saloon I have ever been in." Warner described Bob as "a neat-dressed cowboy hanging around the bar like he wanted to talk to me. I liked his looks and sidled over to him, and we begun to buy drinks for each other."

6

AND THEY'RE OFF

Telluride, *not a cow town,* didn't give a hoot about the busted cattle bubble, or much else. Every sundown, there was an excuse for mindless celebration. Setting the scene for his first encounter with Bob Parker in his memoir *The Last of the Bandit Riders,* Matt Warner describes a routinely raucous evening in an unidentified place that is most likely the Cosmopolitan Club, a high-end watering hole about which those two would at the very least have heard tell. The Cosmopolitan had everything you might want in an old-time Western saloon: a large portrait of a large, naked lady behind the bar, a roulette wheel, a brass rail to set your boot on, mounted deer heads with antlers on which people other than cowboys, who never took off their hats, could hang their hats. It also featured the kind of Western cliché characters Warner normally eschewed: "lily-fingered gamblers, silk-hat confidence men, pasty-faced bartenders, and pimps that parted their hair in the middle." That night, though, he didn't mind mingling with people he felt looked down on him for being a scruffy, ill-educated cowboy. Warner needed to see a man about a horse, and until he accomplished that goal and settled matters to his satisfaction, folks could think of him as they wished.

Warner's urgency related not to the buying or selling of an animal but to the arrangement of a race. An admirer of fast horses and the flashy, well-heeled men who hovered around them, he had come to town with a mare named Betty, whom he wanted to match against the local champion du jour, whomever that might be. Warner had supreme confidence in Betty, an unprepossessing mongrel he had bought for what was probably a bargain price a year earlier from a rancher in the outlaw-friendly environs of Brown's Park. He'd at first thought of her as nothing more than a fun little side project—a way for an outsider like him to dabble in the frontier version of the so-called sport of kings. But the more he trained her, in his secluded lair up in the La Sal Mountains on the Utah-Colorado border, the more of an athlete she showed herself to be, and before long, he and his sidekick, the occasional jockey Johnny Nicholson, considered her "the fastest thing on four feet"—if not the second coming of Fashion, the elegant female champion of the hoity-toity Long Island turf. With a droopy-eared, mouse-colored speed machine like Betty, he knew, a man could make himself a ton of cash.

Racing was extremely popular across America—it and boxing were the only spectator sports of any note back then—but Colorado had a reputation for being a particularly horse-crazy place; the Kentucky of the West minus the lush bluegrass. Runners, trotters, and pacers competed at fairs and festivals; neatly manicured tracks with well-appointed grandstands coordinated their schedules to create a months-long "professional" circuit; and newspapers in places like Leadville and Durango carried results and stable gossip from Epsom Downs in England, Coney Island in Brooklyn, and other far-flung racing hubs. Beyond that, and at least as much fun, were the unscheduled and not-exactly-legal races that came about when horse owners challenged one another over drinks, or in front of ladies—and threw down large sums of money along with the gauntlet. Publicized by word of mouth, and often requiring passing a bribe to local lawmen in lieu of proper licensing, these off-the-record events attracted thousands of pilgrims who often made a picnic of the day and enthusiastically joined in the "punting," winning and losing not-so-small fortunes to bookmakers and one another. In short, whether above or below board, "a horse race then," Warner wrote us, "was the biggest event in the West."

Warner was by necessity a below-board guy, owing to his status as a budding bandit. Once he had Betty trained tight as a banjo, he went looking for a foil in the form of a man who thought he had an unbeatable horse—and Telluride, a mere day's journey from his hideout and brimming with haughty "sportsmen" temporarily rich from their mining ventures, beckoned. The newcomer had only to make a few polite inquiries before he found himself on a barstool beside a man he would remember, more than fifty years later, when he sat down to write his life story (quite possibly on another bar-stool), only as Mulcahy. The man's strapping young stallion, whom everyone called simply "the Mulcahy colt," had lately been beating all comers, and, just as Warner had hoped, his owner jumped at the opportunity to race against an unheralded mare—female horses then being considered generally inferior in terms of strength and fortitude. Each man put up $500 and, because Warner had run out of cash but wanted to make things still more interesting, his pants. (Warner said he simply couldn't stop himself from betting his trusty "weather-beaten, double-bottomed" dungarees against "a fancy pair of dude pants I wouldn't be seen in.") Odd things happened in the Old West, especially as the evening wore on.

If Warner was trying to look gullible for purposes of clinching the wager, it wouldn't have been much of a stretch. Born Willard Erastus Christiansen in tiny Ephraim, Utah, he, behind the Amer-icanized alias and the vaquero bravado, was really just another poor Mormon lad with dreams of having a more exciting life than his (in this case, Danish) immigrant daddy. This was, he confessed in his book, his first trip to Telluride, or any town big enough to bustle, and, with an assist from his ghostwriter, he admitted being dazed by the "gambling dives, dance halls, and board sidewalks where thousands of strange, crazy people . . . swarmed, pulled amazing scads of money out of their pockets . . . and tricked, robbed, shot, and stabbed each other to an amazing extent." Yet despite his claims, Warner was hardly a complete naif—he'd already worked the Betty hustle a few times out in the boondocks, and his $500 grubstake came from robbing stores and rustling Mexican cattle, usually in the company of a hardened criminal named Tom McCarty. While he wasn't exactly a sophisticate, he was a natural-born con man who knew how and when to let his inner yokel shine when that worked to his benefit.

Even Bob—who happened to be standing nearby, eavesdropping—fell for the technique and thought Warner was getting in over his head with a Telluride smoothie. "I know the Mulcahy colt; it has never been beat," he told his fellow saloon patron as soon as they struck up a conversation. "You're going to lose." Seeing an additional opportunity, Warner asked if he wanted to back up his opinion with a bet. Bob said he didn't have much money on him, "but I'll bet everything I got, which is three saddle horses, my saddle, bridle, chaps, and spurs." Warner took the wager, putting his own "personal riding outfit" against Bob's motley collection of animals and gear. It was just another bar bet made by two guys who were plumb out of money. As they shook hands on their deal, though, Warner surprised his new acquaintance, and perhaps himself, by asking if Bob would like to serve as a judge for the race.

"You don't mean that," Bob said. "I'm a stranger, and I'm betting against you."

Warner dismissed the objection. "I know a square-shooting cowboy when I see one," he said. "I'd rather have you for a judge, even if you owned the Mulcahy colt, than trust one of those city pimps or gamblers."

Our boy Bob certainly did make a good impression.

———

We'll never know all the details of the race between Betty and the Mulcahy colt. No newspapers accounts exist, and Warner himself supplies only scattered details of the event. "All Telluride and the surrounding country turned out," he wrote, but whether they watched a sprint or a marathon, and whether it transpired over an oval or point-to-point course, he doesn't say. We do know, though, that the Mulcahy colt was a strong favorite in the betting, and, at the finish, "the most surprised crowd I ever saw" watched Johnny Nicholson bring Betty home a confident half length ahead of her panting rival. The margin of victory had been carefully calculated, Warner said. "I told Johnny to beat the Mulcahy colt just enough so there wouldn't be any dispute among the judges—I didn't want to discourage future races by showing what Betty could really do." Though most of the spectators had lost money on the outcome, the crowd apparently accepted the contest as legit. "As soon as they could get their breath," Warner wrote, "they cheered the winner like the good Western sports that they was."

Bob was a good sport, too. Minutes later, he appeared before Warner holding his saddle, from which his chaps, gun, and spurs dangled. "Here they are, kid," he said. "You won 'em fair." Warner, however, waved him away, saying he should consider them compensation for serving as judge and "handing me the race just like I trusted you would." Knowing that was nonsense and that Bob would keep insisting, he abruptly changed the subject—with another unexpected proposition.

"How would you like to be my partner, and [run] match races all over Colorado?"

According to Warner, Bob looked "startled, surprised, joyful, and doubtful all at once."

Some things in life actually do live up to expectations. For the little gang of hustlers who took Betty around the state, matching her against local phenoms wherever they could, and always winning, the next eighteen months proved to be every bit as fun and as profitable as they had hoped. They beat a mare called Gypsy Queen at Durango, another horse known as Cavanaugh Stud at Mancos, and many other local champions. At the start of the tour, Bob replaced Johnny Nicholson as Betty's jockey, a move that gained him a measure of fame, as he demonstrated what a bold yet gentle rider he was. Like Ennis del Mar in Annie Proulx's short story "Brokeback Mountain," "he possessed a muscular and supple body made for the horse." Bob, it was said, was able to guide a galloping thoroughbred mostly with subtle shifts of his weight, and without tugging on the bit or using a whip, an approach that Betty and the other mounts they'd brought along with them seemed to appreciate and responded to enthusiastically.

He certainly caught the attention of two young girls, Josie and Ann Bassett, when in the spring of 1888 the hunt for racing opportunities took the little caravan to Brown's Park, a notorious outlaw refuge in the northwestern corner of Colorado. "I thought he was the most dashing and handsome man I had ever seen," said Josie, who was fourteen at the time, in an interview many years later. "I was such a young thing, and giddy as most teenagers are, and I looked upon Butch as my knight in shining armor." In a nostalgic piece her sister Ann published in *Colorado* magazine in the 1950s, the "Queen of the Rustlers," as she was known in her prime, described a race in which Bob—"a slender, brown-haired young fellow, quiet and unobtrusive"—rode a sorrel gelding owned by Charlie Crouse, a prominent local rancher as well as the breeder of the estimable Betty. Bob's opponent on that occasion was a black mare from Vernal, Utah, who had beaten every challenger between there and Brown's Park. While the names of the horses escaped her after nearly six decades, Bassett did recall that both had their enthusiastic backers, who made their way to the remote valley in large numbers to see them compete. "Racing fans may assemble in greater numbers at Churchill Downs," Bassett wrote, "but never could they have gathered at spur [sic] of keener interest and excitement. Betting ran high, and the atmosphere was taut." Bob, she said, scored a "glorious victory" with Crouse's gelding on the grassy, point-to-point "Indian course" and was "hailed with enthusiastic acclaim." She also noted that all the approbation he received seemed to mean little to him. After taking a quick supper with his friends, Bob, though he never ceased to be affable and appreciative of the backslaps he was getting, skipped the postrace festivities and went directly to bed.

In Ann's opinion, Bob's tendency to keep an even keel only added to his luster. "I never saw [him] dance or get drunk, or carry a gun in sight. I am not presuming to say he was not an outlaw later. But what I do say is I had seen him many times before and after he was called an outlaw, and he was at all times a well-mannered fellow." Josie, meanwhile, observed those same traits in a less favorable light. "He was more interested in his horse than he was in me," she said, "and I was very put out by that. I went home after being snubbed by him and stamped my foot on the floor in frustration."

I don't think Bob Parker was really such a goody two-shoes. This is likely another case of a good story—saintly behavior on the part of a raffish brigand—beating out the more shaded, less fascinating truth. Over the years, each sister accused the other of being an exaggerator, and both seem to have been correct. They liked the attention they received from the newspapermen and historians who trekked to their remote ranches for interviews, and they touched up their own life stories here and there, especially in regard to their education and their relationships with prominent men, to make sure they'd be mentioned in their accounts. While it's true that quite a few of Bob's contemporaries did comment on his good manners and relative sobriety, Matt Warner, who knew him better than most, certainly didn't see Bob as an ascetic or all that different from other cowboys. "After we had won a race . . . we would trail around to every saloon, gambling dive, and dance hall in the town and treat the whole population till the community just about had all of its money back," Warner wrote. "Talk about howling, rip-roaring times; we sure had 'em."

Other credible reports of Bob being drunk and disorderly also exist. If he was indeed giving the Bassett girls the brush-off on his first trip to Brown's Park, it just might have been because they were so young. (Ann was only ten.) Also, the Bassets over time contradicted themselves on the subject of Bob's susceptibility to seduction. Ann says elsewhere that a few years after his 1888 visit, he became "my Brown's Park beau." Meanwhile, Josie, late in life, told a story of how when Bob was hiding in her father's hayloft following "the death of one of his rich uncles" [outlaw code for having pulled off a heist], he would plaintively call down to her, "I'm lonely up here! Come and keep me company. What am I going to do to keep from being bored?"

"Well," said Josie, "all I can say is that I didn't let him get bored."

For reasons that probably had to do with wanting a fresh horse, either to travel on or to flesh out his and Warner's racing operation, Bob got the notion, as they crisscrossed southwestern Colorado in June 1888, to finally reclaim Cornish. That was the colt he'd left with a rancher on the San Miguel River when he'd come into the state from Utah four years earlier. Of course, by that time, Cornish was a colt no more, and the ranch owner, whose name we don't know, seems to have barely remembered the young man who had appeared unexpectedly one day and left the animal in his care before quickly moving on with his two buddies. Bob almost certainly had not been paying for Cornish's upkeep in the interim, and now that he wanted him back, he and the rancher had to settle the question of how much was owed—or, for that matter, which one of them at that point owned the horse. For Bob, who seems to have retained some kind of proof of purchase, perhaps in the form of a bill of sale, the matter was simple and his patience for disputation short. After a brief, frustrating exchange with the rancher, he rode back to the man's barn, snapped a lead shank on Cornish's bridle, and led him away.

That hardly settled the matter, though. About a week later, Bob was arrested seventy miles north of there, in the town of Ophir, Colorado, on a warrant sworn out by the man who had cared for the horse. From there he was taken in cuffs by the sheriff to a rather tumbledown jailhouse in Montrose, the county seat. In a brief item, the local paper, a snarky weekly called the *Solid Muldoon*, reported his detention and dismissed him as a "horse marine," meaning an incompetent thief.

With no public records extant—and the *Solid Muldoon* more interested in making strained wisecracks than reporting the news—what happened next is hard to say. But because a second snippet about the matter didn't see print in the paper until some eight months later, and we have evidence of Bob being places other than the Montrose jail in the interim, it seems reasonable to assume that someone signed a surety bond allowing him to go free until a designated date in late February or early March 1889, when he was "bound over" for trial. This was the usual way justice worked in the Old West, where because of too few judges and too many miles between towns, cases moved along slowly and defendants were given a long leash. Still, it wasn't just the honor system that kept people connected to the courts; the threat of forfeiting bail money and of being designated a fugitive also served as incentives—as did, for some, the prospect of clearing one's name. Bob, in his typical fashion, wanted not just to protest his innocence but also to express his outrage at being accused. What, *him* steal something? What about his gol-darned bill of sale? Just as when he had gotten into trouble as a teenager for taking a pair of overalls from the store in Beaver, Utah, he felt insulted by the charge, and relished the chance to wave his piece of paper in some lawyer's face and stalk off proudly. There was no way that Bob Parker, with his thin skin and performative personality, would ever miss his day in court.

In the time between Bob's arrest and trial, he and Warner did their best to resume their excellent adventure, which in their eyes was not a confidence game so much as good cleanish fun—entertainment for the common folk, who loved to gamble, especially on horses. No one was forced to bet against Betty, after all, and most of what they extracted from their marks got pumped back into the local economy when they bought drinks, gambling chips, and whore visits for half the town as a way of celebrating. Nowadays we'd call it a win-win situation. If you were young and carefree, as they were, it was a rather glorious way of life, one too good to last—as they found out when they reached Cortez, Colorado, and the chemistry of their little crew began to curdle.

Cortez, in the far southwest of the state, wasn't much of a town and still isn't. In 1888 it was basically a bunch of dormitories thrown up a year or two earlier to house men digging ditches meant to divert the Dolores River into the Montezuma Valley so that farmers could grow crops and raise animals to feed the area's miners. Cortez did not have decent restaurants or comfortable hotels, but because this was Colorado, it did have horse racing, and it was at those races, on the Fourth of July, that Bob and Warner ran into Tom McCarty, the professional rustler with whom Warner had ridden on cattle raids into Mexico. Despite his shady resume (McCarty had even served time in the Nevada State Prison for robbing the railroad station at Elko), he was the classic hale fellow well met—handsome and personable, with piercing gray eyes that were often remarked upon. At first, the two old compadres, who were also former brothers-in-law (McCarty had been a neglectful and abusive husband to Warner's sister Teenie, who'd died in 1881), couldn't have been happier about the coincidence. "We drunk the saloon dry treating each other and set 'em up to the crowd," Warner wrote.

At the end of their long evening, McCarty invited the two of them, plus Johnny Nicholson and Betty's unnamed caretaker, to his cabin in the mountains eight miles outside of town, so they could rest up and plot their next venture. This seemed fortuitous—they were coming off a long ride—but the next day, after hearing more of their hilarious stories about separating suckers from their money, McCarty made it clear that when it came time for them to pull out, he wanted to go along with them.

That made things awkward. McCarty was like them in several important ways: he loved fast horses (he'd been working as a jockey at the races in Cortez) and, though not a Mormon, had spent much of his childhood in the same desolate Circle Valley region where the Parkers had settled, counting the days until he was old enough to go see the elephant. Beyond that, he was, for a criminal, definitely on the cerebral side, believing that a clever, well-plotted escape was often the difference between a successful outlaw and a penitentiary inmate.

Yet the dissimilarities between them and McCarty were too big to ignore. At thirty-five he was in a fundamentally different stage of life than Bob and Warner were at twenty or so, and even more important, he lacked a critical something that the other two both obviously possessed, albeit to varying degrees: a conscience. McCarty may have been cheerful and companionable compared with some of the barbarous loners you'd find along the Outlaw Trail; he may have believed that it was usually better, for practical reasons, to outsmart people rather than outgun them. But his heart was cold and his gray eyes strangely vacant. The prospect of taking him into their group no doubt gave them pause.

The first trouble came soon after they took off with McCarty from his mountain retreat, headed for . . . well, that was the question: Where to now, boys? Because word about Betty was spreading, and their ability to get up races seemed to be diminishing by the day, they wound up steering their caravan toward a tumbledown

Navaho village in an area known as McElmo Gulch. They guessed, correctly, that the Indians there, living apart from white society, had probably not yet heard of their mare, and, being proud of their own horses, they'd jump at the chance to beat her and in the process cash a nice bet. The McElmo Gulch Indians didn't have any legal tender to speak of, but they did have a half-blind pony known as White Face whom they greatly esteemed, and after a brief conversation, they agreed to bet the horses against each other, winner take both, along with a pile of their homemade blankets against a certain amount of the white men's bills and coins. Knowing that lots of blankets would probably be involved in whatever deal they negotiated, Bob, Warner, and McCarty had brought an empty buckboard to haul away their winnings. When the Navahos noticed the vehicle, they laughed at the white men's presumptuousness.

No one was laughing after the race, though, which Betty won easily—so easily that the Indians immediately realized they'd been hustled and refused to pay up. Bob, trying to dispel the mounting tension, put on a big smile as he tried to explain the rules. "White man win White Face," he said. "White Face belong to white man." But when one of the Indians started to lead the pony back to the village, McCarty wrestled the young brave to the ground and began beating him with a short braided riding whip that he kept tied around his wrist. Warner said he was appalled by McCarty's actions. "A man couldn't do a more foolhardy thing than that," he wrote, noting that "there was maybe two hundred bucks, squaws, and papooses there" staring down the five members of his party. It looked like the white men's best option "was to slide out of there without undue delay and keep going while the going was good." The half-blind pony and the blankets could stay right where they were.

McCarty wasn't done overreacting, though. A minute or so into the standoff, he whipped out his pistol and shot an Indian who had moved in a way he thought suspicious. Bob and his companions then pulled their own guns and braced for a counterattack—but instead of coming toward them, the villagers turned their backs and focused on their fallen comrade, whose life was ebbing away. It was strange, Warner said, but the Indians seemed to instinctively sense that enough blood had been spilled, and they would "rather not pay the price of a frightful loss of life" over a mere horse race. While the white men stood watching, they "lifted the dead man on his pony like a sack of flour, tied him there, and rode away silent."

That sad incident and the onset of winter brought the racing tour to an end. It was just as well; despite all their success on the track, everyone was flat broke and in the mood for something different. But what might that be? "Times being now rather dull," McCarty wrote in his memoir, *Tom McCarty's Own Story: Autobiography of an Outlaw*, "we thought it time to make a raid of some sort." With that vague goal in mind, the troupe rode northeast toward Denver, where there was money to be had. But now they traveled without Bob Parker, who had a court date in Montrose that he very much wanted to keep.

7

GETTING IN DEEPER

ot long after they arrived in the Mile High City, McCarty and Warner robbed Denver's First National Bank. While the caper was technically successful—they got away with $21,000—outlaw scholars have always struggled to make sense of what happened in the stodgy stone building on Sixteenth and Larimer on the morning of March 30, 1889, as it was reported in the *New York Times* and several other papers. Why, for example, did the robbers go out of their way to trick the bank president into coming from his office several blocks away to witness the crime? Why did McCarty, disguised as a crazy old coot, wave around a beaker of "nitroglycerine" (actually mineral oil) and threaten to blow up the bank instead of just whipping out his gun and demanding money? And why did Warner say yes when asked by a teller if he'd accept a $10,000 bill, a form of currency used only in interbank transfers and virtually unpassable in the outside world? By some accounts, the bizarrely complicated scheme was the brainchild of one Jim Clark, who happened to be the town marshal in Telluride. (Semi-outlaws were everywhere.) But whatever its origins, it was more a comedy of errors than a daring heist. Both McCarty and Warner left the story of the Denver robbery out of their memoirs. Butch was fortunate to have been elsewhere.

Not that he was doing such a bang-up job of staying focused and keeping things simple as he prepared to defend himself against the charge of horse thievery. Butch's goals, as he returned to Montrose, Colorado, for his day in court, were decidedly grandiose. He didn't just want to win his case; he wanted to bend the system to his will, to be pronounced innocent in a way that would underscore the absurdity of Robert LeRoy Parker, of all people, being charged in the first place. What did he have in mind, exactly? He probably didn't know, but if, after pronouncing him innocent on all counts, the judge rose up on the bench and delivered a pro-Bob (and poor Bob) stem-winder that ended with the prosecutors slouching off in irons toward the very cell that he had recently vacated—well, something along those lines would have suited him nicely.

Of course, no such thing was likely to happen, and no such thing did, which ticked him off mightily. Bob, as it turned out, was in particularly high dudgeon in late March or early April 1889, when he left the Montrose courthouse following his trial. Because the legal records are lost, and the newspaper coverage was (no doubt to his chagrin) all but nonexistent, we don't have many details beyond those in the family legends. But it's fairly clear that while he was not found guilty, he was also not exonerated as resoundingly as he would have liked. It's possible that the proceedings just fizzled; perhaps the rancher who'd accused him of stealing Cornish never appeared to press his claim, or a lack of witnesses or evidence caused the judge to bang his gavel and say "Case dismissed—next?" Or perhaps Bob was simply tried and acquitted in an expeditious and/or routine manner that to him felt anticlimactic. All we can say for certain is that the defendant was so deeply dissatisfied with the outcome that instead of taking his two horses and leaving town in a celebratory state of mind, he stomped back to his jail cell and pouted.

Word of Bob's arrest had reached Circleville, Utah, but news of his trial result did not arrive before his father set out on a ride of more than 150 miles to provide what support he could for his son. (Bad breaks like that were the story of Maxi's life.) According to family lore, when the senior Parker finally reached the jailhouse in Montrose, he found his son sitting in a cell with the door swung wide open, reading a magazine. Shrugging off the absurdity of the situation (by then, nothing Bob did surprised him), Maxi came right to the point, saying, according to Lula Betenson in her book *Butch Cassidy, My Brother*, "Come with me. Your mother has never been the same. We need you."

They certainly could have used his help back home. Ann Parker had just given birth to her thirteenth child: the future author Lula. Writing in old age (and in a state of simmering rage at Hollywood for not paying her a dime for the family story), she says that Bob briefly considered coming back to Utah. Then, remembering how constrained he had always felt on the farm, even when there were only six or seven other people sleeping in the Parker cabin ("Closed in, nothing he could get his hands on, no money, no excitement"), her brother, says Lula, shook his head, pressed a few gold pieces in Maxi's hand—"for Ma"—and turned away.

It was, as far as can be told, the last time father and son would speak.

Not long after that sad parting, Bob abandoned his jail cell sit-in and made his way to McCarty's cabin in the Mancos Mountains, where he found him and Warner batting around the idea of robbing Telluride's San Miguel Valley Bank. In his massive collection of wild conjecture self-published under the title *Butch Cassidy: The Untold Story*, Kerry Ross Boren says that the heist was all about getting revenge and restitution for investors who'd been flimflammed by the bank's president, L. L. Nunn—a group that he claims included Bob's father. Maxi supposedly had lost several thousand dollars thanks to Nunn's financial shenanigans, which had left the institution teetering on the brink of insolvency. Since the elder Parker, who spent his life scratching out an existence as a subsistence farmer, never had anything like that kind of money, and Nunn's bank was operating firmly in the black, it's hard to see any basis for Boren's fable, beyond his chronic dissatisfaction with the commonly accepted facts. In reality, the principals, after the elaborate prank they'd pulled in Denver, were of a mind to keep things simple this time—no costumes, no props, no scripted lines—though Warner still insisted that they wanted to make a statement as much as they wanted money. "One of the big things that drew us into this adventure was the chance it offered us to satisfy the old cowboy grudge against city smart alecks," Warner wrote. "We would ride right into town and show 'em who was the smartest."

Notwithstanding the robbery at the Denver First National Bank, Warner, in his book *The Last of the Bandit Riders*, describes the San Miguel Valley job as their first bank robbery, a decision (probably made by his ghostwriter) that allows him to talk more naturally about how it felt to graduate from the ranks of the common rustler. The prospect of stealing money as opposed to livestock, he says, both excited and scared them. "The adventure seemed so great it purty much took our breaths away," Warner wrote. "All of us had outlaw records and was proud of 'em and bragged to each other about 'em. But none of us had done anything yet that had put us clear outside the law . . . and put us in a position where the only way we could live was rustling and robbing. We still had one foot on the safe side of the law and got the biggest part our living from sources recognized by the law. Now we plan a robbery that may bring that big change where a man passes clear over from the condition of a half outlaw to that of an outlaw who has to depend entirely on outlaw operations to live and finds it almost impossible to get back again on the safe side of the law." Besides not referencing the Denver robbery, this passage also omits any mention of McCarty's record as a murderer and horse thief (to say nothing of his status as an ex-con). The story is neater and more dramatic that way. Beyond literary considerations, though, it probably also comforted Warner to see himself, Bob, and McCarty as true compadres—all in the same boat as they prepared to enter a lengthy stretch of rapids.

———

Preparations for the San Miguel Valley robbery took several months and, because they seem to have already blown their money from the Denver job, had to be carried out while the three made a living as ranch hands at various local livestock outfits. In early May 1889 or thereabouts, Warner and McCarty hired on at the infamous Carlisle Cattle Company, sixteen miles from the border, near Monticello, Utah. Cheerfully brazen about its reputation as a den of thieves—a newspaperman once said that to get a job there "a man had to have robbed at least three trains"—the Carlisle ran about five thousand head of mostly rustled cattle on public land illegally cordoned off with barbed wire and overseen by a pair of sketchy English brothers who flew a skull and crossbones over the bunkhouse. Ranch hands, including Bob's brother Dan, had a standing order to shoot anyone who came by to retrieve his stolen animals or attempt to herd sheep on the property (to hardcore cowmen, as we've seen, a disgusting offense). As eager young outlaws, Warner and McCarty felt at home in such a setting, and in their spare time fashioned buckskin moneybags ample enough to carry thousands of dollars in stolen loot—gear that would serve them well in the San Miguel robbery. They also built a fake haystack big enough to sleep four husky fugitives. If any of their equally shady coworkers noticed what they were up to, nobody blabbed about it.

The job of casing the bank fell naturally to Warner, who, since his earliest days in Telluride, had been fascinated with the neat little wood-frame building on Colorado Avenue, midway between Fir and Pine Streets. "I didn't know before that there was anyplace in the world with such rich trimmings and furnishings," he wrote.

The San Miguel Valley was the smaller but by far the prettier of the town's two banks, all done up in exquisite mahogany, brass, and marble fixtures meant to convey prosperity and security. Warner, having quit his job at the Carlisle after just a few weeks, dallied many an hour in that cool refuge from the town's dusty streets, "studying the layout," he wrote, and watching "piles of money" being pushed and pulled through the windows by mine executives, gamblers, and prostitutes. Each business day, he noticed, was built around distinct morning and evening rushes. "I decided," he wrote, "that the time to rob it was at noon, any day, when most of the clerks was out and there wasn't many customers in there."

Noon on Saturday would have been the absolute slack water of the banking week, a time when you might have to wake up a clerk to show him your gun, but the trio decided not to strike then because a certain mine payroll usually arrived on a Monday morning and significantly swelled the coffers. It was Bob who took note of that weekly windfall in his capacity as the "outside man," charged with studying the streets and planning the crucial early portion of the escape. Streamlining the process of getting the team out of the narrow valley in which Telluride sat was a challenge he spent more than a month addressing. One important task was the recruitment of a fourth man to hold the horses, so their riders wouldn't have to stop and untie them from a hitching post. But Bob made his job much more difficult than it had to be when he came up with a stylish maneuver that he decided just *had* to be incorporated into the plan.

The idea was pure Bobby Parker, a throwback to the childhood days on the Circleville farm, when he put on shows for his neighbors. While the other robbers could get back aboard their horses any way they pleased, Bob decided that he would remount by forgoing the trusty stirrup and making a vaulting leap from the rear. This circus maneuver, though it was sure to elicit oohs and aahs from witnesses, and might even save a few seconds, could also result, if either he or the animal moved wrongly at the critical moment, in his landing in the street and maybe breaking an arm or ankle, or at least losing more time than he stood to save. Such a trick would also necessitate several weeks of training that were best done, he knew, slap-dab (as the cowboys said) in the middle of town, under the same crowded, noisy conditions that would be in effect on the day of the heist—an activity sure to arouse suspicion. Still, because he was riding an especially fine horse at the time, a "dapple-brown" thoroughbred gelding, Warner said, that had been given to him by a typically smitten rancher whom he'd worked for briefly, and had a hunch that both he and the animal could rise to the challenge, he forged ahead. One Telluride resident, a Mrs. John Hancock, told a newspaper later that she found his daily equestrian activity down by the train station to be more than a little fishy, but if she tipped off the authorities, nothing happened. The law in that town, let us not forget, was ultimately represented by Marshal Jim Clark, who had probably helped plan the Denver First National Bank robbery. Clark, in fact, had arranged to be "away on business" on the appointed day. His hefty fee for the strategic absence was $2,300, to be paid out of the stolen funds and left under a designated log along the escape route.

———

Bob was neither Butch nor Cassidy yet, but he was inching up on the name. Harry Adsit knew him then as *Bud* Parker, a sign that the metamorphosis was in progress. Adsit was the prominent Colorado cattleman who had hired Bob to work at his place, the Spectacle Ranch, and then regretfully accepted his resignation when he felt that he had to focus on the bank job. In 1912, talking to a reporter for the *Dolores (Colorado) Star*, Adsit recalled Bob as "above average in height" and having "good features, sandy hair, piercing blue eyes, and a rapid-fire way of talking which later served him well. He cared not at all for liquor or cards," Adsit noted, "although he occasionally held the candle while the boys played poker on a saddle blanket in the open." As they sat around the campfire, Bob—or, rather, Bud—"would declare that he would make a mark in this world. And he did."

When after only two months at the Spectacle Ranch Bob fed him a lie about needing to go back to Utah to help his struggling parents, Adsit had sighed and told him to take his pick of the ranch's saddle stock. He no doubt knew that Bob, with his keen eye for horseflesh, would choose the obvious standout, the big bay gelding, and that his parting gift would thus be strikingly out of proportion to the length of time he'd served. The other wranglers would surely cock an eyebrow at that. But Adsit, like most infatuated people, didn't care about gossip. He was, as we shall see, still not done bestowing favors on a man he hardly knew.

McCarty may have been the busiest of the robbers in those months leading up to the Telluride caper. His task was to set up the relay of horses that would allow the three of them, plus their in-town horse holder, to outrun the inevitable posse. McCarty, a stickler when it came to escape tactics, wanted fresh mounts at five places along a westward route. These stations, he decided, would be separated by a mile or so at the start, and then by increasing distances as they got farther from town and the posse's horses grew increasingly tired. That meant he needed to find five trustworthy men to escort the five teams of animals to the appointed places—specks on the map called Keystone Hill, Hot Spring, West Fork, Johnston's Horse Camp, and Mud Springs—and a total of twenty horses. But not just any twenty. McCarty wanted stout, thickly muscled sprinters for the earlier, more closely bunched stops, and rangy distance runners for the later stages. Assembling this bespoke herd was no easy task, but McCarty relished the challenge of creating the right mix of animals and the chance to outwit their pursuers.

Bob, Warner, McCarty, and their hired horse holder slept somewhere in Telluride on July 24, the night before the heist. At about ten o'clock the next morning, they got their horses—who were decked out in silver-studded bridles and saddles—from a downtown livery stable and rode them slowly to a saloon across from the San Miguel Valley Bank. The men were as sharp-looking as their mounts, Warner tells us, with "silver spurs, five-gallon hats, red bandannas, flashy shirts, chaps, and high-heeled cowboy boots." The idea was to dress "top-notch, cowboy-style, like we was going to a dance instead of a holdup." Their appearance, says Warner, "was more than just pride and vainglory. There was policy and protection in it. Cowboys always dressed top-notch when they went to town on account of the girls they expected to tangle with. If we dressed that-a-way, we would be just some more cowboys riding in town to see the girls."

Inside the saloon, they each took a seat near the window, ordered a cigar and a glass of whiskey, and tried not to make obvious that they were keeping an eye on the bank. At about ten thirty, they saw the chief officer, Charles Painter, exit the building to run an errand. Perhaps other workers were out sick that day, or robberies were truly not a concern, because as unlikely as it seems, the executive's departure left only one employee, the teller, inside the bank. As soon as Painter passed by their window, the trio paid their tab, then moseyed across the street, nodding and smiling at townsfolk who indeed seemed pleased to see such a crew of clean, well-dressed cowpokes. Then they stopped for a moment in the doorway to pull their bandannas around their faces, and went in.

The job itself was fast and a bit brutal. McCarty gave the teller a check with very small handwriting, and when the man bent over to read it, McCarty grabbed his head from behind and slammed it into the counter, pulling out his revolver at the same time. The teller said later that he was told to keep quiet or suffer "the pain of instant death." While that was happening, Bob and Warner gracefully vaulted the railing that separated the public and private areas of the bank and began stuffing whatever money they saw into the cowhide bags that Warner and McCarty had made at the Carlisle Ranch. To handle the gold and silver coins on the counters, they used the toy shovels that banks in those days had lying around for that purpose. In a minute or two, they had pulled together all they could carry and were out the front door with $22,350.

The inside part of the robbery could not have gone much better. "The whole thing was done so quietly and smoothly," Charles Kelly wrote after talking to some eyewitnesses, "that considerable time elapsed before the alarm was spread and a pursuit organized." Their getaway, however, was a tad ragged. Bob, making his crowd-pleasing leap, managed to land squarely in the saddle but lost his hat in midflight. Then a moment later, McCarty, noticing the teller had disobeyed orders and followed them to the front door, shouted at the man to get back and fired at his feet. The shots startled the fourth man's horse, causing it to rear and nearly throw him. As the gang galloped away, they fired their pistols randomly into the air in order, said McCarty, "to intimidate the people we would meet." The tactic worked. Warner said he thought they'd "see the town explode in our faces with everybody in creation shooting at us." Instead, the citizens, apparently not yet aware that the bank had been robbed, "just looked on paralyzed, helpless, and dumb." Said McCarty: "This city crowd is like a bunch of babies."

Their escape, though, was just getting started. At about the five-mile mark (probably just before the third relay station), Mc-Carty's mount began limping and had to be pulled up. Fortunately for them, while they discussed what to do, a man came by driving a wagon pulled by two horses. They waved him down and told him they were going to take one of his team, but that they would pay him for it. The outlaws might not have coalesced into the Wild Bunch quite yet, but they were already showing that gang's habitual kindness to the bystanders who got caught up in their crimes—and by doing so gaining the gratitude and usually the loyalty of their not-so-victimized victims. When they left him, the man with the wagon wished them well and tipped his hat.

There was no shortage of traffic that day on their escape route along the old Keystone Road. Almost as soon as they got going again, they galloped past Harry Adsit and another man—probably his partner, Robert Porter—who'd been traveling slowly in the opposite direction. Adsit was startled and confused. Why were they spurring their horses so hard? Why was Bob hatless? Yet as always, he said later, he was pleased to see them.

"Hello, cowboys!" he called out. "What's your hurry?"

The four flew by in silence, unable to believe their bad luck at being seen by someone who knew at least two of them. "Hell's fire!" Warner quotes Bob as saying. "That feller will turn our names in as soon as he hears about the robbery!"

McCarty, as usual, had a stronger reaction. "Damnation!" he said as they galloped onward. "Why didn't I think to shoot them interfering coyotes?"

Warner, for his part, said he felt not anger but sadness. "Just that little accident made all the difference in the world to us the rest of our lives," he wrote. "It give 'em a clue so they could trace us for thousands of miles and for years. Right at that point is when we broke with our half-outlaw past, became real outlaws, burned our bridges behind us, and had no way to live except by robbing and stealing."

8

ROBBERS ROOST

The four fugitives needn't have worried so much about being seen. Those were not exactly hellhounds on their trail.

As Harry Adsit and his equally bemused colleague rode on past Bob Parker and company, the big picture of what was happening out there on the Keystone Road started coming into focus. The first thing Adsit noticed, he told a newspaperman many years later, was the sunlight glinting off a passel of Winchesters about a mile down the highway in the direction they were headed. Such a large band of rifle-carrying riders (based on the expense reports later filed to the county, there had to have been at least fifty of them) could, he thought, have meant only one thing: a posse was in hot pursuit of the four men who'd just nearly run him over.

Adsit's first instinct was to exercise caution, so that he and his partner, Porter, would not get caught in a crossfire between the deputies and their prey. The words of the then-popular English poet Owen Meredith—"Tis more brave to live than to die"—came to his mind unbidden, he said, for Adsit was an agriculturalist and a businessman (as well as an ex-seminarian who had studied to be a

Catholic priest in his native New York) and thus quite far out of his element in such dangerous situations.

The sheriff who was leading the posse was no swashbuckler himself, as Adsit couldn't help noticing when they met a few minutes later. James A. Beattle, a thirty-six-year-old mine speculator who had been hastily conscripted into the service of justice in Marshal Jim Clark's absence, was, said Adsit, "not an aggressive Wild West officer." As such, he was a fitting leader for the misfit crew of temporary deputies he'd pulled together in a half hour or so after the teller at the San Miguel Valley Bank sounded the alarm. Adsit, in his 1912 interview, dismissed the posse as a bunch of "clerks and others who would not have ridden well in a covered wagon." Beattie, perhaps realizing he was overmatched—and, though only a few miles from town, already weary of the chase—seemed eager to pass the torch of law enforcement to Adsit, who admitted he'd encountered a quartet of hell-bent horsemen only a few moments earlier.

"Here—lead out!" Beattie said, thrusting a rifle into his hands. But instead of acting on the sheriff's order, Adsit paused, pushed back his hat, and posed a question. What had the alleged perpetrators done, he wanted to know, and had they hurt anyone in the process? When a posse member piped up that they had robbed a bank but fired only at the feet of the teller to discourage him from following them, Adsit let another moment pass, then eased his mount around and began traveling in the direction of the criminals—but at a languid canter that said more about his distaste for confrontation and his high regard for "Bud" Parker than his passion for law enforcement.

———

It can be said without fear of contradiction that the initial part of the chase lacked for tension and suspense. While the deputies under Adsit's direction were dragging their hooves, the outlaws, thanks to their system of relay stations, covered a truly impressive amount of territory: more than eighty miles during their first twelve hours on the lam. They got so far ahead of their pursuers that they were able to stop occasionally—first to count and divvy up their loot (Adsit said he found $500 and $1,000 money wrappers strewn by the side of the trail), then to sample the international cuisine on offer in the melting pot that was the Wyoming Rockies. The first day, they cadged a hearty lunch from a young Italian couple, Giovanni and Clementa Sagrillo (Bob was said to have praised the woman's polenta), and took dinner with a kindly Norwegian woman named Mrs. Olren at the congeries of cabins called Johnston's Horse Camp. With no lawmen in sight, they took their time getting to their next relay station, where they would spend the night. After receiving their horses, the wranglers walked them around a bit in various directions, creating a tangle of false trails for the posse to puzzle over the next day.

Playing tricks on their pursuers was part of the fun. At least once, they walked their mounts across slick rock with gunny sacks tied over their hooves so their tracks would vanish. On another occasion, when they spotted the posse far below them, at the base of a small mountain they were about to summit, they took a stray Indian pony they had recently come upon, brought it, says McCarty in his memoir, "to the brink of the hill, fastened quite a large brush to its tail, and gave it a scare." The animal took off down the hill "with the speed of an engine," and "the noise caused by the breaking and snapping of dry timber made it sound as though we had an army of men and were all making a charge at the posse." According to Warner, "We could hear 'em yell, 'There they go!' 'That's them!' 'Don't let 'em get away!' And their guns roared and blasted. Then we could hear the clatter of their horses' hoofs pursuing that pony back in the direction of Telluride. We nearly choked to death laughing."

That poor first posse left with nothing to show for its efforts except the brown thoroughbred that Bob had ridden to the robbery and on the first miles of the escape. (Sheriff Beatty had found it wandering near one of the relay stations and claimed it as his own.) That night, with no one tracking them for the time being, they felt secure enough to make a fire; upon rising at four in the morning, they had hot coffee and bacon drippings for their corn-pone, soul-satisfying luxuries for men on the move. It was still too soon, though, to declare victory. Although they'd wound up with less money than they'd hoped for—their haul of slightly more than $22,000 suggests that the usual Monday payroll never did arrive after all—they had taken enough to keep the law fixated on them at least for a while. A $500 reward for their capture, dead or alive, piqued the interest of local bounty hunters, just as it was supposed to, and would make future campfires problematic.

Phase two of the chase would, in fact, prove to be a very different experience for the fugitives. When Adsit and Beatty moved out, a more professional bunch of pursuers moved in and generally made their lives miserable. Back in Telluride, a deputy sheriff named Wasson had started keeping close tabs on Billy Madden, the saloon keeper, with an eye toward cracking the case. Six days after the heist, he noticed Madden leaving town with a fully loaded packhorse. Wasson followed him discreetly for several hours until Madden met up with one George Brown, a cohort of Tom McCarty's who had once served as the groom for the speedy mare Betty. As they transferred the packs from Madden's horse to Brown's, the deputy moved in and arrested the pair, then took them in cuffs to the Telluride jailhouse. During the patdown, he found on Madden a note from his half brother Bert, who some witnesses had identified as the fourth man on the operation, asking for provisions to be brought to a drop-off point in the Mancos Mountains, perhaps a half day's ride away. The deputy then formed a second posse and led it to the location described in the letter. Even if Bert Madden wasn't the one who held the horses, Wasson knew, he might have worked at one of the relay stations, and thus be an accessory to the crime and a possible source of information. When the lawmen reached the designated spot, though, the only thing they found was a note nailed to a tree warning them not to push their luck and to return home immediately.

By that time, at least three or four posses were tracking the robbers as they made their way toward Moab, Utah, in search of, as one newspaper columnist put it a few years later, "pretty Mormon girls and wine from the native grape." Moab was still a long way off, though—perhaps too long for the mysterious fourth man, who dropped out at this point, leaving a core group who, needing to buck up their increasingly beleaguered spirits, began referring to themselves as "the Invincible Three."

In his landmark 1998 biography of Butch Cassidy, Richard Patterson does an almost too-thorough job of detailing the robbers' escape route following the Telluride heist. The obscure map points he cites—Roan Cliffs, Green River, "Whipsaw Flat, down near Thompson Springs," Diamond Mountain, Cannon Ball Mesa, Robbers Roost—at first boggle the mind, because those places were largely unknown outside of a small circle of condors and rattlesnakes, but they eventually become a kind of poetry. *Whirlpool Canyon, "a branch of the old Spanish Trail north of La Sal Junction," Vermillion Creek, Zenobia Peak, Cisco, Dry Valley, Crescent, Solitude.* Where the litany ultimately fails is in its ability to convey a sense of how awful the going was at ground level; how hard it was on men and horses. "In the daytime, we would sweat, fry, or sizzle under the hot desert sun, or ride for whole days with our clothes soaking wet in rainy weather," Warner wrote. He called the long scramble over the Colorado moonscape "hell proper."

What hurt most of all, though, were their feelings. "We had no idea how taking money from a bank would stir up the whole country against us and lay a dragnet for us in every state and county in the West," wrote Warner. They didn't like thinking of themselves as the bad guys. On July 4 McCarty stood on a mountaintop and, through field glasses, looked longingly at the fireworks display going on in Mancos, wishing he were back there with his old buddies.

They slept uneasily in a damp cave one night, and another night—after crossing the border into Utah and making their way back to the Carlisle Ranch—in the fake haystack McCarty and Warner had assembled just a few weeks earlier when they were young and carefree; it was hot and stuffy in there. Feeling perhaps that the narrative could use a refreshing jolt of female energy at this point, our old friend Kerry Ross Boren, that inveterate spicer-upper, says that Bob and the others had their first encounter with Ethel Place during their stay at the Carlisle. The stunning twenty-three-year-old, newly arrived from her native Ireland and supposedly still going by her real name of Laura Etta Capel as she conducted a worldwide search for her aristocratic father, had the ranch hands' hearts so aflutter that they were taking as many as two baths a month, Boren maintains—as usual, without citing any sources.

Feeling pressed by their pursuers, the three men spent only one might in Moab, staying in a hotel owned by a crusty Mormon widow named Mary A. "Maw" Darrow, who smoked a corncob pipe and was said to get only mildly upset when the Carlisle Ranch crew fired their guns in her dining room. Checking out before sunrise, they made their way to the ferry dock on the Colorado River, crawling the last hundred or so yards on their bellies "like night-prowling animals," Warner says, in case the area was being staked out by deputies. They drew no fire but found the four ferry keepers asleep by their barge on account of the early-July heat. Lester Taylor and his sons, whom the robbers knew, made a good living taking horses and people across for fifty cents each. But after Warner woke them, the oldest boy, Jick, refused to go until the sun came up, saying the river was still too high from the spring runoff to attempt the trip in darkness.

The robbers didn't like that response. "Our business lies rolling," Warner said, gesturing with his gun barrel toward the far bank.

Poppa Lester got the message and said, "Come on, boys. We'll put them across." When they reached the other side, Warner gave him one of the $20 gold pieces that had been taken from the Telluride bank.

The Taylors never forgot the generous gesture. When some thirty-five years later (during the Prohibition era) a couple of them found themselves in a speakeasy that Warner was then running in Price, Utah, and saw that he didn't recognize them and so wouldn't serve them alcohol, they made as if to leave. "Matt," one of them said as he got off his stool, "it's like we once heard you say, our business lies rolling!" Warner furrowed his brow for a moment—then roared with laughter. The Taylors drank all night for free.

About that $20 gold piece.

The Invincible Three threw money around because they wanted to be thought of as big sports and friends of the little man, but they also didn't mind having their burden lightened as well, if only by the weight of a single double eagle, as the coin was then known. As Warner says in his book, "the strangest thing of all was about that money we carried in belts next to our skins—ten thousand dollars in greenbacks and coin is amazingly heavy." On summer days, he said, "we would sweat like butchers. The sweat would roll down our bellies and backs, and the hard, heavy money belts would gall a raw ring clear around our bodies, and the money got heavier and heavier and the sore rawer and rawer every time we rode, till we thought we couldn't stand it any longer." Warner admitted that on several occasions "one or the other of us let loose and acted like a crazy man, swore like a trooper, pawed at his belt, and threatened to tear the damned thing off and throw it away." Nobody ever went quite that far, though.

———

A few days later, as they reached Whipsaw Flat, they got their first glimpse of a posse in two weeks. Looking through his field glasses,

Warner said, "I seen a deputy sitting on a horse just like me looking at me with field glasses just like I was looking at him." The lawman was actually one of six who soon began galloping in their direction. Spurring their horses away, the outlaws ducked into a natural gateway in a line of cliffs—and, said Warner, soon ran "slap-dab into a straight wall a bird couldn't fly over." They'd gotten themselves trapped in a box canyon. "They'll never take me alive!" McCarty shouted. Then, without exchanging another word, the three unslung their Winchesters, turned their horses, and rode hard toward their only way out—the same canyon "door" through which they'd entered. At the very least, they expected a hailstorm of gunfire from the men who were chasing them—but instead all they got was silence. As best as the outlaws could figure, the deputies had afforded them too much credit, figuring they would never be dumb enough to get themselves boxed. Assuming they'd be coming out the *other* end of the canyon, the lawmen had ridden around there, to an exit that didn't exist.

While the robbers may have felt momentarily exhilarated by that adventure, their horses were on their last legs. Bob, not for the first time, rued the day he'd had to leave behind the extraordinary thoroughbred that Harry Adsit had given him. Adsit said it was around this time that he got a letter from "Bud" that said, "Dear Harry: I understand the sheriff of San Miguel County is riding the dapple brown colt. I want you to tell Mr. Sheriff that this horse packed me one hundred and ten miles in ten hours across that broken country and declared a dividend of $22,580, and this will be your order for the horse. Please send him over to me at Moab, Utah, at the first opportunity." Adsit didn't follow Bob's orders precisely, but after getting the letter, he did go to James Beattie and ask that the horse be returned to him, since it bore his brand. But the sheriff declined, saying that seeing as how he hadn't been reimbursed by the county for his expenses, he was keeping the horse—and added that Harry's friend Bob Parker would have to find himself another mount.

For their immediate transportation needs, the trio turned to a band of friendly Ute Indians who lived along the White River in Colorado and always had horses for sale at fair prices. In exchange for their three sore-footed animals and a small stack of double eagles, the Indians gave them three decent but green replacements. The robbers had barely strapped on their saddles, though, when they spotted still another posse on the horizon, and hightailed it into Brown's Park, 160 miles to the west. There the reliable Charlie Crouse provided them with a secluded cabin "among thick pines and cedars near a spring," said Warner. For the next few days, they would do little besides sleep and play poker. In one game, Warner said, Bob drew three queens and pushed his money belt into the pot. Warner did the same and turned over four jacks—causing Bob to whoop with glee at the prospect of finally being free of his belt. Warner was having none of it, though. "I told him I would shoot him if he tried to make me carry another dollar of the damn stuff, so he took it back again."

Their idyll was eventually interrupted by one of Crouse's ranch hands, who knocked on the door to say that a posse was at the main house, three miles away, asking questions. The robbers hurriedly grabbed provisions and set out for what Warner called "the greatest natural rock fortress" in America: the world-class collection of canyons, mesas, and gorges known as Robbers Roost.

The Roost sits in a particularly remote and desolate portion of southern Utah. At its center, Robert Redford tells us in *The Outlaw Trail*, is "a five-mile circular flat surrounded by lookout points" that is reachable, even today, only by horse or mule. Around its perimeter, "it provided outlaws with caves in which to store their weapons, with bunkhouses, saloons, and such 'essentials' as disguised hollowed-out trees for the posting of letters and messages." If you knew where the natural springs were, you could survive there indefinitely, albeit on a diet of water and rustled beef. But "many lawmen brave or foolish enough to penetrate the refuge were lost in the mazes or perished from thirst." As Patterson says in his *Butch Cassidy* bio, "The Roost took care of its own."

The decisiveness they showed about heading there—they proceeded directly to a relatively cozy corner of the region that Warner describes as "a fine place with water and grass and shade on top of a high mesa at the end of a steep, crooked trail"—makes it clear that they'd discussed the move in advance. The only question, as Patterson notes trenchantly, is why they didn't go sooner to a spot so well defended from pesky lawmen and so much closer to Telluride than Brown's Park and several other stops on their itinerary. Patterson surmises that the delay may have had something to do with the hundred degree afternoons that occur routinely in the high desert in mid-July, and the likelihood of lawmen instinctively lining the paths to such a obvious hideout. To those good guesses we might add the fact that the money, besides weighing them down, was burning a hole in their pockets. "While we was frying, freezing, starving, and depriving ourselves of every comfort and pleasure of existence, here was all that stolen money in our belts that would buy anything we wanted, and we couldn't go anywhere or contact anybody to spend it," Warner wrote. The only thing most outlaws preferred to the thrill of stealing money, let us not forget, was the feel of it running through their fingers. And Robbers Roost was not exactly a shopper's paradise.

They stayed there from the summer of 1889 to some unknown date in the fall, or at least two of them did. If Parker family legend can be believed, Bob, perhaps in September of that year, attempted to make a trip back to his boyhood home in Circleville, about 150 miles to the southwest. His sister Lula says in her book that after months on the run, he was toying with the idea of going straight, helping his father on the farm and living a simple, anonymous existence. If that's true, it wasn't the first or the last time he would feel a strong tug toward the right side of the law. But, she says, "the closer he got to home, the weaker he felt" about his yearnings, and at a fork in the road just outside Beaver County, "his heart failed him," and he turned onto a path that would take him north of his native grounds. He knew he wasn't cut out for the hardscrabble rancher's life, Lula said, and he couldn't abide the idea of breaking from his parents a second time.

What he, in fact, needed to do, he realized during this long, solitary ride, was to distance himself from his family, start a new life—maybe with a new name. His state of mind made an accidental encounter with his kid brother Dan in the hamlet of Milford, Utah, a day or so later a less than pleasant experience. Dan, who had talked himself into a minor role in the Telluride heist as a wrangler at one of the relay stations, now tried to pitch himself as a permanent member of Bob's nascent gang. But Bob shook his head and said Dan was too slow and too stupid—basically too easy to catch. His reaction sounds uncharacteristically cruel, but Bob's grand-nephew Bill Betenson says in his book *Butch Cassidy, My Uncle*, that this "was Robert's way of protecting him from a dangerous life." It may have also been an honest assessment. A few months after Bob's rejection, Dan took up with a third-rate desperado named Bill Brown, and by the end of that year, he was on his way to federal prison in Detroit for robbing a stagecoach carrying the US mail.

———

Not long after he returned to the Roost, Bob went for supplies into Green River, Utah, a busy little stop on the Denver and Rio Grande Railroad. By then, all three of the Invincibles had seen their names in the newspapers in connection with the Telluride robbery and were trying to lay low; they thought for some reason that Bob was the least likely to be recognized, but no sooner did he walk into the general store than he bumped into an old acquaintance from Circleville. They had a brief, awkward conversation that left Bob with the impression that the man might report the encounter in hopes of sharing in a reward. Sure enough, back at the Roost a few days later, they spied a four-man posse coming from the direction of town, but also noted that the lawmen had taken a wrong turn and were heading out to, as Warner wrote, "rough, broken country where a bird could get lost and there wasn't a drop of water."

Bob and Warner, worried that the men were likely to die, tracked them down and, from a distant promontory, signaled them by firing their Winchesters into the air and pointing in the direction of a potable spring. While Sheriff Tom Fares, his deputies, and their horses drank their fill, Bob and Warner stepped out from behind a boulder with their pistols drawn. They took their guns and, because they were the Invincible Three and liked to do things with a little panache, the sheriff's pants and saddle. The old cowboys who were still chortling over the tale in the 1940s always noted that Sheriff Fares was rather sore between the thighs when he and his posse finally made it back home.

9

FRIENDS AND NEIGHBORS

Butch Cassidy and the Sundance Kid comes to a famously inconclusive conclusion, which may strike you as either refreshing for such a superslick Hollywood production or cowardly in its inability to commit. But the beginning of the film is something to behold, by general consensus a master class in expository mainstream cinema. Following the credits, the titular twosome appear, successively, looking leathered but perfectly preweathered, like expensive cowboy boots. Screenwriter William Goldman, believing that "screenplays are structure" and "the first fifteen minutes are the most important," skips over all the backstory about Mormon roots and Sundance's early life amidst stodgy Pennsylvania Dutch Lutherans and centers on what he sees as the obvious "spine" of the story: the bromance of the fully bloomed banditos.

The movie starts in medias res, with a series of short scenes that deftly sketch a pair of scoundrels so charming we'd follow them anywhere. That they are going places is never in doubt because the Cassidy character, while supremely comfortable in his own skin, comes off as nevertheless chronically restless, not just in terms of physical surroundings but also about his career. "I'm over the hill," Paul Newman (as Butch) tells Robert Redford (as Sundance), about seven minutes in—and the implication is that he would still be in his prime if he had chosen a road more traveled. The dialogue isn't brilliant (as Goldman admitted), but in the first four scenes, it is freighted and fraught; every utterance has a meaning, and all the talk tilts toward internal conflict, the hardest thing for movies to portray.

The genius of what was Goldman's first original screenplay (which in the final product is inseparable from George Roy Hill's direction and the actors' acting, because movies are always a team sport) is that we see not just the West changing before our eyes (that it was getting ever harder to be an American outlaw was the theme of that first quarter hour, Goldman has said) but also the Western movie. *Butch Cassidy* is not just about the external challenges the protagonists face—the "super posse," the Pinkertons, the mutinous gang members, and the poker opponents who swear they've been hornswaggled—it's about our doomed yearning to know one another fully or to truly know even ourselves, about "our hopeless and terrible and, sadly permanent loneliness," Goldman said.

John Wayne would probably have asked where the damn Indians were. Many in "the business" would not have approved of, or maybe even understood, the film's never explicitly articulated message. The wonder is that the team behind *Butch Cassidy* not only succeeded in packing such airy, ambiguous ideas into a popcorn-friendly buddy picaresque but also hit a bull's-eye that Goldman, who was always very ambivalent about library research, wasn't even aiming for, by achieving historical accuracy. For even if the film is for the most part silly fiction, and the final freeze-frame disappoints, *Butch Cassidy* did in the end get two very big things right: that Butch Cassidy was a man of abundant, fate-shaping charisma and that he could never stay put.

His constant movement was, it would seem to most reasonable people, I think, an attempt to scratch some kind of deep psychological itch. We can see this playing out just as starkly, if not quite as neatly as in the screenplay, in the next part of our narrative. When the Invincible Three woke up one morning in the autumn of 1889 and, after wolfing down their usual can of cold beans and bacon, realized, en bloc, that the quiet had deepened, that the tree line was now merely treelined and that the posse had gone home, the chase was officially over. They could exhale and finally imagine life in the somewhat longer term. For Warner and McCarty, that meant getting drunk and getting laid. The first thing Bob did, however, was to say that he wanted to go his own way, at least temporarily. He had a rancher friend in Wyoming named Brown, he said, and he reckoned he would bunk with him for a spell. (This may well have been Marion Francis "Mike" Brown, a small-time rustler and general hell-raiser whom Bob had worked with at the Embar a few years earlier and who was eventually shot dead by his wife, but we don't know for certain. The name was a popular outlaw alias.)

Wyoming, in any case, was the best choice in the tristate area for all three of the robbers, who were well known in Utah and wanted dead or alive in Colorado, even if they weren't still being actively pursued there. So they headed off, and stayed together until they were a mile or two outside Lander, the small (population, 737) saloon-studded seat of newly founded Fremont County—at which point Warner and McCarty waved their hats and rode on toward the distant sound of a tinkling piano, while Bob peeled off to reacquaint himself with the dependable rhythms of ranch life.

He was too skittish, though, too caffeinated by his new life of crime, to settle in anywhere, and only a week or two later, he migrated from Brown's ranch to Brown's Park, that outlaw-friendly valley where Colorado, Utah, and Wyoming tentatively touch. There he worked for his old booster Herb Bassett, one of the region's biggest beef producers, ostensibly as a farm hand but really as a kind of professional houseguest who spent most of the day reading. Bassett's home library was nearly as famous as his ridin', ropin', and rustlin' duo of daughters, Josie and Ann, would someday be—and, besides, he was the local postmaster, which meant mountains of magazines could always be found stacked in the supply room. In 1889 these would have surely included mainstream staples such as *Frank Leslie's Illustrated Newspaper* (brimming that year with woodcuts depicting dramatic scenes from the Johnstown Flood), the *National Police Gazette* (a semimonthly mélange of sex scandals and sports), and *Harper's Weekly* (which, in its October 12 issue, ran a brief article on the natural and economic wonders of Bolivia that may well have planted a seed).

And yet as much as he may have enjoyed dipping into Mark Twain, Arthur Conan Doyle, and possibly even the beautiful sixteen-year-old Josie, this period, too, was punctuated by intermittent wanderings—mostly trips north, toward the site of the current town of Dubois, Wyoming, where he was apparently scouting locations for a horse breeding business of his own. At some point, after he found a tumbledown old trapper's cabin on a tributary of the Wind River called Horse Creek, he simply quit coming back to Bassett's house, and the transition was complete; he had once again moved on. But how to account for the pull of this prototypical Podunk? Horse Creek was indeed a strange destination for a genuine "people person" such as himself—so remote, one resident wrote, that you could ride around the countryside for several days without seeing any of your "next door" neighbors. Yet for reasons we can only guess at (it was an excellent locale for raising horses, his second favorite species?), Bob had loved those lonely, undulating grasslands of the upper Wind River ever since he first encountered them on his "year abroad" in the mid-1880s, even if the price of them could be measured in the thing he loved most: human companionship.

And the Wind River community loved him back—for his cheerfulness, his generosity, and his willingness to take folks as they came, no small thing in a part of the country where some spoke Swedish, some Shoshone, and some barely spoke at all, at least not about the dark thing that had driven them so far from civilization, to start anew. Robert Waln, a farmer who claimed to have known Bob, described him in the 1960s as "a most pleasant guy to meet—friendly, congenial, and ready and willing to hold up his end of the rope." (The highest compliment an old-time Westerner could bestow.) Women competed for his attention and, in later years, bragged about being what today we'd call his main squeeze. But while he apparently attended a number of Friday-night church dances in Lander and environs and may have even gone on a few moonlight horseback rides, it seems he never squired the same maiden twice, adhering as always to his policy of being more than a little squirrelly when it came to the fair sex.

Of course, the whiff of mystery that he exuded only added to the intrigue. Eugene Amoretti Jr., scion of the wealthy Lander family whose holdings included one of the town's bigger banks, liked to tell the story of how Bob, then brand new to the area and a stranger to him, came in one day looking every inch the typical, trail-dusty cowboy—and opened an account with a deposit of $17,500. Their meeting marked a quintessentially American moment: the son of a Lancashire millworker (Bob) and the son of a Venetian aristocrat (Amoretti's grandfather had been an aide to Napoléon I) striking up a high plains friendship that would keep going, even after Bob, suddenly flat broke, went to work barely a month later on the Amoretti family's sprawling EA Ranch, mending fences, branding cattle, and doing all the usual cowboy stuff for $1 a day. Bob's fortunes would always surge and tumble like the Wind River rapids, but his relationships were generally placid. One of his closest pals from those Wyoming years was Christian Heiden, the German immigrant mentioned in chapter 2, who, at the age of sixteen or so, drove the stagecoach between the microscopic hamlet of Embar and the aspiring town of Meeteetse (not yet known as the ferret capital of the world) to help his family get by. Heiden admired

Bob's "wicked-looking Colt .45 with a big wooden handle," and idolized Bob himself, who would often make the trip with him, Heiden said, just for the fun of it, sitting in the shotgun seat, the two passing a bottle and laughing frequently as they bumped along the road adjoining the Greybull River, perhaps stopping at lunchtime to fish for trout. No one who saw them then, merrily cooking their catch on a stick, would have taken them for the pair of suicides they would both in time become.

———

There are, the astute student of outlaws will note, basically two types of stories told about Robert Leroy Parker. The first kind are the ones that, because they mix a bit of grit in with the glorification, tend to instantly ring true. In this category, we can confidently place Heiden's remembrances, which show Bob to be a friend of the little man and supportive of the still-wet immigrant. Heiden gives us a Bob we can believe in, one who'd gladly waste an afternoon getting wasted in the company of another agreeable young man: a flawed figure but, still, in a way, inspiring, for stepping off life's treadmill when the mood struck and imbibing the yarrow-scented air—a kind of backwater Anthony Bourdain. Amoretti's description of Bob, meanwhile, also fits here because it paints a realistically ambiguous picture of a man smart enough—or at least bold enough—to acquire a breathtaking amount of money ($17,500 was the equivalent of about $350,000 today), but also foolish (or unmaterialistic) enough to piss it all away. The wonder is how Bob managed to lose so much so quickly so often. We know, based on the testimony of his contemporaries, that it was, from a practical standpoint, virtually impossible for a wealthy man to *spend* his way to bankruptcy in nineteenth-century Wyoming, even if he always bought drinks for the house and overtipped his whore, as the older men advised. Land was cheap and sometimes absolutely free if you went in as a homesteader, so you couldn't really lose a bundle in real estate, the way investors sometimes did back east. Outside of Lander and a couple of other towns, as a crusty old cowboy known as Pistol Jack Rawson told an interviewer in the 1920s, there were only "four places where anything could be bought" in the entire northwestern portion of the state, "and about the most any of them carried were hootch, overalls, gloves, and a few plugs of tobacco with some cans of peaches and corned beef."

And yet for all of those built-in protections against insolvency, Bob's tendency to toggle throughout his adult life between prosperity and the daily grind of herding cows and breaking broncs has, I think, a simple explanation: he had been bit hard by the gambling bug, the same affliction that kept so many more ordinary cowboys in a state of indentured servitude, and the only addiction in those parts that approached the epidemic proportions of alcoholism. With gambling, all (bad) things are possible. There was no natural limit to the fortune a man could drop in just one night of faro, Bob's favorite game, even in a second-rate sin city like Lander or a third-rate one such as Meeteetse or Thermopolis, towns that, as they said in those parts, couldn't have a parade because there would be nobody left to watch it. And at the card tables, Bob seems to have been a mere mortal, teased but never truly favored by the gods of fortune: in the end, just another poor victim of arithmetic bucking the odds and blowing his grubstake.

I say "seems to have been" because, apart from a couple of self-aggrandizing yarns Warner tells in his book about beating Bob at a horse racing bet and then in a poker game, there are virtually no accounts of our hero suffering significant gambling losses. The legend of Butch Cassidy has coalesced in such a way over the last 130 or so years as to leave the connection between the financial peaks and valleys unexplained. We never hear of him failing and flailing, just zigging constantly between brigandry and grunt work, and we are left to draw our own conclusions, if, in fact, we even notice the discrepancy. In a way, this really is not so surprising; there would never be a market for stories in which Bob came off as ordinary and weak. What people yearned for was an example of a man who basically had life licked; a role model who could show them something about their own potential or at least protect them from their oppressors.

We can best see that desire smoldering in the second kind of stories told about Bob, the ones that are all sunlight, no shadow, and tend to sound like the teller was not merely claiming that Bob was more competent and interesting than most people you meet but was rather the kind of teetotaling Goody Two-shoes who might have helped Lord Baden-Powell found the Boy Scouts if he wasn't so darn busy robbing trains and banks. The immediate effect is either astonishment or skepticism, depending on the listener. As noted earlier, many of these tales cast Bob as a Robin Hood figure and in this way resemble myths and legends passed down through the ages and across continents about what historians call the Noble Robber: the "bad man" who helps the needy. One story that journalists and historians found circulating in the Big Horn Basin and environs circa 1925, when they started in earnest to gather information about the all-but-vanished Wild West, was an account of how George Cassidy—as Bob had, in fact, been known in those parts until, for reasons that remain unclear, he metamorphosed into Butch—had ridden hundreds of miles through a fierce snowstorm to bring influenza medicine to a neighbor named Margaret Simpson for her sick children. It didn't matter that one of Mrs. Simpson's sons said later that he couldn't remember the flu ever being a particular problem in that vicinity—or that the story bore a striking resemblance to contemporaneous newspaper reports about Balto the Siberian husky, who had led a team of sled dogs bringing desperately needed diphtheria antitoxin from Anchorage to Nome, Alaska. Old-timers insisted that Butch Cassidy had actually performed that courageous deed some thirty years earlier.

Had he?

Before we address that question, let us consider another tall-sounding tale told at around the same time by the aforementioned ranch man Robert Waln: an account of how our guy saved a young wrangler from a bully. It seems that one day when the cowboys at the Rocky Mountain Cattle Company were huddled in the bunkhouse to wait out a thunder storm, an obnoxious fellow called "Dusty" Jim McCloud got bored and tried to prod a teenage kid into a gunfight. George Cassidy, Waln said, quickly intervened, preventing the boy from getting hurt or killed. "You big four-flusher!" Cassidy supposedly said to McCloud, using a card-playing term that deserves revivification. "If you want a gunfight, just step outside where you got plenty of room to shoot, and I'll take you on!" Rather than face down George, known to be a marksman of the first water, Dusty Jim retired to the ranch office, drew his salary, and rode off into the sunset, shamed and defeated.

Among those who study banditry in an academic environment, it is generally conceded that the less shaded Noble Robber stories—that is, the ones, like the two recounted, that posit the subject as a kind of secular saint—reveal more about the teller than the subject. The historian Eric Hobsbawn has written that since time immemorial, propagators of such yarns have tended to be low-level soil tillers who are hungry for hope—hope "that justice is possible, that poor men need not be humble, helpless and meek." The heroic characters they create—either from whole cloth or by embroidering upon the perceived virtues of actual humans at large in the community—can tell us much about the inner workings of a nineteenth-century Wyoming farmer. But that really doesn't help outlaw historians very much. What Cassidy-heads need to know is how much hard truth is contained in those second kind of stories. The big question is, did the boy born on April 13, 1866, in Beaver, Utah, really grow up to be an extraordinary human being?

Oddly enough, the answer, it seems, is yes, he sure did. I say "oddly enough" because we live in a cynical time and the scholars in this discipline tend to be such sourpusses, disinclined to admit that their obsession is worthy of admiration. And, of course, it's complicated. Some of the stories told about Bob/George/Butch are obviously pure fiction—wishful thinking in narrative form—and many mix fancy with fact. But take the tales as a body of work, comb out the blatant nonsense, and you'll see that if you were a downtrodden rancher, or a struggling storekeeper, or a desiccated, wind-whipped Westerner who needed a champion to dream on, the flesh-and-blood Butch Cassidy gave you a lot to work with. He was a good guy, a *curiously* good guy, a friend to you and the bane of your oppressors—a kind of hero, really, at a time when something like war was brewing between the haves and the have-nots of the intermountain West. Even if he didn't take from the rich and give to the poor, directly.

Margaret Simpson would not need to be told any of this. Almost as soon as he arrived on Horse Creek, the fellow who'd christened himself George Cassidy began appearing at her doorstep on Jakey's Fork, just over four miles distant, to cheerfully help the forty-three-year-old housewife with her chores. She repaid him by just as cheerfully playing the role of surrogate mother to a twenty-three-year-old man. (In terms of average life expectancy, she was a senior citizen, and he was middle-aged.) His first Christmas on Horse Creek, Margaret and her husband, John, invited him over to celebrate with their family and other neighbors. George Cassidy showed up early with an armful of presents for their six children, including a bolt of cloth for their teenage daughter Ida, who, he'd noticed, liked to sew—items he'd no doubt purchased in Lander, a seventy-mile ride in each direction. He also had with him, in typical Cassidy fashion, a textbook example of bad company in the person of Al Hainer, a nondescript-looking fellow whom he introduced as his new business partner. Upon entering the Simpson house,

Hainer went directly to a corner and sat there by himself for the rest of the day, saying almost nothing. More about him ahead.

Margaret Simpson wasn't just throwing a holiday party for the locals at the end of 1889: she was helping alleviate the grinding medieval grimness of the upper Wind River, where, until she came along, December 25 was just another day to milk the cow and cross off the calendar. She seemed, perhaps more than a tad optimistically, to be declaring the area suitable for human habitation—officially settled. Her inclination to make the world a lighter, happier, more hospitable place was definitely something George Cassidy could get behind. In the 1920s, a writer named Frederick Bechdolt interviewed several people who claimed to have bellied up to the Simpsons' groaning board for that pivotal Yuletide feast. They all got wide eyed when remembering the occasion. Young Cassidy, it was said, exhibited "a spirit of frolic" of a sort rarely seen on the frontier, performing for the kids but also getting the attention of the adults. "Before dinner was on the table, those who had grinned in silence were beginning to laugh out loud," Bechdolt wrote. "The children hovered close about him. In the afternoon, there was an eggnog, and then they had games. There are old-timers who tell to this day how the cowboys of Wind River roared with laughter, and how the children shrieked with mirth, and how Butch Cassidy set the pace, with his tow-colored hair in wild disorder and his puckered blue eyes blazing."

That Christmas marked the beginning of a very harsh winter in the Basin—not as bad as the Big Die-Up of 1886–87, perhaps, yet for a good number of people and livestock, dangerous bordering on deadly. Cattle, unable to reach vegetation through the thick ice rime, began eating one another's tails. To keep their barnyard animals (and thus themselves) alive, some residents took to feeding them shreds of deer jerky mixed with straw padding from under their carpets. Might this have been the frozen season when George Cassidy carried influenza serum to the Simpson family? Possibly, but a deeper dive into local folklore reveals another, similar story about the distribution of medicine that may well be closer to what actually happened. (As hagiographers know, there is usually a lusterless truth hiding behind the miracle.) In this version of events, it was Margaret Simpson who made and perhaps sold the elixirs—homeopathic remedies for fever, coughs, and sniffles, concocted out of herbs and roots in accordance with an old family recipe—and George Cassidy who braved the blizzards and freezing temperatures to make sure her "cures" didn't go to waste. Told this way, with the serum flowing in the opposite direction and the Balto-esque heroics turned down a notch, it's a more mundane tale: no lives hang in the balance, the profit motive enters the picture, and so on. But even in this version, George Cassidy is still being selfless and doing all he can to help folks, including the Wind River invalids, for whom he must have been a sight for rheumy eyes.

Bob's specialness can be believed because it comes down to a pattern of behavior. Just as his standing up for a kid against the bullying of Dusty Jim McCloud was foreshadowed by his defense of George Streeter, the boy with the bedroll, a few years earlier, his overarching role as a friend of the downtrodden was worked out long before in the cabin in Circleville. As the oldest child in a crowded household from which the parents were often absent, Butch from an early age had to fashion himself into a benevolent authority figure, ready to referee any dispute, restore balance among the weaker and stronger, and sometimes impose justice. He also played the harmonica, read aloud from storybooks, and otherwise kept the growing brood—and himself—entertained. In the end, it was the usual things—nature and nurture—that made him the extraordinary fellow that he was.

10

THE EQUALITY STATE

It is hard to understand exactly what George Cassidy was up to from 1889 to roughly 1894, a stretch of time that the scholars, using a term that tips you off to their lack of clarity on the subject, refer to simply as "the Wyoming years." Was he trying to go straight and get the law off his back (again)? Was he doubling down on his decision to go the outlaw way? With a little research, you could make a decent case for either proposition, and sometimes, as you sift the evidence, you have to wonder if he even knew himself.

Let's start with what seems fairly certain. Cassidy remained fidgety, moving about the territory (and then, after June 1890, the state) so frenetically that at some point he just gave up pretending to have a permanent address and started getting his mail at the home of Margaret Simpson (who, being the Earth Mother/community-organizer type, served as her area's first postmaster). As usual, he visited godforsaken places that had picturesque names (Lost Cabin, Hole-in-the-Wall, Mail Camp) and reeked of turpentine and resin. (According to the historian Bernard DeVoto, most of the West smells that way, on account of the sun-warmed sage. DeVoto won the Pulitzer Prize, so I'll have to take his word for it;

my own nose begs to differ.) He went to Sheridan, Wyoming, in 1890—we know because he was fined $1 for public intoxication by its justice of the peace—and several times to Lander, too. While visiting the seat of Fremont County, according to a man who claimed to know him there, Butch "and several exuberant fellow spirits" hitched four unbroken horses to a stagecoach "filled inside with rouged women" and then hopped on top as it went "reeling down the street to the banging of their six-shooters and the shrieking of the female passengers." On a separate occasion, Butch, Al Hainer, and another man careened down Lander's Main Street in a buckboard "until they ran afoul of a hitching rack in front of Coalter's Saloon" and were thrown from the wrecked vehicle. This is quite a lot of reeling and careening for someone who is said by many to be abstemious—and I haven't mentioned yet that twice during these Wyoming years, he accidently injured people (not seriously) while offering to remove the legs from their chair or the hat from their head with his pistol.

He may have also have gone to Texas for a spell and to Nebraska. He traveled practically everywhere, it seems, but back home to Circleville—not even cleaving to the family in 1890, when his brother Arthur, another part-time jockey, died after falling off a horse at the Fourth of July races in Telluride. In truth, by then, he may no longer have been welcome at his parents' place. When interviewed by the *Beaver (Utah) Utonian* for a story about Arthur's death, the Parkers described their deceased son as their eldest, showing perhaps that they no longer publicly acknowledged Dan and Butch, as a convict and a wanted man, respectively, both sources of shame, even to Jack Mormons like them.

Butch's wanderings seem to have reflected his curious employment history. He held more jobs during this period than anyone has ever been able to count, cowboying at, among other places, the Embar, the Two Bar (a different one than he'd worked at a few years earlier), the Pitchfork, the 4H and EA Ranches, a spread belonging to a notoriously cranky fellow named Charlie Ayers over near Dixon, Wyoming, a gigantic place owned by one Tom Beason over near Opal, the Rocky Mountain Cattle Company, and the Quien Sabe over on Hoodoo Creek, which was owned by an Englishman named Wilfred Jevons, who killed himself after losing everything at the gambling tables one night in Meeteetse. George Cassidy may have even worked one winter as a butcher in the coal mining town of Rock Springs, Wyoming, a job at which he is said to have acquired the nickname Butch. (It was a rare moniker, just then coming into vogue, connoting a tough guy and sometimes, though not necessarily, connected to butchers, but this explanation seems more likely than Matt Warner's cockamamie story about his being named after a balky rifle.) His sister Lula said that the housewives of Rock Springs loved the sight of him smiling over his bloody apron and the fact that he "gave good measure" when weighing their meat.

But while his heart—and his thumbs—may have been in the right place, Butch "walked pretty much on the wild side" in Rock Springs, according to one local historian, "spending his spare time drinking and gambling in the town's numerous saloons and paying far more attention to the ladies than was his custom." One story has him breaking up a barroom brawl there and in the process saving the life, or at least preserving the proboscis, of a prominent lawyer named Douglas Arnold Preston, who will soon weave back into our tale. The general thrust of the Rock Springs stories, though, is that he made a supergood impression, as usual. Butch might have settled in there for a spell, but no, not him. As soon as the spring thaw came, he was gone.

What was his hurry? He certainly wasn't the sort who had a hard time staying employed. Tom Beason joined a veritable chorus of ex-bosses when he said, a few years later, that Butch was probably the best worker he'd ever had. "He could drive nails by shooting bullets at them," said another cattle baron. "A fine hand!" said still another. Besides being so adept with horses, ropes, and guns, Butch had a reputation for never stealing livestock from the person who was currently signing his paycheck, a real distinction in those days when everyone in the cow business was suspicious of everyone else. Who *wouldn't* be sorry to see such a man move on? If a foreman or an owner ventured to ask Butch why he was leaving so soon, and offered to rectify any problems, Butch probably dusted off his go-to sob story about being needed back in Utah on the family farm. That always made for an easier breakup: *It's not you, boss, it's me.* It also made the terms nonnegotiable. In any case, he couldn't tell the truth—which was that he had to keep moving because, rightly or wrongly, he felt like he was being pursued by the law. A young woman who saw him at a church dance in Auburn, Wyoming, at around this time said he didn't two-step even once that evening and instead kept shooting nervous glances at the front door.

It was a tense time in Butch's windswept corner of the world. Ranchers large and small still reeled from the Big Die-Up of four years earlier, when more than half of the cattle perished over the course of that merciless winter. Boarded-up store windows and abandoned mansions were common sights now, as the biggest industry in the West wobbled. The exclusive Cheyenne Club, once a posh gathering place for barons with a taste for marble-topped commodes, diamond cuff buttons, and $2 Cuban cigars, was all but abandoned, its twin tennis courts left to the tumbleweed. As one Irish visitor to Wyoming wrote in his diary in 1888, "Cheyenne dull and doleful. Surely the glory has departed. The cattle kings are gone, and Cheyenne must settle down to the humdrum life of a farmer town." After years of struggling, the once-confident English and Scottish syndicates had started pulling out—along with Montana's best-known beef-producer, Granville Stuart, who one day upped and moved to Butte and became a librarian. Desperate to generate cash and downsize their operations, the big ranchers had for a time pushed too many cows toward the slaughterhouse, driving down the price of beef (from a high of $35 to around $5 a head) and making their futures less certain still. What worried them most, however, was the steady influx of homesteaders who, for a $10 filing fee, could claim a 160-acre hunk of the public land on which the growers had been illegally but traditionally grazing their animals at no cost. The settlements, which broke up the flow of the landscape with barbwire fences and snatched away the precious water sources, seemed to sprout on a daily basis. To cattlemen, the formal land-application notices filling the Wyoming newspapers read like obituaries for a business to which they felt they had given birth. They weren't just strapped; they were emotionally wounded.

The needle was moving, and well on its way from Displeasure to Panic in 1889, when Butch arrived on the upper Wind River with his vague plan about starting a horse breeding business with his pal Al Hainer. To influential groups such as the Wyoming Stock Growers Association (WSGA), placing blame seemed of paramount importance, a priority far above understanding what was actually happening out there on the range. The way they saw things, the problem wasn't the too-long winters, the lack of rain, or the rapacious bankers and railroad barons who were threatening to put them out of business by charging excessive rates for loans and shipping; rather, it was the cowboys—like Butch—and the homesteaders who, they were sure, rustled from them with increasing frequency and nose-thumbing sass. By 1890 or so, cattlemen were using the terms *rustler* and *settler* interchangeably, often at meetings where they discussed harsh methods of dealing with the parasites previously known as neighbors and hands. If and when their minds ever cleared a bit, and their animosity flagged, the newspapers controlled by the WSGA would stoke their passion with stories of mavericks and strays as well as many head of well-herded and clearly branded cattle being siphoned away. A new breed of men who called themselves "stock detectives," and had services to sell, were also standing by to fan the ranchers' fears. Not only were rustlers robbing them blind, the detectives insisted, but the local courts were obviously rigged in favor of the common thief and would not convict anyone of stealing livestock. They noted that only about two out of ten accused rustlers were ever found guilty. All this and their dwindling bank balances made the ranchers feel that if they had any chance of surviving, they had to act fast and take the law into their own hands.

What almost none of the cattlemen ever stopped to consider, though, was the question of whether a rustling renaissance was actually under way. As I've noted, a certain amount of pilferage had always taken place on the open range, but the numbers were relatively small and the injuries for the most part offset by the big stealing from both the small and the big as much as the small stealing from the big and one another. Cattle counts always seemed to come out more or less even from one roundup to the next. Virtually every modern historian who has looked into the Wyoming "range wars" of the early 1890s has found no evidence of any fundamental change in this ebb and flow after the Big Die-Up. Even in Johnson County, Wyoming, the supposed epicenter of the epidemic, researchers don't see a rise in rustling, just a spike in paranoia brought on by poor market conditions and conspiracy theorists such as the WSGA's "kept press" and the stock detectives. If the Western courts weren't convicting people of rustling, the historians have noted, it wasn't because the judges and juries sympathized with the thieves; it was, rather, because they couldn't find any credible evidence of these crimes. At bottom, the whole brouhaha about cattle rustling was just a runaway rumor—albeit with the destructive force of a runaway train.

Knowing that the accusations were baseless makes the cattlemen's decent into depravity look especially pathetic. Aggrieved ranchers lashed out on multiple fronts, posting rewards of up to $20,000 for people convicted of rustling, but in practice settling for those merely suspected of the crime; callous bounty hunters executed dozens of innocent people. Cattlemen also blacklisted some cowboys, while forcing others to apply for homesteading grants—which they were then expected to "sell" for $1 to their employers. When some of those wranglers evidenced second thoughts about turning over their prime 160-acre parcels, they were promptly shot, hanged, or drowned.

The killings, at first sporadic and secret, became more frequent and more brazen over time, as crimes that go unpunished will. In July the pro-rancher *Nebraska State Journal* proudly presented a story, datelined Cheyenne, that told how a "reckless prairie virago of loose morals" known as Cattle Kate had been lynched along with her boyfriend James Averell. The four-man party that came to her cabin on the Sweetwater River claimed she had been trading her favors for stolen cows, accumulating a small but growing herd from area rustlers. Prostitution was legal in Wyoming at that time, and no one had actually looked into how the couple got their animals, but the paper's reporter noted nevertheless, "It is doubtful if any inquest will be held, and the executioners have no fear of being punished. The cattlemen have been forced to [do] this, and more hangings will follow unless there is less thieving." The problem with the story was that key elements weren't true. No one had ever before referred to the twenty-eight-year-old Ellen Watson as "Cattle Kate," she was not a prostitute, and she possessed a valid bill of sale for her livestock—which in a heavy Scottish brogue she had desperately insisted on showing to her accusers. "Fortified with liquor" (as a subsequent story pointed out), the self-appointed executioners botched both the hangings, turning them into slow-motion strangulations, the details of which I shall spare you. Her only crime seems to have been being a woman with a bunch of cows out back; Averell was an equally innocent bystander. The one thing the paper was correct about was that there would be more killings.

Dozens more, in fact, and yet still not enough to satisfy the Wyoming Stock Growers Association—which in April 1892 decided to bring in an "army of invaders" to accelerate the purge. Twenty-three gunmen who'd been recruited from Paris, Texas, got off the train in Casper, combined forces with a crew of twenty-seven Wyoming stock detectives, ranchers, and newspaper reporters who'd been invited to come along, and went looking for people to kill. The first name on their hit list was that of Nate Champion, a Texan himself who had organized a group of small ranchers to push back against the WSGA and who had been involved in various minor disputes with some of its members. Champion, a well-liked former cowboy who ran a herd of just two hundred cattle, had survived an attack a year earlier when four stock detectives stormed his cabin in the Hole-in-the-Wall region in the middle of the night and ordered him at gunpoint to come with them. Pretending to stretch as he got out of bed, he had instead grabbed his pistol and begun blasting away. Three detectives had run for their lives, dragging the fourth, who died of his wounds a few weeks later.

Now the Johnson County invaders came calling with at least forty armed men at the cabin that Champion used as his ranch headquarters on the middle fork of the Powder River near Kaycee, Wyoming. After they quickly captured two of his crew members and killed another, Champion held them off single-handedly for seven hours (while keeping a diary that is worth reading) before he jumped through a back window with a pistol in one hand and a knife in the other and was finally shot dead. A Chicago newspaperman embedded with the invaders pinned a sign to his body that said, "Thieves Beware!"

So where does our boy Butch fit into this not-un-Hollywoodish picture?

There is a difference of opinion on that.

The thing to keep in mind when we contemplate the so-called range wars—if only because the historians tend to forget it themselves—is that they took place on two tiers. Cattle got most of the ink because they were not just the number one commodity in the

West but also vitally important in Chicago, New York, and everywhere in between as food and a source of employment. But horses mattered tremendously, too, in and out of the beef business. Apart from railroads, which were in short supply west of the 100th meridian, they and mules were the only meaningful engines of transportation until the automobile arrived in the early 1900s. But they also were in a very real sense—like cars and clothing, but unlike individual cows—a medium of communication; a way to signal something about your personal taste, financial position, and social rank. Whereas with cattle only the sheer number of the horned beasts attested to your wealth and, by extension, to your worldly wisdom, the sight of just a single well-conformed, spiffily groomed, nicely tacked-out stallion could intimidate another man or titillate a woman. Horses had powers that cattle just didn't. Which made them, generally speaking, more valuable than any other animal in the West and—when you factor in that they were often left unattended for weeks on the open range and relatively easy to move around the landscape in large numbers—as stealable as apple pie.

But were they being stolen in any significant number? Or were the losses, as with cattle, largely a figment of their owners' fear? Without a doubt, many ranchers who raised horses, exclusively or in combination with cattle, thought that rustling was on the rise. "Horse stealing is going on worser and badder and more of it," the manager of the Dilworth Cattle Company, in Red Lodge, Montana, wrote in a personal letter in October 1891. "There is hardly a horse man but that has not lost heavily." By early 1892, ranchers in Montana and Wyoming were claiming that between four hundred and five hundred horses were missing, and one stockman said he had suffered $24,000 in losses. Rewards of as much as $400 a head were being offered—petulantly, one must assume, because that was far more than most horses were worth. "The whole country is infested with rustlers and their sympathizers!" said the *Livingston (Montana)*

Enterprise. Within a few weeks, the estimate of stolen horses in those two states had jumped to a thousand. The sheriff of Park County, Montana, O. P. Templeton, pooh-poohed those reports, calling them exaggerated and saying it would be "next to impossible" to "run off so many horses without attracting attention."

Still, this situation did seem to be somewhat different from what was happening on the cattle side of the ledger. *Something* was causing corrals to go empty and horses carrying Wyoming brands to be cropping up everywhere from Utah to North Dakota. Even though the horsemen were probably inflating the numbers in order to elicit public sympathy and justify their hiring of "regulators" to hunt down suspected rustlers, there did, in fact, seem to be a loosely organized syndicate of thieves working a kind of relay system to move the stolen property. "Separate and distinct from the organized cattle rustlers of the border of Wyoming," said the *Billings (Montana) Gazette*, "is a horse rustling gang who has been operating on an extensive scale." Working in concert, these men filched horses that had been left out on the range, then passed them along two or three times before selling them in various far-flung towns across as many as seven Western states. Pretty easy work, it was, and safe, too, so long as you just kept moving.

Might the protagonist of our tale, the nascent local legend named Butch Cassidy—a man who'd always been a little horse crazy and a little on the make—have been part of this group? The evidence was circumstantial but strong. It had to do with the way he lived and the company he kept at a time when horse stealing was a hot topic. His very rhythms were incriminating. Butch would work someplace for a month or so, disappear, then reemerge in the company of some grifter like Jacob "Jakey" Snyder (a convicted rustler with whom he ran a small ranch for a while), Billy Nutcher (a soon-to-be fugitive who dealt in stolen horses), or Al Hainer—flashing a big wad of cash, or with $20 gold pieces braided into his horse's tail. Then he'd go broke, and the cycle would repeat.

I know what Butch would want me to say. Sitting here in Brooklyn, I feel the weight of his glare from wherever he is now; the big ranch in the sky or whatever: How could I even *think* he was guilty of such shenanigans? *Him* a horse thief? Ridiculous!

But Butch can protest and argue his case all he wants. What mattered more than whether he was actually involved in stealing horses was that a certain trio of prominent ranchers was stone cold certain that he was.

11

CAPTURED

The person *Butch Cassidy had* to worry about first and fore-most in 1891, when the big ranchers started trying in earnest to scrub him from the landscape, was a tall, wiry, bushy-bearded, and exceedingly intense native of Sangamon, Illinois, named John William Chapman. A local newspaper known as the *Stinking Water Prospector* (after the Stinking Water River, since inexplicably renamed the Shoshone) gave the size of Chapman's ranch at 1,300 deeded acres and his herd of "horned stock" at 2,000, numbers that set his sole proprietorship squarely within the "Big Cattle" class. He'd left Oregon, which was getting too crowded for his taste, for Wyoming in 1878, and, since settling in the extreme northwestern corner of the territory, had become one of its most successful horse breeders. Chapman's secret was husky Percheron stallions, which he crossed with local mongrel mares, producing an all-purpose steed able to pull a plow through the distressingly dense Wyoming sod and look good doing it. He made a small fortune selling those horses at a penny a pound.

If you thought Oregon was too congested in the mid-nineteenth century, you probably weren't the party-animal type, and Chapman wasn't. He spoke little to his wife, Alphia, or anyone else. (They had no children.) He fervently loved Jesus but relished the remoteness of his ranch house, which stood fifty miles from his nearest non-Indian neighbor. Alphia, it was said, did not see another white woman for two and a half years after they moved in, and the Indians she encountered, or spied from a distance, probably frightened her. The Indian Wars were still ongoing at that point, and if you noticed the deer stirring, you took it as a sign that one or another of the local tribes was on the move, and you went home and bolted the door. Ten years later, though—in the period now under discussion—the Indians had been more or less subdued, and the situation wasn't quite so pioneer-y. You worried about other things, like the dramatic drop-off in deer.

All was basically fine at the Chapman ranch, though, until the latter part of 1891, when some of his horses started disappearing— first in twos and threes, then in herds of tens and twenties. When that happened, Chapman got blazingly angry.

So upset was the ranch owner, in fact, that he traveled the countryside, seeking out his fellow humans. Talking with people wasn't easy for Chapman, but he wanted to see if other ranchers had incurred similar losses or picked up any information about thieves. The answers, as it turned out, were yes and yes—and in these conversations, the name of Butch Cassidy surfaced early and often.

Perhaps that was to be expected. People talked about Butch. Remember how it was frequently said that he had a reputation for not stealing from his current employer? We ought to be impressed by that, and not just because it demonstrates loyalty. It also demonstrates his place in the local culture as something of a celebrity. It was the rare cowboy who had a reputation for *anything* in those days when ranch hands were for the most part regarded as cogs in a machine that ultimately spit out rib eyes and pot roasts. The very vastness of the open spaces worked against the idea of celebrity, but Butch overcame that. Many who had not met him knew him by his ripening reputation as a man set apart by his skill and mag-netic personality; they had started associating his name with acts of derring-do—acts, in other words, like rustling from the Cheyenne Club set—and looking up to him as the baron-bedeviling rogue they themselves might have become if they had only been just a bit bolder by nature or not gotten married at age seventeen and taken on obligations. When people ran out of Butch stories to tell, they just made up more, often exaggerating his assets to express their esteem. Even Chapman, a virtual hermit, knew very well who Butch was and was said to admire him greatly in spite of his own strong feelings about rustlers. This put Chapman in a strange posi-tion, emotionally speaking, because as his investigation proceeded, he came to realize that if he was going to strike a blow against horse thieves, he would ultimately need to track down and arrest Butch. While no one thought that Butch was anything but a small part of the problem in terms of the number of horses he was handling, putting a flashy, name-brand rustler like him behind bars might have a chilling effect on the ongoing epidemic of theft. It would also allow the barons to pound their chests over their prowess as man hunters, for you had to be pretty damn slick to catch Butch Cassidy. This was the downside of being Butch: everything you did got magnified, as did the reaction to everything you did, and people made an example of you.

Chapman's search for Butch almost ended before it got going. The scuttlebutt said that the outlaw was holed up with his eternally morose pal Al Hainer on Alkali Creek, a relatively short distance from Chapman's ranch. What Butch saw in Hainer—a drunk and a skunk if there ever was one, with shallow, dark eyes and a scraggly, red beard—we'll never know. But Butch was always nonjudgmen-tal to a fault, and, during this period, they were inseparable part-ners in crime. When Chapman reached the tiny cabin where they'd supposedly been staying, he saw that the inside walls were covered with sketches of cattle brands as well as various ways those brands might be altered. It was a true den of thieves. But the most recent occupants had already vamoosed.

A few days later, while making his way through the Owl Creek Mountains, in the central part of the state, accompanied by two livestock detectives that the WSGA had thoughtfully provided him, Chapman encountered a rancher named John Thomas, who said he had seen Butch with a half dozen or so horses bearing the brand of the giant Pitchfork Ranch; he and Hainer, Thomas said, had been heading southeast, bound, they'd told him, for Evanston, Wyoming, more than two hundred miles away. Later that day, when Chapman stopped for supplies at Fort Washakie, a clerk at the Shoshone tribal agency there confirmed Thomas's story. Butch's going in that direction made sense. Evanston was a stop on the Union Pacific Railroad and a magnet for rustlers, who sold their stock to unscrupulous brokers, who then quickly moved the cows and horses onto eastward-bound trains. It was a long way to ride for six horses that weren't even your own, especially with winter coming on, but Chapman and his companions were game for the expedition. ("Plenty of powder and lead is the only thing that will break the gang up," said the *Red Lodge [Montana] Picket.*) Chapman would spend several weeks in and around Evanston, asking questions and adding helpers to his search party, but ultimately he failed to find Butch and Hainer. In mid-December, disappointed but feeling confident that the coming snows would contain them until he could resume his hunt in the spring, Chapman headed back home, stopping along the way to discuss the situation with his fellow Butch aficionados Jay Torrey and Otto Franc.

———

In most ways, those two and Chapman were not exactly peas in a pod. Torrey, the owner of the massive Embar spread, was a classic American success story—he'd put himself through Washington University Law School in Saint Louis as a fatherless teenager by selling newspapers—and an enlightened entrepreneur who bestowed scholarships upon his employees' children and provided free medical care for anyone injured on the job. In 1893 he would send his entire crew of thirty cowboys to the Chicago World's Fair so they could see the pretty girls in the Javanese village, the pretty girls in the Irish village, and ride the Ferris wheel. That same year, after winning a seat in the Wyoming State Legislature, he promptly became Speaker of the House.

Otto Franc was, in terms of personality and background, something between the uneducated, staunchly religious Chapman and the sophisticated, liberal-minded Torrey. A member of the German royal family, Count Otto Franc von Liechtenstein, to use his official name, came to the Big Horn Basin on a hunting trip in 1876 (the year General George Custer was killed there by the Sioux) and fell in love with the region. The land in those days still teemed with deer, elk, bear, and, most obviously, buffalo, which the professional hunters, with their Sharps rifles, killed by the hundreds until there were no more left. For the first few years after he started the Pitchfork Ranch on the Greybull River in 1878, Franc could—and did—shoot buffalo from his living room window, especially if he saw the bulls rubbing themselves against his precious fences.

Franc almost perfectly fit the stereotype of the cranky old cattle baron eager to fend off rustlers by any means necessary. He ran his ranch the way German chancellor Otto von Bismarck ran the Reichstag, sometimes dabbling in casual cruelty. When his saddle mare died of old age, he ordered his cook to feed it to his men and tell them it was beefsteak; while they ate, he walked among them and laughed. Another time, when he discovered someone was stealing butter from his springhouse, he rigged up a shotgun with a string so that it would fire if an intruder opened the door. Asked by an employee if that punishment wasn't "a little severe" for such a minor offense, Franc replied, "A man who would steal your butter would steal your ranch next time."

What these diverse men had in common, besides an interest in the cattle business, was an obsession with rustlers in general and Butch Cassidy in particular. Since Butch had worked at the Embar on two separate occasions, once in the mid-1880s and again only recently, Torrey knew him best and admired him most, and no doubt for that reason thought more than the others in terms of rehabilitating him so that he could someday return to the range, and maybe even the Embar Ranch, as an honest cowboy—but not, of course, until he'd learned his lesson. While the three never concerned themselves with any other individual rustler, they were all intent on sending Cassidy to prison. Butch seemed to excite them in ways they might not have understood themselves. Anyway, again, the downside of charisma.

Chapman, after wintering at his secluded ranch, resumed his search for Butch and Hainer before spring had truly arrived—before March, even. A man less consumed by the task at hand would surely have waited. The mountain trails were still treacherous, the snows still deep enough for him to consider riding as far as he could toward Evanston, then walking the rest of the way in snowshoes. He just had to keep going. The range wars of northern Wyoming were coming to a head just then. That army of Texas "stock detectives" would a few weeks later "invade" Johnson County, and the big ranchers were working themselves, and one another, into a foaming hatred of rustlers real or imagined. On February 6 the *Livingston (Montana) Enterprise* carried the headline "War on Rustlers—War on the Horse Thieves Will Soon Be Vigorously Begun in North-Eastern Montana and Northern Wyoming—Beginning of a War of Extermination!" On March 2 Franc, in his understated way, wrote in his diary: "I start for Billings to attend a meeting of the Stockmen of Northern Wyoming to consider ways to protect ourselves against the rustlers." He would take with him rifles and ammunition—"a veritable arsenal," one newspaper called it—which he would distribute to men in the field so that they could shoot suspected horse and cattle thieves on sight.

In early March Chapman and four unofficial deputies arrived in Auburn, Wyoming, 130 miles north of Evanston, and began checking out reports that Cassidy and Hainer had made their way there during the winter. It took a couple of weeks, and maybe a memory-stirring double eagle or two, but they eventually learned that the pair had hired a girl of about twelve named Kate Davis to run errands and bring them supplies from town. Chapman and company kept an eye on Kate, and when they saw her heading into the mountains on Monday, April 11—two days, by the way, after Nate Champion was killed by the invaders in Kaycee, Wyoming—they followed her from a distance to a combination ranch and sawmill at a place called Stump's Creek.

It was early morning, but Hainer was already up and outside, standing with a few other men watching logs being cut while he sipped coffee. One of the "regulators" in Chapman's party, Uinta County deputy sheriff Robert Calverly, a stout, heavily moustached man of thirty-six, came up behind them with his gun drawn, put his hand on Hainer's shoulder, and told him to come along quietly, he was under arrest. Hainer, abashed and ashen faced, did what he was told, and when Calverly asked where Cassidy was, he said, "In the cabin." Calverly then took Hainer a short distance into the woods and tied him to a tree.

Butch, by that point, seemed aware of what was happening and stepped out the back door of the cabin just as Calverly was coming in the front. "Stop, I have a warrant for your arrest—come with me!" the deputy shouted.

"I'll be damned if I do!" Butch said.

In a letter written many years later, Calverly recalled that Butch then reached into the overalls he was wearing over his regular clothing, pulled out a gun, and said, "Let's get to shooting!" The first thing he did, though, was to try to grab Calverly's gun. Meanwhile, another member of the posse named Al Cook somehow got between them, and the confrontation turned into a three-way wrestling match.

Calverly said that at one point he had the barrel of his revolver "almost touching Cassidy's stomach," but when he snapped the trigger, the gun misfired. He then snapped it three more times with the same result. On the fifth pull, the gun fired, and a bullet grazed Butch's forehead, drawing blood and knocking him to the ground where, said Calverly, "he made no further resistance."

While others attended to Butch, Calverly and Cook holstered their weapons and went around the property looking for stolen horses. The initial reports said they found eight, all but one belonging to the Greybull Cattle Company, a ranch that Otto Franc managed for a New York socialite friend of his named Archibald Rogers. Meanwhile, Cassidy sat on the ground, Calverly said, loudly bemoaning the injustice of being accused of horse thievery.

That much, of course, was only to be expected. What is striking is that as Butch babbled on, saying, according to one newspaper, "that he preferred death to prison," John Chapman—his relentless pursuer—knelt beside him on the cabin floor, tending silently to his wounds.

12

ORDER IN THE COURT

I t took *Butch a good* six weeks to recover from his arrest-related injury. In the meantime, he and Hainer languished in their shared cell at the Uinta County jail in Evanston, awaiting transfer to the bigger, more penitentiary-like lockup in Lander, the seat of Fremont County, two hundred miles to the northeast. There they would receive further processing as prisoners, get a chance to talk to their respective lawyers, and finally learn the amount of their bail—not that they stood much chance of being able to make it. They certainly couldn't afford lawyers, which is why the first thing any lawyers they hired were likely to do was to ask the judge for a continuance—that is, a postponement—of several months. The stated reasons given in such cases usually had to do with the purported need to collect evidence or witnesses, but everyone knew that often enough the delay was really just to give the accused a chance to scrape together some cash. The poorer you were in the West, the slower the wheels of justice moved, for better or worse. Butch and Hainer—despite the fact that they would be depicted by the prosecution as cunning and successful horse thieves—were so poor that they requested and got a whole year to come up with enough money to pay their lawyers.

We don't know much about the Uinta County hoosegow beyond that it was a bare-bones facility constructed five years earlier by a Saint Louis company that specialized in manufacturing budget-priced prefab human cages. (It's still in business.) Butch's and Hainer's fellow inmates consisted of a half dozen other men whose crimes were listed in the handsome, leather-bound jail register as "assault with knife," "stealing clothing," "burglary," and "crazy." On April 24, ten days into their stay, Otto Franc wrote in his diary, "I go to Wood River to swear out a warrant against two horse thieves who are arrested in Uinta County and have a TL horse in their possession." (The thieves were Butch and Hainer, of course. Wood River was a hamlet about six miles from his ranch house. TL was, for some reason, one of the brands of the Greybull Cattle Company.) Beyond that, absolutely nothing appears to have happened in their case for two months.

Theirs was not an unusual set of circumstances. The criminal justice system in Wyoming at that time was more Little Rascals than proper English common law. Courts tried to look all official and whatnot, issuing continuances, injunctions, and writs of replevin (for the restoration of personal property) like they were going out of style, doling out prison sentences, and even sending men to the gallows, but they were basically a slapdash, make-believe version of what anyone who had studied jurisprudence back east had come to expect. Many judges considered an appointment in the West to be a suicidal career move—"a form of exile," one legal historian has written—and many who did work there, because the pay was so low and bribes so frequently proffered, turned out to be neither overly bright nor particularly honest. A constant, low-grade chaos also reigned: a fair percentage of people ignored the subpoenas they were served because they could not read them or didn't want to snitch; illegal, off-the-books deals were routinely struck by prosecutors to obtain evidence; and too many cases culminated in jailbreaks, with the accused either disappearing forever or being recaptured and remanded by a torch-carrying mob to the care of "Judge Colt" or "Judge Lynch." Butch and Hainer's case in some ways got off to a typical start. Seven of the eight horses taken as evidence upon their arrest seem to have vanished, perhaps into some court clerk's corral; months of mind-numbing incarceration passed before they were formally charged with a crime; and the official records have them arriving in Lander, the site of their trial, on June 11, two weeks *before* they were officially released from the Uinta jail. As an added touch, both of their names were misspelled—as George Cassady and Albert Hayner—in the court record.

Yet whenever it was that they actually got to Lander and hooked up with their lawyers, things did become more orderly. Hainer was represented by Coker Fifield Rathbone, a thirty-one-year-old auburn-haired go-getter fast gaining political influence as publisher of the *Fremont County Gazette.* He probably came to his ne'er-do-well client via Butch's attorney, Douglas Arnold Preston, a wily veteran of the Wyoming courts and a future state attorney general also connected to the newspaper business through his then-current wife (the fourth of five), Cora, editor of the *Wind River Mountaineer.* Preston, you may recall, was the lawyer Butch was said to have saved from harm in a bar fight in Rock Springs a year or two earlier. Bald and plain-looking but in conversation a colorful sort, he represented (and under the system then in place, sometimes prosecuted) murderers, thieves, con men, and adulterers in the kind of lurid cases that the press adored. He also fancied himself something of a political reformer; at the Wyoming Constitutional Convention of 1890, Preston delivered an old-fashioned stem-winder arguing for a woman's right to mine coal, a liberty that many ladies were surprised to learn they'd been seeking.

Butch and Hainer would very much need good lawyers because the trio of ranchers pitted against them wasn't fooling around. Otto

Franc—who may or may not have remembered first meeting Butch in a bar eight years earlier, when Franc was circulating a petition to build a bridge over the Greybull River, and Butch was happy to sign it as Robert Parker—eagerly embraced his role as the official "prosecuting witness." Jay Torrey, although he had no formal involvement in the case, let it be known to the presiding judge, Jesse Knight, perhaps over drinks at a saloon adjacent to the courthouse, that he very much wanted to see Cassidy put away for a spell. (Like Franc, he seemed from the start utterly agnostic about Hainer.)

When, on July 15, an attorney for Fremont County filed an information (the rough equivalent of an indictment) asserting that Butch and Hainer "unlawfully, knowingly, and feloniously did steal, take, and carry away, lead away, and drive away" a horse from the Greybull Cattle Company on or about October 1 of the previous year, the value of the animal was set, significantly, at $40. Why the case suddenly seemed to center on a single horse we don't know, but because said horse was purported to be worth more than $25, the charge remained grand larceny. This in part justified the relatively high bail of $400 that was set for each man at the same hearing. As expected, neither could come up with anything near that amount, so Rathbone and Preston, who presumably had chits they could call in, arranged for four Lander businessmen to kick in money for what's known as a surety bond. It was, in the end, not all that big a favor, since Butch couldn't be considered much of a flight risk. Given his overwhelming desire to make his case, clear his name, and publicly denounce his accusers as mean-spirited morons, there was little doubt that he'd be back in court in Lander on June 19, well rested, freshly shaved, and ready to assist in his own acquittal.

But while Butch didn't have any intention of running from the law, neither did he avoid trouble during the interregnum. On March 6, 1893, an Embar cowboy spotted him and his friend Billy Nutcher riding a pair of horses belonging to Jay Torrey's ranch on the open range near Meeteetse. The cowboy told the foreman, who told his brother, who had just been appointed deputy sheriff at a salary of $900 a year. The eager young lawman tracked down the pair and served them summonses to appear in court on May 27. It was an odd little charge that they faced: not stealing but merely riding horses that didn't belong to them. Was this part of Torrey's pattern of wanting to be hard on Butch but never really *too* hard, of always playing the Dutch uncle? It's difficult to say. What we do know is that while Nutcher failed to keep his court date, Butch appeared dutifully, pleaded guilty, and paid a $25 fine. For once, he didn't argue that he was innocent and that the officer who'd brought him to justice had lost all semblance of common sense. Maybe he was feeling confident about the more serious case that was still pending and didn't want to mess things up.

On the evening of June 20, the first day of Butch and Hainer's trial for stealing a $40 horse, *tout* Lander turned out for a party at the home of the district court clerk. It was the unofficial kickoff of the annual summer court session, the kind of lemonade-and-elderberry-punch event at which you could make endless small talk or sidle with someone to a more private area and strike a deal that would seal some poor sucker's legal fate. The *Fremont Clipper* noted that attorneys Preston and Rathbone were present, along with prosecutors James Vidal and M. C. Brown; Judge Jesse Knight; former chief justice of the Wyoming Supreme Court Willis Van Devanter; and Otto Franc, who, the paper explained was "not an attorney, simply an honorary member of the company," even though he was sometimes called "Judge." Van Devanter, now a powerful lawyer in Cheyenne, had come to town to defend a businessman client in a civil suit and also talk to Franc about the Cassidy trial. He had been one of a team of prosecutors who had convicted Butch's brother Dan Parker of robbing the US mails, and so he knew a thing or two about the defendant called Cassidy, starting with his real name. Outwardly, the legal eagles at the party seemed relaxed and sociable, and the *Clipper* reported that the entertainment was "most pleasant, consisting of games of cards, tiddle-de-wink, etc."

But, in fact, the Wyoming ranchers were increasingly worried about what was for them a symbolically important case. Van Devanter had told Franc that he didn't think a jury would convict Cassidy, an extremely likeable sort who had a halfway decent story about having bought the allegedly stolen horse from his friend Billy Nutcher. Did the ranchers have a backup plan? Actually, they did. The morning after the party, as Butch and Hainer sat down in court for the second day of their trial, they were served with a second warrant, sworn out by Franc the previous afternoon, that accused them of stealing another horse, this one from the Z-T Ranch, owned by a wealthy Englishman named Richard Ashworth, on August 28, 1891, a few months before the other alleged theft. If the men of Big Cattle didn't succeed at their first attempt to convict Butch and Hainer—or maybe even if they did—they would try, try again.

There were no court stenographers in those days—not in Wyoming, anyway—so we can only piece together what was said during the June 1893 trial from the sketchy notes in whatever remains of records and the spotty newspaper coverage of the trial. Things got off to a shaky start for the defense team of Rathbone and Preston when Judge Knight denied their request for another continuance, this one until the following month, so that two cowboys who claimed they'd seen Butch and Hainer purchase the allegedly stolen horse could be located and brought in to testify. Clearly, Knight felt that things had already been postponed long enough. He also overruled the lawyers' objection to the second arrest warrant, which had caught them by surprise. Preston and Rathbone had argued that the charge amounted to double jeopardy, but Knight pointed out that while the animal in question came from the same string that the pair had in their possession when arrested, it was a different horse owned by a different man. Whatever the verdict in this case, they would be back in court.

It is difficult to see how the initial trial consumed three days. The prosecution went first, as it always does. In flat, matter-of-fact tones, and without embroidery, M. C. Brown, a former judge, gave what the *Fremont Clipper* called "a short argument" laying out the story of how the defendants had been tracked to the sawmill on Stump's Creek, how Butch had vigorously resisted arrest, and how the horse carrying the Greybull brand had been found nearby. Then he sat down and let the defense speak.

Handing off the narrative to each other at key points, Preston and Rathbone unspooled their slightly more elaborate version of the tale. In August 1891, they said, Butch and Hainer had run into Billy Nutcher at a place in the Big Horn Basin called Mail Camp. Nutcher told them that about a year earlier, he'd bought three nice stud horses—a bay, a sorrel, and a gray—from a man in Johnson County. He'd lost track of the animals on the range for a while, then found them again just recently—but if he'd ever had any use for them, he didn't now, he said, nor did he have any convenient place to keep them. If Butch was interested, they could be found, for the time being, in a corral on a farm just a few miles from where they were standing. When Butch asked about proof of ownership (as any careful person might in those days, Preston noted), Nutcher assured him that he had a bill of sale for the animals, which he would dig up later if they were to make a deal. Did Butch want to take a look at the horses? He did. Since his Utah days, Butch had always dabbled in horse trading, and these sounded like the kind of already-broken stallions that would make for a quick sale. They repaired to the farm and struck a bargain on the spot. That was the last time the defendants had thought about the ownership of the animals, their lawyers said, until Deputy Calverly had stuck a pistol in Butch's stomach.

The defense team then rested, having kept their argument spare and straightforward, and neither offering evidence nor calling any witnesses, including the defendants. The only person they expressed disappointment at not being able to examine in open court was Nutcher, who hadn't honored the subpoena—but his not showing up, they maintained, was no big deal. Their basic argument was that their clients were innocent until proven guilty, and the prosecution had rested without making a credible case. It took the jury just two hours to come to the same conclusion and find Butch and Al Hainer not guilty.

———

Would the second trial be anything more than a replay of the first? The court proceedings started the way they usually did in Wyoming—which is to say by being postponed. Judge Knight automatically granted both sides a continuance until the fall of 1893, and then the date was pushed back again until June '94 because of the crowded docket. In the meantime, the Wyoming range war had played itself out, with a posse of small-time cattle raisers cornering the fifty-odd invaders brought in by major meat producers on ranch near Crazy Woman Creek. President Benjamin Harrison had to send in troops from nearby Fort McKinney to save the Texans.

In the wake of that embarrassing denouement, a rough version of peace would be negotiated between the large and little ranchers—but in 1893, when Butch and Hainer were having their days in court, tension between the two sides was still palpable, and cowboys were still getting shot, sent to prison, or stripped of their stock. In November of that year, just as his second trial was being postponed yet again, Butch himself got big-footed out of several horses he legitimately owned in partnership with Hainer and Jakey Snyder. The animals were seized while grazing on a ranch that had once belonged to Billy Nutcher, who was then having his property foreclosed on by several banks. Feeling, with justification, that his rights were being trampled, Butch in January 1894 filed the first in a series of lawsuits aimed at various individuals involved in the settlement. In the end, the horses were sold to repay Nutcher's debts before Butch's complaints could be addressed. He filed an appeal and at least one other suit, but his case seems to have gotten lost in the system. As he waited for his next trial, it was likely with a fresh sense of how powerful entities would always be able to manipulate the justice system as they pleased.

In retrospect, Butch and Hainer should have known something was up when the authorities didn't wait for them to come to Lander for their second trial but instead went out to get them a few days early, just to make sure they'd be present. In early June '94 Lander sheriff Charles Stough rode 130 miles to escort Butch from the Cowboy Saloon in Meeteetse. Intent on doing everything by the book, Stough formally advised Butch that he was charged with stealing a horse worth $50 and asked him to surrender his two pistols and come along with him. Prisoner 144, as Butch was officially known, did so without hesitation.

"Butch was a gentleman" the whole way, the sheriff said, noting that he did not have to be handcuffed. Stough also made a separate trip to round up prisoner 145, Hainer, who was back in the upper Wind River region, fifty or so miles north of Lander. Hainer went with him just as willingly but refused to turn over his gun. "I won't give it to you till we get to Lander," he said. "You will have no trouble with me." Stough didn't, and when they got to the courthouse, Hainer said, "Well, Charlie, here it is. Now, the reason I didn't give you the gun was because there were some men laying for me, and I wanted a chance, which I would not have had if you had all the guns." Hainer never did say whom he was worried about, but some of the scholars believe it may have been Butch, who was starting to suspect his partner of cooperating with the opposition.

The prosecution had a different look and feel the second time around, thanks to its new lead attorney, twenty-six-year-old William Lee Simpson. Billy, as the local folks called him, was the eldest son of Margaret Simpson, the woman who had taken such a shine to Butch when he first showed up in northern Wyoming. Billy had been present at the Christmas dinner of 1889 where George Cassidy had brought gifts for his family and kept everyone entertained. He had socialized with Butch on many occasions since then and also knew Al Hainer. Billy's brother Alva wrote in his memoir that Butch was still coming by the Simpson home on Jakey's Fork when he was out on bail awaiting his trials. If this hadn't been a small town in Wyoming in the 1890s, where everyone was in some way connected to everyone else, Billy probably would have been under pressure to recuse himself. By the time the second trial came around, however, he had seen more of the sausage making that passed for Western justice, and claimed that he had no compunction about leading an effort to send family friends—including his mother's personal favorite—to the penitentiary. He made it sound like he was guided by a sense of duty and fairness, but the truth was that by then he'd already forgotten his roots as the son of hardscrabble Wind River stock growers and cast his lot with the cattle barons.

It's tough to be too hard on Billy, though. Quick on the draw and even quicker with his liquor, Simpson—whose son Milward would one day be the governor and whose grandson Alan K. Simpson would represent Wyoming in the US Senate for eighteen years, from 1979 to 1995—was a conniver and survivor who personified the rough-and-tumble politics of those times. Unable to afford law school, he had taught himself the basics ("a huge accomplishment in a largely bookless land," he said), then served a brief apprenticeship under Douglas Preston before starting his own practice and running successfully for county prosecutor. His temper was volcanic. In later years, Billy would shoot a supposedly insolent banker in the ear (the man survived) and fatally pistol-whip a disgruntled constituent who accosted him on the street. In both instances, he was acquitted of criminal charges, but when he died in 1940, Wyoming newspapers ran no obituaries, apparently feeling that an accurate accounting of his life would embarrass his family. After his cemetery rites, as the mourners dispersed, a boulder rolled down a high mound of displaced dirt and crushed his casket. "Well, that will keep old Billy from getting to the bar tonight," one of his grave diggers said.

At the time of Butch and Hainer's second trial in June 1894, though, Billy was just entering his prime as a lawyer, and by all accounts, his energy was evident as he presented a much more fulsome prosecution than the defendants had faced the first time around from M. C. Brown. The distinguished Judge Brown was in the courtroom, though, along with, said the *Cheyenne Daily Leader*, "several leading lawyers from other parts of the state" and "Judge" Jay L. Torrey, to lend moral support. Once again, records are sketchy, and the newspaper coverage was curiously slight—discouraged, perhaps, by powerful men who didn't want to rouse the rabble should they succeed in their mission of putting Butch away—but it seems Simpson called as many as eleven witnesses, including Otto Franc; John Chapman; the arresting officer, Robert Calverly; "Arapaho Dave" Blanchard (a "half-breed" who said he'd seen George Cassidy acting suspiciously), and Richard Ashworth (the owner of the allegedly stolen horse), to back up the state's version of events. Simpson had a simple story to tell—a sketchy, fly-by-night sort of fellow had been found with a horse bearing another man's brand—and he was leaving nothing to chance.

When it came time for the defense to make its case, Preston did the talking for the team, and once again fell back on the story that Butch had bought whatever horses he had from (the still missing) Billy Nutcher. This time Preston called four witnesses, all of whom testified to Butch's sterling character. He was also prepared to enter into the record a much discussed but hitherto unseen piece of evidence: the bill of sale that Nutcher had passed along to Butch, to prove that he had not stolen the horses but, rather, purchased them from a man in Nebraska. Preston was actually waving around the envelope that contained the document, promising to tear it open and reveal the key to Butch's innocence, when he noticed in the courtroom the very Nebraska horse dealer who was supposed to have signed the invoice; the ranchers had brought him in to testify that he had never done business with Nutcher and that the document was a fake. Preston stopped speaking for a moment, then moved abruptly to a different line of attack as he slipped the envelope into his suit pocket.

The trial may as well have happened a thousand years ago, so sparse and fuzzy are the details, thanks to the overly casual record keeping of the court. The defense seems to have rested on Monday, July 2, with the jury reaching its verdict late the following evening. Because the next day, July 4, was a holiday, and many involved in the trial had drifted away, expecting a longer deliberation, Judge Knight said the verdict would remain sealed until Monday morning, the ninth. It would not be a quiet weekend. In a 1939 letter to Charles Kelly, author of *Outlaw Trail*, Billy Simpson wrote that early on that Sunday morning, "an attempt on my life was made by Al Hainer, a Mexican by the name of Armento, and a half-breed by the name of Lamareaux, who jerked me off of my horse in front of the livery stable at about sun-up and attempted to get me inside of the stable. They were all drunk and all defendants being tried at that term of court, except Lamareaux. I was riding a rather wild horse and . . . I held to the bridle and turned the horse around, and he kicked Lamareaux up against the stable. That gave me an opportunity to get my six-shooter, which was between my overalls and my other clothes, and they all disappeared into the barn." At that point, Hainer began beating Arapaho Dave Blanchard with a pistol and a rope. While all this was happening, Billy Simpson's future wife, Maggie, stood across the street from the stable, screaming.

Sheriff Stough heard the commotion, jumped on his horse, and galloped toward the scene. He and Simpson then proceeded to the Fremont Hotel, where Jesse Knight was staying. When they told him what had happened, he revoked Hainer's and Cassidy's bail on the spot and ordered them to be held in the town jail until the reading of the verdict. Simpson, the sheriff, and the judge also discussed a rumor then circulating about a gang of about ten "strangers"—"Matt Warner and his outfit," Simpson said in his 1939 letter—who were said to be camped on "a little stream about a mile from town," biding their time until they would sweep in and carry Butch, and maybe Hainer, too, to safety. That same night, Simpson said, a number of townsfolk gathered in F. G. Burnett's jewelry store on Lander's Main Street "intending to have it out with the outlaws." He showed up and made a little speech there, telling the assembled to be vigilant but sensible and to go home and get some sleep. The rescue of the accused horse thieves never materialized, though one newspaper said that on Monday, some of "Cassidy's friends" tried to push their way into the crowded courthouse after being told there was no more room.

The scene inside was exceedingly tense. "The mayor, the councilmen, and numerous businessmen" all came armed, said one newspaper, as did Judge Knight, Billy Simpson, "and all interested in the court," meaning mostly likely Preston and Rathbone and most of the spectators. Knight hammered his gavel to silence the room, then read the verdict: "We the jury find the above-named defendant George Cassidy guilty of horse stealing, as charged in the information, and we find the value of the property stolen to be five dollars. And we find the above-named defendant Al Hainer not guilty. And the jury recommend the said Cassidy to the mercy of the court." Knight pounded his gavel again and sentenced Butch to two years in the Wyoming State Penitentiary at Laramie. It was in some ways a relatively light punishment for the time (the maximum was ten years), and yet more than a wrist slap, since the jury had mysteriously and perhaps mistakenly reduced the value of the horse he'd stolen to a mere $5—considerably below the $25 minimum for grand larceny. Actually, strictly speaking, Butch's conviction was illegal, since he had been charged with a different, more serious crime than the one he was found guilty of, and his sentence was too severe for such a small theft. You could see this as a complete and utter miscarriage of justice, or, if you were familiar with the Wyoming court system of that era, a Monday. Douglas Preston immediately filed a motion for a new trial, but Judge Knight turned it down without comment.

Otto Franc, for his part, had no complaints about the outcome. Writing in his diary that night and working in a reference to another rustler he had testified against at the same court session, he wrote: "I return from Lander; the Wind Mill is up and pumping water into the tank near the house; At Lander I had Winkle convicted of killing one Pitchfork Bull and Cassidy for horse stealing."

13

INSIDE STORY

On a sunny summer's day, the Wyoming State Penitentiary, set out on four scrubby acres of the Laramie plains just west of town, looks almost welcoming—as well it might, since it is a tourist destination these days: a Victorian-era house of pain with a gift shop, informative signage, actors in gray-and-white prison stripes (to help you get a sense of what the place was like back in the day; picture a man sitting on the edge of a cot, head in hands), self-guided tours, everything you might expect at an official historic site except a robust throng of tourists. To be fair, crowds are generally hard to come by anywhere in Wyoming, the least populous state in the union, with 544,000 people sprinkled over some ninety-seven thousand square miles. You'd have to be a Fox News personality giving out big ol' belt buckles to draw even a gaggle. (Wyoming is also the reddest state in the union.) In Butch Cassidy's day, there were some 55,000 Wyomingites, one for every seat in today's Yankee Stadium, about 115 of whom were confined at any given time in this collection of deceptively friendly looking buildings erected in 1872, and abandoned, for all penal purposes, thirty years later, when the inmates packed up their shackles and moved to Rawlins. The prison in the 1890s was about 99 percent male and about 85 percent rustlers, but in other ways, it had a diversity of which twenty-first-century brochure writers seem proud. People came from all over the world, it seems, to make brooms and bricks here for ten hours each day, to sample the bread and water, and to be chained occasionally to the ceiling. They came from Europe, Mexico, Canada, and China, as well as, of course, every dusty little corner of Wyoming. Their numbers included Protestants, Catholics, Jews, and Mormons, as well as those listed as "religion: none," like Butch. And they were all going to be absolutely fine, every last one of them—so long as they didn't speak to one another, fall out of the lockstep formations that were required when they moved about the grounds as a group, or fail to keep their cells "in perfect order."

But the place wasn't simply awful or simply anything. Prisons are a reflection of the communities they serve, and the people of Wyoming in those days seem never to have quite figured out how mean they really wanted to be to those who violated the law. Early white settlers didn't necessarily relish the idea of locking up people—they were, after all, a pretty rough bunch themselves—but once a court system evolved, they had to find a place to put those who were found guilty. At first they tried sending prisoners to nearby army forts, which tended to have secure rooms, but after a while, the commanders of those forts complained about the practice, as people to whom you send prisoners eventually will. Plan B was to consign convicts to the Detroit House of Correction, the nearest federal facility, almost 1,300 miles away. The authorities were still doing that to some extent in the 1880s—Butch's brother Dan, you will recall, was sent there for robbing the US mails and was still there when Butch arrived in Laramie—but the cost was burdensome ($1.25 per man per week), and, besides, in order to be a real, grown-up state, one had to have a pen of one's own. So the governor petitioned Congress, which appropriated funds for the construction of the facility in 1870. Because the original territorial penitentiary remains today almost perfectly intact, we can see that its design reflected the desire of Wyoming's early image shapers to stress the sunny and the modern over the dim and the dank. Just as nineteenth-century Russia emulated Europe, nineteenth-century Wyoming aspired to be Pennsylvania or Massachusetts: that is, humane, sophisticated, secular. When it came to building a prison, though, striking the balance between civility and severity proved tricky. Their enlightened thinking and their fierce Old Testament instincts never got beyond the strange-bedfellows stage. You can see it in the buildings, which were essentially torture chambers constructed of bland, light-colored limestone with a pinkish sandstone trim. The time capsule still embedded in the prison's cornerstone, dedicated in 1873 to "evil doers of all classes and kinds," contains a bottle of Old Crow.

Butch arrived there on Sunday, July 15, 1894, too late in the day for both the Sabbath church services and the weekly washing of the prisoners' underwear. (Only the latter was mandatory.) After getting his picture taken and filling out his Bertillon card (Alphonse Bertillon was a French police officer who pioneered a method of measuring and debriefing criminals for purposes of classification), he probably went directly to his otherwise unoccupied five-by-seven-foot cell. The still-existing card says, "*Age*: 27; *Nativity*: New York City; *Occupation*: cowboy; *Height*: 5'9"; *Complexion*: light; *Hair*: dark flaxen; *Eyes*: blue; *Wife*: no; *Parents*: not known; *Children*: no; *Religion*: none; *Habits of Life*: intemperate; *Education*: common school; *Relations Address*: not known; *Weight*: 165 pounds; *Features*: regular, small deep-set eyes, 2 cut scars on back of head, small red scar under left eye, red mark on left side of back, small brown mole on calf of left leg, good build." After a supper of "simple fare" such as soup or hash, he probably crawled into his canvas hammock and fell asleep.

The trip there had been exhausting. Butch and five other incoming inmates, one of them a sixteen-year-old horse thief named

Charlie Brown, had traveled, in the company of three guards, first by wagon from Lander to Rawlins, a bone-jarring 125 miles, then by train to Laramie, an almost equally jangly 100 more. When the warden, William Adams, met them at the Union Pacific station in Laramie that afternoon, he was shocked to see that prisoner 187, alone among the others, was not wearing shackles. Butch had said they would not be necessary, and, as usual, he'd received the benefit of the doubt. "Honor among thieves, I guess," was how he explained it to the warden. What Adams didn't know was that the night before the group had set out for Laramie, Butch had been allowed to stay in the Lander home of his prosecutor, Billy Simpson—more specifically, in the room of Billy's sister Ida.

But if Butch had received the ultimate going-away gift bestowed by kind ladies since time immemorial, there was nothing classic about the way he'd spend his time behind bars. The Wyoming State Penitentiary prided itself on being an early advocate of the Auburn system, named after a penitentiary in upstate New York that had, the officials there felt, come up with a radical way to make convicts "physically and morally" better. The basic idea was to strip prisoners of their identity, so they could create a new and improved one in the few hours each day they were not making brooms. Under the Auburn system, an inmate didn't just *have* a number, he *was* a number, which was substituted for his name during his entire incarceration. Outlaw scholars sometimes argue over whether Butch got his nickname in prison or at the butcher shop in Rock Springs, Wyoming—his Bertillon card bears the word, but it seems to have been scribbled in belatedly. Yet whatever he called himself or was called by his fellow inmates while at Laramie, to the guards and warden, he was never anything other than 187.

It was not, apparently, a number very often spit out in anger. Butch was a model prisoner, though, as always, he mixed freely with bad company. Of course, it wasn't hard in that environment to find the kind of incorrigibles who kept the disciplinary system humming. For briefly escaping via a tunnel he'd dug with a spoon, the aforementioned Charlie Brown was cuffed to the ceiling of "the dungeon" for ten days, then forced to wear a ball and chain for four months. William T. Wilcox, a professional portrait painter turned burglar whom Butch knew from his time in Sheridan, was "deprived of candles, tobacco, and reading materials for ten days for leaving his cell without permission," and later given four days in "the dark cell" for "burying in cell floor a false moustache and duplicate keys to cell door." In an institution where you could be subjected to fifteen minutes of drenching by a high-pressure water hose for sassing the guards or "failure to air and dust bedding twice a week," escapes were an everyday occurrence. The very first prisoner ever placed in the Laramie Territorial Penitentiary in 1873, a "stout built" young murderer "with a poor education" named Richard Scott, promptly ran away and was never seen again. "Escape from the penitentiary had an air that could be described as gamelike," says a present-day brochure—but it was not a game Butch chose to play, even though the prison took away the part of life he seemed to like best. "You will not be allowed to converse with each other," said a sign near the entrance to the main building, "only outside when working, and in regard to your work."

Butch, like all the other prisoners, rose at five thirty each morning, marched to the dining hall for a breakfast of "hash or stew," then put in five hours of work, either in the broom factory, the candle factory, the blacksmith shop, or on the prison farm. In the winter, he might have cut ice from a pond. The midday meal consisted of "roasted or boiled meats, fresh-baked breads, and vegetables," followed by five more hours of labor until it was time for the so-called simple fare. Everyone had to be in his solitary cell and asleep by seven thirty.

There *were* some amenities. The prison library contained 1,200 volumes, you could smoke or chew in your cell as long as you cleaned out your spit box, and, until the state leased the prison to a private operator who was interested primarily in profit, some university classes were taught. A month before Butch arrived, Warden Adams had arranged for a traveling company to present a comic operetta in the prison yard, and two months into his stay, the prisoners staged a rodeo in which Butch probably participated. At Christmas, you got a chicken dinner, a slice of pie, and a cigar.

One of the more curious things about the Wyoming state prison is that virtually none of its inmates served his full sentence. Even the worst-behaved among them—like John Madden, a rustler who'd beaten the warden with his own cane during a 1891 prisoner uprising—got some time off for "good behavior," if only a single day's worth of symbolic mercy, to send them out into the world on a positive note. Those partial pardons, however, had to be requested, and sometimes pushed for diligently by an ally on the outside who might petition politicians and prison officials. In Butch's case, it's interesting to see who worked for a reduction in his two-year sentence—and who didn't. His parents, for example, took no action on his behalf, even though (or perhaps because?) they were then in the midst of a campaign to get his younger brother Dan out of prison. The Parkers had written many letters to congressmen from Wyoming and Utah pointing out alleged technical errors in Dan's prosecution and even hired a lawyer to petition President Grover Cleveland to free Dan, who was four years into what they argued was an overly severe life sentence for mail robbery. It wouldn't be until 1897 that Dan finally received a pardon, from President William McKinley. Perhaps Maxi and Ann never pushed for Butch's freedom because, after seeing how long the process took, they felt he would have finished his two-year sentence before they could spring him. On the other hand, as Butch's biographer Richard Patterson notes, it's also quite possible that they never even knew he'd been arrested. They had fallen out of in touch with him, after all, and as far as the courts and the newspapers were concerned, he was George Cassidy, *Parents: not known.*

As for those who advocated for his early release, Butch wanted no part of them. On Monday, February 25, 1895, Jay Torrey himself came calling at the prison to visit Butch. Torrey wanted to gauge just how contrite he was feeling a little more than seven months into his stay. If he was willing to admit his guilt—and perhaps even agree to talk to young and impressionable cowboys about staying on the straight and narrow—the rancher and newly elected state representative would be willing to push the governor for a pardon. Torrey's star was then on the ascent; he had just come from a gala White House reception for the army and navy overseen by President Cleveland, and only a year later, he'd be discussed as a possible vice presidential candidate on William McKinley's first ticket. (If he'd gotten the spot, he would have become president when McKinley was assassinated in 1901.) Torrey's very presence must have caused a stir at the prison—but Butch, still resentful about the rancher's role in his conviction, refused to see him.

Butch had only somewhat less hostile feelings about another adversary turned booster, Judge Jesse Knight. On September 28, 1895, Knight typed an unsolicited six-and-a-half-page letter to Wyoming governor William A. Richards asking him to release Butch ahead of schedule. "Cassiday" had been much on his mind, the judge told the governor, as well as being a concern of Uinta County sheriff John Ward, who, after visiting him recently, came away feeling he ought to be pardoned. "Cassiday is a man that would be hard to describe," Knight wrote, "a brave, daring fellow and a man well calculated to be a leader."

After recapping for Richards the story of Butch's arrival in "the Lander country" with Al Hainer in 1889 and his 1894 conviction for horse stealing ("Judge Torrey, as well as some of the leading men of that country, being interested in the prosecution"), Knight then went on to make a convoluted, though obviously heartfelt, series of apologies for errors made by him and the prosecution in Butch's second trial. Although he never mentioned his most egregious mistake—allowing Butch and Hainer to be convicted of a crime for which they'd never been charged—he did tell the governor that he hadn't explained certain things to the jury properly and admitted he'd been mistaken in denying Douglas Preston's motion for a new trial.

What Knight's extraordinary letter conveyed most clearly was his sincere and somewhat fatherly concern for Butch. At the end of the trial, he wrote, "I talked to Cassiday a long time," telling him, "he was a man calculated to be a leader" but that he needed to be "sentenced to a reasonable term of imprisonment" lest he "return to Fremont County and prey upon the public." Summing up his plea for a pardon, Knight said, "Cassiday has gone and served a portion of his term and been an exemplary prisoner. . . . What I particularly desire is that he be given his citizenship. I would be glad," he wrote, "to assume part of the responsibility."

No record exists of a reply by Richards, nor are there any documents at Laramie relating to Butch's pardon. What we do know is that on January 19, 1896, the day Butch was released, the governor was at the prison to wish him well, lie to him about how splendid he looked in his state-issued new suit of clothes, and advise him to henceforth behave himself within the borders of Wyoming. He was getting out six months early.

2

14

ELZY

*A*ngus "Bud" McIntosh, *the assistant* cashier at Idaho's Bank of Montpelier, always called it the unluckiest moment of his life, and it was easy to see why. At precisely 3:13 p.m. on August 13, 1896, he said, right after he'd recorded his thirteenth transaction of the day, the depositing of a check for $13, a strapping fellow with a bandanna tied around his face suddenly appeared in front of his teller's window, pushed a canvas sack into his cage, and told him to fill it with money. Even though the man brandished a pistol, McIntosh tried to put him off at first by burbling something, in his heavy Scottish burr, about being fresh out of cash. But the robber only got angry, called him "a goddamn liar," and hit him very hard on the head with the barrel of his gun. Stars swirled, tears welled; poor McIntosh thought he was a goner.

In the West, though, your luck could change very quickly. From a spot near the front entrance, a voice suddenly rang out, telling the robber to *"leave that man alone!"* It wasn't the sheriff because Montpelier, an odd little town with distinct Mormon and gentile districts, was too small to have a sheriff. The speaker, unknown to McIntosh, sounded like the man who had just assaulted him, a bit angry as well as a bit bandanna muffled. *Could it be*, McIntosh wondered, *that I am being defended by* another bandit?

As it turned out, he was. Witnesses would say later that the man who'd stationed himself by the front door was sandy haired, somewhat on the stocky side, and obviously the leader. Even in that tense moment, with his gun drawn, he'd managed to calm down the customers and make it clear that while he and his friends—a group of three if you included the nervous-looking fellow standing outside with the sorrel packhorse—wanted to steal as much as they could, he didn't want anyone to get hurt.

Something was happening in Montpelier that day, something more than just another a robbery. Those nicely dressed boys were not really the Wild Bunch yet, but a hierarchy was being worked out there on the floor of the bank for everyone to see. On a peaceful summer afternoon in Idaho, a gang was born.

One of its trademarks would be careful planning. The Montpelier job had actually started a month earlier. Realizing they needed to become familiar with the bank and the town, and get the citizens accustomed to the sight of them, the three principals—Butch, Elzy Lay, and Henry "Bub" Meeks—had taken jobs on the nearby ranch owned by a Swiss-born man named Samuel Emelle, who also had a jewelry shop on Montpelier's Washington Street. This gave them an excuse to come to town, where they could case the bank and, while having a drink or two of whiskey at the general store just across the street, become a regular part of the scenery.

After eighteen months of quietly nursing his resentments in prison, Butch seemed to be feeling good about jumping back into the outlaw life with both feet. He'd pulled together a fine little team of accomplices. Bub Meeks would one day fling himself from a watchtower at an insane asylum, attempting suicide for neither the first nor last time, but for now, he was known in the bandit community as a six-foot-two gentle giant who happened to be very good around horses, a quality Butch always respected. Meeks had raised and trained the spunky little pack mare, who, once they'd loaded her down with stolen money, could be trusted to trot along after them untethered, a neat and quite useful trick. As for Elzy Lay, he was, in Butch's opinion, the outlaw equivalent of officer material—a handsome, smart, fellow book reader (he always kept one or two in his saddlebag) who by now Butch considered his closest confidante—especially since he'd cut off communication with Al Hainer, whose acquittal he now saw as a reward for turning state's evidence.

The kerfuffle involving McIntosh notwithstanding, Butch and Lay usually worked together exceedingly well. "If he and Cassidy had been entrepreneurs, I'm sure they would have been a great success," Lay's grandson Harvey Murdock (who'd met Elzy a couple of times as a kid) told me shortly before his death in 2017. "I'm sure they would have made more money than they did as outlaws." If they'd been on a football team instead of an outlaw crew, Meeks would have been the lovable equipment manager; Butch, the genius coach; and Lay, the hearthrob quarterback, owing to his physical grace and what one of his daughters called his "striking dark eyes that radiated charm."

Two years younger than Butch, Lay was the son of a Civil War veteran who farmed in Ohio before moving his family west. As a young man, he'd had found excitement as a partner in the Gambling-Hell Saloon near Fort Duchesne, as well as the kind of old-fashioned highwayman who stepped out from behind boulders to rob travelers, and, it almost goes without saying, a rustler. How he and Butch met is not known, but biographer Patterson thinks they connected in the mid-1880s when both were staying at the Bassett ranch in Brown's Park and Lay invited Butch to participate in a scheme distributing counterfeit money coming down from Canada.

Early on, he and Butch discovered they had similar values. When negotiating for a horse, for example, they would, as a goodwill gesture, always give the owner $5 or $10 more than his asking price. Once when they got roaring drunk and shot up a saloon, they came back the next day and, with heads throbbing, counted the bullet holes and gave the owner a silver dollar for each one. Meanwhile, back at the ranch, they liked to keep their sort-of girlfriends Josie and "Queen Anne" Bassett guessing about whose beau was whose. According to one neighbor, the sisters once had a "knock-down-drag-out" over which one had first dibs on Butch.

Many of the scholars think that *Butch Cassidy and the Sundance Kid*, though widely considered to be one of the all-time great buddy movies, gets the buddies seriously wrong. While Harry Longabaugh, aka the Sundance Kid, went through an awful lot with Butch and was there at the bitter end, it was Elzy Lay who ranked overall as Butch's true bestie. No one in the intermountain West would have thought otherwise until the movie came out. Harvey Murdock told me that when he and Butch's sister, Lula Parker Betenson, emerged from the Salt Lake City premiere of the film in 1969, they were still scratching their heads about all the stuff Hollywood had added and subtracted but especially the conflation of Lay and Longabaugh in the character of Sundance. While they waited outside the theater, hoping (in vain) to greet Robert Redford and Paul Newman, Lula said to Murdock, "Looks like they made over your granddaddy into the Sundance Kid."

"I know," Harvey said. "But I guess they figured who would want to go see a movie called *Butch Cassidy and Elzy Lay*?"

The summer of 1896, when the outlaws arrived in Montpelier, was a tumultuous time in America, three years into the ruinous Panic of 1893 and one month into a presidential campaign—William McKinley, who represented the Eastern Establishment, versus William Jennings Bryan, a.k.a. The Great Commoner—that felt like a struggle for the nation's soul. In southeastern Idaho, meanwhile, it was haying season. Most folks were out in the fields that sunny afternoon, leaving the streets of little Montpelier nearly bereft of horse and foot traffic—just the way Butch and company wanted it.

Even if you planned things as patiently as they did, though, you never knew how a bank or train robbery would play out. Seemingly simple heists got botched and stymied all the time. In 1892 Butch's future partner Harry Longabaugh had, with several others, attempted to rob a Great Northern Railway train near Malta, Montana, but because no one on board knew the combination to the safe, they realized only about $65 in total. Whether Butch was aware of that or even knew who the Sundance Kid was at this point, the scholars can't say, but either way, he and his friends couldn't afford to have the Montpelier robbery result in one of those comically small hauls that newspaper readers first snickered about, then read aloud to their companions.

Whatever happened in Montpelier, the pot was going to be split more than three ways. Besides the principals, a minor outlaw named William "Curly" Harris, who wasn't along for the heist but had served as a kind of consultant in the planning stages, was due to receive a portion. A much bigger chunk, in all likelihood the lion's share, would go to Butch's old compadre Matt Warner, who was just then down on his luck in a serious fashion: facing the hangman's noose, in fact, for killing two men around Vernal, Utah. It's a long story, and Warner's ghostwriter in 1937 made it even longer to fill pages after Warner died prior to the book's completion. Let's just say for now that Warner in 1896 needed a lawyer like Douglas Preston, whose price for trying to save a man from the gallows was about $3,500. Butch was basically pulling the Montpelier job for him.

———

The robbery itself was not a complicated affair. As Butch kept the half dozen or so customers calm, Lay scrambled to scoop up every last paper dollar in McIntosh's drawer, then went into the vault to grab additional bills before finally sweeping any remaining gold and silver coins off the counter. He stole everything he could see, even the Winchester rifle that McIntosh had standing in the corner by his work station. He took so much—$16,500 in cash, as it turned out—that he needed to make several trips out to the horses, with Butch clearing a path among the customers for him each time. Lay put the paper money in his own saddlebag and strapped the dozen or so sacks of gold and silver pieces to the riderless sorrel horse. When he and Meeks finally swung into their saddles, Butch told the people in the bank to stay quiet and not leave for ten minutes—then dashed out the door himself. The robbers at first proceeded slowly down Washington Street so as not to attract attention, but when they reached the town limits, they spurred their horses into a gallop, with the pack mare keeping up as best she could.

It wasn't much of a chase. The closest thing to a law enforcement official in Montpelier was a part-time process server named Fred Cruickshank, who owned neither a gun nor a horse. He was working that day at the dry goods store two blocks from the bank, folding overalls, and when word of the robbery reached him, he climbed aboard his trusty (if already obsolete) high-wheeled penny-farthing bicycle and took off in the direction of the robbers. (If the movie had to have a bicycle scene, this would have been a better one than Newman riding Katharine Ross around.) Cruickshank was forced to stop pedaling when he ran out of street, though, while the robbers continued on the trail that would have them across the border and into Wyoming in fifteen miles.

Summoned by telegraph—an innovation that was already making the Western outlaw an endangered species—the county sheriff, M. Jeff Davis, and his deputy, Mike Malone, rushed the ten miles from Paris, Idaho, to Montpelier, formed a posse, and set off in pursuit, but the seven or eight civilians they'd sworn in turned back as soon as they heard gunfire. Davis and Malone kept going—until they realized that the robbers had planted fresh horses at relay stations along their escape route, and they had no chance.

The trio's big worry in the initial stages of the escape was not that they'd get caught but that they might outrun their money. By day two, the poor sorrel, who had been laboring under her considerable burden almost from the start, was nowhere in sight. Thinking they had put too much trust in Meeks's mare, Butch and Lay grew sullen. But as they sat around their campfire that evening, with Meeks, jolly as ever, droning on about how Robin Hood once rescued one of his merry men from the sheriff of Nottingham, Lay caught sight of a tiny copper-colored speck down in the valley and let out a whoop. It was indeed the intrepid sorrel. When she finally staggered into their camp a half hour later, they stripped her of her cargo and, as a member of Meeks's family tells the tale, stood back, and laughed as "she rolled gratefully in the red dust."

While all this was happening, the newspapers scrambled to construct the inside story of what one had called the "bold and daring" Montpelier heist. Good information was hard to come by. Initially the robbery was attributed to Tom McCarty and his gang by, among others, the Pinkerton Detective Agency, whose chief Denver operative, while not officially involved in the case, opined that the crime was too well planned to be the work of any other outlaw. Just as unhelpful was Sidonia Emelle, wife of the jeweler who'd employed the robbers on the family ranch; she thought that one of them might be named Frank. When even a $500 reward produced no leads, the *Idaho Mountain Express* groused that the robbers were probably off somewhere "playing stallion poker or feeding the tiger in some city" with the stolen loot. It took a few weeks, but lawmen and journalists finally found themselves a reliable source: Matt Warner's wife, Rose.

Rose Morgan had been a fourteen-year-old Mormon lass "with

eyes that plumb got me from the first," Warner says in his memoir, when the two married about ten years earlier. It was never a happy union, though, because of his alcoholism, his outlawry, and his penchant for domestic violence. Warner once kicked her so brutally that she needed to get her leg amputated. Rose hated her husband and wanted to tell the world everything she knew about him—and also about the man who wanted to help him beat the rap: Butch Cassidy.

Suddenly the newspaper accounts of the Montpelier robbery were detail rich and dead-on accurate, at least by the standards of the Old West press. On Wednesday, September 9, the *Salt Lake Tribune* devoted its entire front page and much more to what its banner headline called a "Most Desperate Plot Unearthed." The report named Butch, Lay, and "Bob" Meeks as the perpetrators and noted that they had robbed the bank to pay Warner's legal fees. Laying the foundation stones for the Wild Bunch myth, it called them "notorious outlaws" and "desperados of the first water" who had a "perfect organization" and a "bold plot to set [Warner] free at the point of pistols" if court proceedings didn't seem to be going his way.

But Rose wasn't finished helping the authorities. Besides serving as a source of information, she agreed to take part in a "honeypot" scheme designed to lure Butch into Vernal so that he could be arrested for the Montpelier heist. At the request of the sheriff, she sent word to him that she'd appreciate a visit and added that if he came by to talk to her, he could have "anything he wanted." Butch saw through the ploy, though, and on August 25 responded with a letter that was promptly published in the *Tribune*:

Mrs. Rosa Warner, Salt Lake;

My Dear friend.

Through the kindness of Mrs. Rummel [Rose's mother], I received your letter last night. I am sorry that I can't comply with your request, but at present it is impossible for me to go to see you, and I can't tell just when I can get there. If you have got anything to tell me that will help your Matt, write and tell me what it is, and I will be there on time. I can't understand what it can be, for I have heard from reliable partys that you did not want Matt to get out, and I can't see what benefit it would be to you unless it was in his behalf. I may be misinformed, but I got it so straight that I would have to be shown why you made this talk before I could think otherwise. But that is neither here nor there, you are a lady and I would do all I could for you or any of the sex that was in trouble, of course. I am foolish (Which you have found out), but it is my nature and I can't change it. I may be wrong in this, but if so I hope you will look over it and prove to me that you are all right, and I will ask forgiveness for writing you as I have. I understand you and Matt named your boy Rex Leroy after me, thank you. I hope I will be able to meet you all before long if everything is satisfactory. I [am] sorry to hear about your leg. If I can do anything to help you out let me know and I will do it. Lay and I have got a good man to defend Matt and [his codefendant Bill] Wall, and put up plenty of money, too, for Matt and Wall to defend themselves. Write me here in care of John Bluford [the black barber at the Antler's Saloon in Vernal] and believe me to be a true friend to my kind of people.

George Cassidy

The lawyer that the Montpelier robbery paid for was the dapper Orlando Woodworth Powers, a former member of the Utah Supreme Court. (An in-state lawyer seemed a more politic choice than Douglas Preston, who was from Wyoming.) The version of events he tried to peddle in the late 1896 trial was that Warner had been helping an acquaintance move his mining camp when he got involved in a dispute with two interlopers and shot them in self-defense. Given the strength of the evidence and the popularity of the deceased, though, Powers had his work cut out for him. He didn't help his case with his habit of asking that the trial be stopped, and the ladies in the courtroom escorted into the hallway, every time he thought bad language was about to be quoted in testimony. Nor did his chief strategy—to call upon a series of character witnesses— seem sufficient, especially given his client's character. Under cross examination, Warner's father, Christen Christiansen, admitted that he'd seen Matt only twice in the last twenty years and had no idea what he did for a living.

Worried about the outcome, Butch was said to have smuggled a note to Warner via a man who visited him in his jail cell. According to Charles Kelly, Butch's first biographer, it said "Dear Matt, The boys are here. If you give the word, we will come and take you out." But if that story is true, nothing ever came of the offer.

In the end, Warner caught a break when a witness became less certain about who'd fired the first shot, and the charge against him was reduced from first-degree murder to voluntary manslaughter. Still, he was convicted and sentenced to five years at hard labor in the Utah State Penitentiary. His criminal career was effectively over.

Butch's, though, was just picking up steam.

15

SUNDANCE

For the late William Goldman, author of the screenplay for *Butch Cassidy and the Sundance Kid*, ignorance was bliss. The less he knew about Robert LeRoy Parker and Harry Alonzo Long- abaugh beyond their marquee-ready noms de guerre, he believed, the more freedom he would have to mold the story of those two historical figures into a movie. If he'd done tons of research and then patrolled the set like one of the hardcore buffs who haunts the Old West Rogues website, constantly jumping in front of the camera, waving his arms and screaming, "No, no, no—that never happened!" he might have wound up with a *film*—which doesn't make half as much money. And so Goldman was not ashamed of his know-nothing-ism; rather, he proclaimed it in his book *Adventures in the Screen Trade*. And, as if to show posterity how committed he was to sloughing off his homework, he left in his papers (which he donated to his alma mater, Columbia University) a pulpy old barbershop magazine with an article about Wild West outlaws and a yellowing 1950s Butch Cassidy comic book. *You want to see my sources, smarty-pants?* You only have to remember his Oscar to understand that on some level, his way worked. And yet by never dipping into the archives, and mostly making it up as he went along, Goldman did, in fact, miss a few truly screen-worthy moments—chief among them, I think, the big "Outlaws' Thanksgiving" gathering of 1896.

Allow me to set the scene for what soon became local legend. The place was the Davenport Ranch at Brown's Park. Seated around the big, rough-hewn table were John Jarvie, the extravagantly white-whiskered owner of the area's only general store; the lovely Queen Ann Bassett; and about thirty-five others who had come together to celebrate the holiday. It was a most American gathering, meaning that newcomers from England, Ireland, Scotland, Wales, Germany, Italy, Yugoslavia, Mexico, and Canada were present. In typical Brown's Park fashion, legit ranchers rubbed elbows with outlaws, who ran the gamut from glorified mischief makers to cold-blooded killers—such as Billie Bender, who, with Elzy Lay, stood at the door and took coats. Commanding the kitchen—and rocking his chef's hat—was the tall black bandit Isom Dart, aka Ned Huddleston, aka the Calico Cowboy: a former slave beloved by many despite his constant rustling.

Everyone was on his best behavior, in part, perhaps, because they were all wearing their best clothes. Menfolk sported dark suits with ties and vests, white shirts with high, stiff collars, and "patent low-cut" shoes overfitted with spats—outfits they'd probably bought for the formal photographic portraits that everyone had done in those days by traveling shutterbugs. "If a moustache existed," Bassett wrote many years later, "it must be waxed and curled." Women wore long, tightly fitted dresses with puffy leg-o-mutton sleeves, no doubt sewn at home on their foot-pedal Singer machines based on pictures they'd seen in *Peterson's* magazine or *Frank Leslie's Illustrated Newspaper.* Ann's own dress, made of light-blue silk, featured accordion pleats and a Peter Pan collar (or whatever it was called eight years before J. M. Barrie's play *Peter Pan*). Showing no mercy for the local lads, she let a single reddish-brown "beau catcher" curl fall cunningly across her forehead.

In the notes for a stage version of the evening created by Ann Bassett for a Colorado women's historical society sixty years later, she said that the evening's formal "program" began with an invocation from Jarvie, the Park's unofficial mayor. Then Mrs. Davenport, the "large and billowy" wife of the ranch owner, and a woman devoted to what Ann called "heart songs," sang "Then You'll Remember Me" and "Last Rose of Summer," accompanied on the accordion by Jarvie, who took care not to get his beard caught in the bellows. Next, Josie Bassett—who was by then married, and so wore a frumpy, loose-fitting, dark-green frock—played "The Cattle Song" on her zither, as one does on such occasions, and Ann delivered a recitation on the true meaning of Thanksgiving.

We don't know what Ann claimed the meaning was, but Thanksgiving, even then, was primarily about food, so the feast started as soon as she stopped speaking. A typical dinner in those parts consisted of a slab of mutton cooked in a pan with sourdough biscuits that absorbed the rendered sheep fat—but the Brown's Park holiday menu featured what were already the traditional dishes: roast turkey, chestnut stuffing, giblet gravy, cranberries, mashed potatoes, candied sweet potatoes, creamed peas, celery, olives, pumpkin pie, whipped cream, plum pudding, hot rolls, and salted nuts, with all of the sides brought by the guests. Before the meal could start, though, everyone sat as still as they could in their buttoned-up, whale-boned Sunday best and bowed their heads to say grace in the flickering light supplied by Ann's mother's silver candelabra. The mood was solemn, the prayer quite long. Then, on the amen, the kitchen door flew open with a bang—and Butch Cassidy and the Sundance Kid barreled in.

They were wearing butcher's aprons and balancing large serving platters as best they could. They bowed, they scraped, they proffered nervous smiles. As they moved from guest to guest, drumsticks seemed to drop from the sky, and gravy boats nearly capsized. The very sight of them, trying to be solicitous, struggling not to spill things, Ann wrote, was "a joke to some of us young roughnecks just itching for an excuse to kick each other under the table and grin." Ann especially enjoyed watching Butch attempt to pour hot coffee like a professional. "Butch could perform such minor jobs as robbing banks and holding up pay trains without the flicker of an eyelash, but serving coffee at a grand party, that was something else," she wrote in 1960. "The blood-curdling job almost floored him. He became frustrated when some of the other guests told him it was not good form to pour coffee from a big black coffee pot and reach from left to right across a guest's plate to grab a cup right under their noses. This just shows how etiquette can put fear into a brave man's heart."

The Outlaws' Thanksgiving dinner shows something else, too. It shows Butch Cassidy and the Sundance Kid together for the first time, ever. Which is not to suggest that this was their initial meeting—clearly, based on their familiarity with each other, it wasn't; we cannot glibly say about the duo that what started in comedy ended in tragedy. Still, it is interesting to note that at their first recorded joint sighting, they were behaving less like Frank and Jesse James and more like Laurel and Hardy.

———

While we don't know how Butch and Sundance met, their partnership, in hindsight, seems almost inevitable. Like Robert LeRoy Parker, Harry Alonzo Longabaugh did not get into the outlaw game just for the money it might provide him. Which is saying something, because when he was growing up in the neighboring canal towns of Mont Clare and Phoenixville, Pennsylvania, about twenty-seven miles northwest of Philadelphia, his family seems to have thought about little else, so meager were its circumstances. I don't want to say his father, Josiah, was not a go-getter, but he avoided service in the Civil War because of hemorrhoids—and he never held anything but part-time, menial employment. When Harry, the Longabaughs' fifth and final child, was born, on an unknown day in 1867 (the year after Butch), the family was living in a few rooms on the upper floor of a wood-frame house that backed up to the Schuylerville Canal—on which at the age of eight he would be forced to find employment.

You couldn't have blamed little Harry if he thought he was adopted. From an early age, he was the industrious sort, like his ancestor Conrad Langenbach, who arrived from Germany as an indentured servant in 1772, earned his way to freedom, and fought in the Revolutionary War. The future Sundance Kid was named for his maternal grandfather, Harry Place, a strict Baptist deacon whose surname would later be appropriated by Harry's sweetheart, a mysterious girl of the golden West who may or may not have been christened Ethel.

Sent to work in 1885 with his uncle Michael Langenbaugh (families often chose their own spellings in the nineteenth century), who maintained a fleet of canal boats in Mont Clare, Harry tried not to let his circumstances get him down. He had his dreams as well as his books to sustain him; his biographer Donna Ernst found a record of his paying $1 for a library card that she suspects he used to borrow novels such as *Malaeska; the Indian Wife of the White Hunter*. He also drew inspiration from his siblings, none of whom were slugabeds, perhaps as a reaction to their dad. Harry's oldest brother, Elwood, left home to go whaling on the bark *Mary & Helen*, bound for the Bering Strait. His spinster sister Emma was a partner in a sewing company, McCandless and Longabaugh, which did contract work for the John Wanamaker Department Store. Brother Harvey, a carpenter, helped build the original boardwalk in Atlantic City, New Jersey. And then there was his oldest sister Samanna, who raised five children while keeping the books for her husband's blacksmith business. She was also the family historian, in the sense that she sometimes scribbled notes about her kinfolk on the backs of envelopes and such. On August

30, 1882, she wrote, "Harry A. Longabaugh left home for the West. Left home at 14."

It is always scary to leave home for the first time, but Harry had connections out west—someone who would meet him at the station. A distant cousin named George Longenbaugh had recently traveled by covered wagon with his wife and children to Colorado and now needed help on the ranch he'd acquired outside Cortez. The arrangement worked well for both a homesteader and a boy eager to learn the cowboy arts but still too young to make his own way in the West. Ultimately, Harry would stay with his relatives in Cortez until 1886—two years before Butch came through for the Fourth of July races with Matt Warner and their speedy mare Betty.

Two years is not exactly a near miss, and yet it's possible that Harry and Butch did bump into each other in Wyoming, Montana, or some other part of Colorado, as for the next decade or so, they wandered that lonely part of the world and between them worked at a couple of dozen ranches and ducked in and out of assorted hiding places along the Outlaw Trail. You'd just think that *someone* would have mentioned it if they had become friends. They were, after all, both standouts: well dressed, intelligent, and good-looking, with Sundance being the more attractive of the two by conventional standards, despite a tendency to put on weight and very small feet that turned inward when he walked. Both liked to read and train horses, which made them similar not just to each other but also to Butch's other good buddy Elzy Lay.

Where Butch and Sundance diverged dramatically was in terms of temperament. Butch, as we've seen, was generally recognized as a cheerful sort, and people often said he was the most magnetic man they'd ever met, whereas Sundance, while capable of being charming when he wanted to be, was destined to be remembered by many for his prolonged, sulky silences and frequent foul moods. While he was never a leader, neither was he just another member of the pack. One ranch hand who worked with him at the Suffolk Cattle Company in Crook County, Wyoming, when Harry was only about eighteen, recalled that almost as soon as he'd signed on, he beat up three fellow wranglers who'd argued with him over the best grazing ground for the ranch's horses—"and came very near whipping our Dutch cook for calling him 'Longboy.' After that," the man added, "the cooks and wranglers did not step on his toes."

It was true that no one could survive long in those parts if he acted like a pushover, but Harry was more aggressive than most, and the uneasiness he could inspire sometimes made him, in his own way, almost as memorable a presence as Butch. If those two had traveled the countryside as a duo, people would surely have been unable to resist making the observation that opposites sure do attract, don't they? But, to twist a famous phrase of William Goldman's, nobody said nothing. Until the mid-1890s, adjoining wanted posters seems to have been the closest Butch and Sundance ever came to a meaningful relationship.

Sundance drifted into outlawry the usual way, by first committing relatively small crimes here and there when he saw the opportunity. It wasn't like he was trying to get rich, but if people were going to be less than vigilant about watching their horses or their wallets, why not teach them a lesson? We don't know if it was his first offense, but when he came back to the ranch house at the Suffolk Cattle Company one evening in 1886, a sheriff was waiting to arrest him for stealing $80 from an old man in Lusk, Wyoming, thirty miles to the northwest. Lusk was a wide-open town, famous once as the home of a legendary prostitute known, for her ruffled underwear, as Mother Featherlegs. All the Suffolk cowboys went there to get drunk and fire their guns into the air, but apparently there were limits. Harry took his arrest in stride and didn't resist the handcuffs, but when the sheriff woke up the next morning to take him back to Lusk, he was missing, though the cuffs were still attached to the bedpost. When it came to picking locks, Harry Longabaugh was perhaps not as adept as Harry Houdini, but he was, as we shall see, every bit as intent on setting himself free.

Harry wasn't being opportunistic, though, when he committed the crime that changed his life; he was just trying to stay alive. Toward the end of the Big Die-Up, the brutal and interminable winter of 1886–87 that killed millions of cattle, the ranch in northern Montana where he'd been working had gone bust, and, out of food and money, and forced to sell his saddle, he found himself riding bareback through Wyoming on an all-but-broken-down horse. Desperate and half frozen, he pulled into the Three V Ranch, looking to grub a meal or get hired. We don't know what kind of reception he got there, but on his way out the next day, February 27, 1887, he stole a light-gray horse and a saddle that belonged to a Three V wrangler named Alonzo Craven, as well as a revolver owned by one Jim Widener. As soon as the victims reported the thefts, the ranch manager, a prominent member of the Cheyenne Club and the Wyoming Stock Growers Association named John Clay, organized a search party, and a pack of ten or so Three V cowboys went combing the countryside for, one newspaper said, a "smooth-faced, gray-eyed boy" riding a horse that had a *J* branded on its left shoulder. Why they were so intent on bringing Harry to justice is hard to say. You might think those fellows had enough to worry about, given the depth of the snow and the absence of live cattle they no doubt took note of as they plodded along. Maybe with everything frozen over, they had little else to do—or they felt that depredations of a grifter were among the few things they still had some control over. But for whatever reason, they stalked Harry obsessively, and two weeks later, when they still hadn't found him but had figured out who he was, they filed charges against him in the euphonically named seat of the aptly named Crook County: Sundance, Wyoming.

The sheriff there was James Ryan, a man who for good reasons has avoided enshrinement in the law enforcement hall of fame in

Perrysburg, Ohio. When Ryan heard that Harry Longabaugh had been detained in Miles City, Montana, two-hundred-odd miles to the north, on suspicion of horse theft, the first thing he did was what any lawman would have done: he went to Miles City to arrest Harry and bring him back to Sundance to face justice. His second move, however, was somewhat unconventional. For reasons still unknown, Ryan took Harry on a return trip that had them traveling by Northern Pacific Railroad from Miles City to Saint Paul, Minnesota, then from there to Rapid City, South Dakota, and on from there by stagecoach to Sundance, a distance of nearly two thousand miles. "The route taken by the sheriff would seem to be a rather long one," the *Sundance Gazette* noted dryly. The sheriff and his prisoner never did make it back, though, because somewhere around Duluth, Minnesota, when Ryan was using the restroom, Harry managed to get out of his shackles and handcuffs and jumped from the moving train.

Sheriff Ryan ordered the train stopped and had passengers and crew search the area, but without success. He was the butt of jokes for weeks afterward, in newspapers and saloons, until Harry showed his own lack of shrewdness by drifting back to a ranch in the Miles City area, where he was far too well known to return safely and got arrested as he was coming in from the barns at the end of a workday. A deputy sheriff named Eph Davis and a stock inspector named Smith relieved him of his three six-shooters, said the *Yellowstone Journal*, and "shackled him and handcuffed him with some patent lock bracelets which were warranted to hold anything until unlocked by the key and which the manufacturers offered a premium if they could be opened otherwise." Nevertheless, a few hours later, as the three men slept on the floor of an empty line shack where they had stopped for the night, Harry did get out of the manacles. It didn't amount to anything—in the darkness, the deputy called out, "Kid, you're loose, ain't you?" and Harry, said the *Journal*, "dropped back like he was shot"—but because he was aggravated by the attempted escape, Davis later told the newspapers he was looking into pinning a number of recent crimes on the Kid besides the grand larceny charges he faced for stealing a horse, a saddle, and a gun. Harry was having none of that, though. In a state of high dudgeon, he got off a letter to the editor of the *Sundance Gazette*, in the process demonstrating another similarity to Butch:

> *In your issue of the 7th inst. I read a very sensational and partly untrue article, which placed me before the public not even second to the notorious Jesse James. Admitting that I have done wrong and expecting to be dealt with according to law and not by false reports from parties who should blush with shame to make them, I ask a little of your space to set my case before the public in a true light. In the first place I have always worked for an honest living; was employed last summer by one of the best outfits in Montana and don't think they can say aught against me, but having got discharged last winter I went to the Black Hills to seek employment—which I could not get—and was forced to work for my board a month and a half, rather than to beg or steal. I am aware that some of your readers will say my statement should be taken for what it is worth, on account of the hard name which has been forced upon me, nevertheless it is true. As for my recapture by Deputy Sheriff Davis, all I can say is that he did his work well and were it not for his "playing possum," I would now be on my way south, which I had hoped to do and live a better life.*
>
> *Harry Longabaugh*

Sheriff Ryan arrived on June 19 to take him back to Sundance, this time more directly, on the Deadwood stage. It was a tense trip. As they climbed aboard in Miles City, a newspaper reporter heard Ryan tell Harry that he was "going to land him or his scalp in the Sundance jail," one way or another. Harry, "securely shacked and handcuffed, the shackles being made of steel and riveted with steel rivets," listened politely but gave Ryan "fair warning that he intended to escape and told him to watch him but not be too rough on him."

Back in Sundance (which they reached without incident; score one for Ryan), Harry was indicted on three counts of grand larceny, the crime being defined in this case as stealing something worth more than $80. In exchange for a guilty plea, which he seems to have given only grudgingly, two of the counts were dropped, and, with a bang of the gavel, he was sentenced to eighteen months at hard labor in the state penitentiary. Because of his age—barely twenty—Harry was consigned to the Sundance town jail rather than the big house in Laramie (where Butch would go five years later) in order to keep him apart from hardened criminals who might impede his rehabilitation.

This idea was somewhat laughable, since Harry was not prepared to be a model prisoner. He made many minor escape attempts, and nine months into his sentence, he and a cellmate tried to overwhelm the jailer who was serving them supper. The other inmate escaped briefly, but the Sundance Kid (as the newspapers now called him) was subdued, remanacled, and from that point onward regarded as "a slippery sort" no longer eligible for early release. In a state where almost no prisoners served their full sentence, Harry would get just a single symbolic day off for good behavior. Which made sense because there was no way that incarceration had made him a more solid citizen. After walking out of the jailhouse in February 1889, he took a breath of freedom and, said the *Gazette*, "hied himself into the hills," headed for trouble.

Despite his eagerness to pursue it, the outlaw life would never be easy for him. This was because despite his intelligence, bravado, and skill with horses, Harry was a natural-born sidekick, meaning that his fortunes always rose and fell depending on his boss. Not everyone was Butch Cassidy—in fact, no one but Butch was— and most ringleaders were highly flawed and indeed sometimes cretinous men whom Harry could stand behind only if he crouched very low. Three months after his release from prison, at nine o'clock the morning of May 16, 1889, Harry was holed up with four dismal desperados in a damp dugout on Oil Creek, thirty-five miles south of Sundance, when two deputy sheriffs burst in and, during a tussle, shot to death the supposed brains of the operation, a murderous Kansan named Robert Minor. The details of the incident remain obscure, but the next day, Harry, expressing outrage at the intrusion, issued a public threat of some sort against one of the deputies, James Swisher, saying he would punish him for overstepping his authority. When Swisher swore out a complaint and had him arrested, Harry promptly bailed himself out and headed for Canada—and the orbit of another strong personality.

This was different, though. That man whose company he sought, Cyril Everett "Ebb" Johnson, held the promise of being a good influence on the twenty-two-year-old Sundance. The two had struck up a friendship a few years before in Wyoming, when both wrangled cattle for the same ranch. It was easy to admire Johnson, a native of Virginia, who by then had already driven a stagecoach through the Black Hills, scouted the Dakotas with Buffalo Bill, and served as a hunting guide for the famous writer Owen Wister, who would use him as a model for the central character in his immensely successful novel, *The Virginian*. He'd also impeccably managed a ranch in High River, Canada, called the Bar U. Sundance, meanwhile, had gone to prison for horse stealing and was now on the lam for threatening a peace officer. Still, when Ebb Johnson heard that his old pal Harry had crossed the border and was working not far south of him, cowboying on a ranch and breaking broncos for contractors who were putting in a railroad line between Calgary and Macleod, he invited him to take a job at the Bar U, just as Harry had hoped he would.

Harry made only a semigood impression with the folks of the Bar U. One neighbor of Johnson's thought he was a worthy addition to the outfit. "While he was likely evading the US law," Fred Ings wrote in his 1936 memoir, "no one could have been better behaved or more decent. A thoroughly likeable fellow was Harry, a favorite with everyone, a splendid rider, and a top-notch cow hand." But others thought he was trouble. According to one regional history, "One day, as Longabaugh stepped off a bronc and pulled off the saddle, Herb [Millar, another Bar U ranch hand] saw something glitter. Laying his saddle down alongside the corral, Longabaugh picked up his rope and went to the corral to catch a horse, which gave Millar a chance to walk by the saddle. The glittering object was a hacksaw blade, peeping out between the skirt and the sheepskin lining. Herb knew what that meant." What it meant was that Harry was packing a burglar's tool; the blade would be useful to any rustler who wanted to alter a branding iron or escape from restraints.

A few months later, Millar filed a complaint about Harry with the North-West Mounted Police—for "cruelty to animals." The accusation apparently stemmed from Harry's particularly "American" way of breaking broncos, which Millar found offensive. But a judge dismissed the charge, and Ebb Johnson doesn't appear to have been bothered by it, either. His friendship with Harry seemed as tight as ever. In November 1891, when Johnson married a pretty English lass named Mary Eleanor Bigland in the nearby town of High River, Harry stood beside him as best man, a role he was familiar with playing.

Ranch life could never hold him, though. A year later, he'd be in and out of a deal to be partners in a saloon in Calgary's Grand Central Hotel and ultimately move back to northern Montana. There on the freezing night of November 29, 1892, he, with two compatriots, robbed a Great Northern Railroad train as it pulled out of the tiny town of Malta. The heist, as noted earlier, was a comedy of errors. Because their masks kept slipping off their faces, they were quickly identified—and arrested. Two of the perpetrators wound up serving more than six years in the Montana State Prison, but in the initial confusion surrounding the court proceedings, Harry was allowed to go free.

This was the start of an upward spiral for the Sundance Kid. Before long, he'd meet and strike up a friendship with Butch Cassidy and wangle an invite to the Outlaws' Thanksgiving dinner. He was, it seemed, very close to living the action-packed life he'd imagined when he boarded the train at Phoenixville, Pennsylvania. The dinner party that evening in Brown's Park lasted six hours, after which the guests repaired to someone's house, where they danced till dawn. It may have been at the Outlaws' Thanksgiving that Sundance met the mysterious woman we know as Ethel Place. It's impossible to say for certain—that phrase again, alas—but according to some witnesses, a few weeks later, when the gang, such as it was, headed off to Robbers Roost down in southern Utah, the beautiful Ethel was one of the women who traveled with them and played a role in a winterlong idyll that set the tone for a stretch of excitement—the stuff of which outlaws dream.

Robert LeRoy Parker—the future Butch Cassidy—spent much of his childhood in this cabin three miles south of Circleville, Utah.

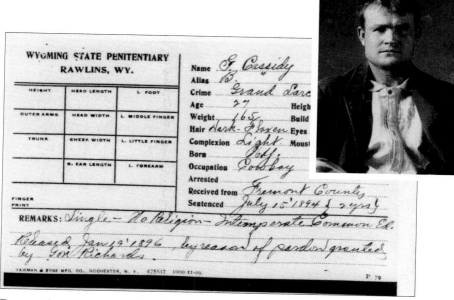

Because he was an avowed enemy of Big Cattle and not just another rustler, Butch Cassidy was sentenced to two years in the Wyoming State Penitentiary for stealing a $5 horse.

Telluride, Colorado, had a reputation for raucousness. "It has ten saloons and plans for a church," said a local newspaper. In 1889 Butch and his boys robbed Telluride's San Miguel Valley Bank and, using a clever relay system that involved planting fresh mounts along the escape route, made a clean getaway.

While attending the wedding of Will Carver (standing, left) in the red-light district of Fort Worth in 1900, the core members of the Wild Bunch took a break to have their picture taken. It would be used in more than a few wanted posters. (From left to right) Harry "the Sundance Kid" Longabaugh, Carver, Ben Kilpatrick, Harvey Logan, and Butch Cassidy.

Harvey Logan, aka Kid Curry, may have had a soft spot for his longtime girlfriend, the Texas prostitute Annie Rogers, but he was, in his early days, a cold-blooded killer in a gang that didn't like to draw blood.

6

Laura Bullion—the girlfriend of Will Carver and then Ben Kilpatrick—was one of several women who traveled with the Wild Bunch and may have even held the horses at a few of their robberies.

Elzy Lay may have dabbled in robbing banks and trains, as well as counterfeiting, but he was, like Butch, a lover of books who carried both novels and nonfiction in his saddlebag.

At the Tipton, Wyoming, train robbery of August 29, 1900, Butch and his gang blew open the express car safe and probably destroyed some of its contents in the process. Still, their haul was estimated at $50,000.

The residents of Sanderson, Texas, were doing the normal thing in 1912 when they proudly displayed the still-warm bodies of two outlaws: Ben "the Tall Texan" Kilpatrick and Ole Beck.

Harry Longabaugh, a.k.a. "The Sundance Kid," told his family that he had married a woman from Texas, and she signed her name as Ethel Place. He and his mysterious bride had this portrait taken during a visit to New York City in 1901, a stopover on their way to Argentina.

Pinkerton's National Detective Agency.

Below appear the photographs, descriptions and histories of GEORGE PARKER, alias "BUTCH" CASSIDY, alias GEORGE CASSIDY, alias INGERFIELD and HARRY LONGBAUGH alias HARRY ALONZO.

Name..George Parker, alias "Butch" Cassidy, alias George Cassidy, alias Ingerfield.
Nationality....................American
Occupation ....Cowboy; rustler
Criminal Occupation......Bank robber and highwayman, cattle and horse thief
Age..36 yrs. (1901)..*Height*....5 feet 9 in
Weight..165 lbs......*Build*......Medium
Complexion..Light..*Color of Hair*..Flaxen
Eyes....Blue.......*Mustache*..Sandy, if any
Remarks:—Two cut scars back of head, small scar under left eye, small brown mole calf of leg. "Butch" Cassidy is known as a criminal principally in Wyoming, Utah, Idaho, Colorado and Nevada and has served time in Wyoming State penitentiary at Laramie for grand Larceny, but was pardoned January 19th, 1896.

GEORGE PARKER.
First photograph taken July 15, 1894.

GEORGE PARKER.
Last photograph taken Nov. 21, 1900.

Name.........Harry Longbaugh, alias "Kid" Longbaugh, alias Harry Alonzo alias Frank Jones, alias Frank Boyd, alias the "Sundance Kid."
Nationality........Swedish-American.. *Occupation*............Cowboy; rustler
Criminal Occupation.........Highwayman, bank burglar, cattle and horse thief
Age............35 years....*Height*........................5 feet 10 in
Weight....165 to 175 lbs....*Build*.........................Good
Eyes.....Blue or gray............*Complexion*...................Medium
Mustache or Beard...............(if any), natural color brown, reddish tinge
Features......Grecian type ....*Nose*........................Rather long
Color of Hair........Natural color brown, may be dyed; combs it pompadour
IS BOW-LEGGED AND HIS FEET FAR APART.
Remarks:—Harry Longbaugh served 18 months in jail at Sundance, Cook Co., Wyoming, when a boy, for horse stealing. In December, 1892, Harry Longbaugh, Bill Madden and Henry Bass "held up" a Great Northern train at Malta, Montana. Bass and Madden were tried for this crime, convicted and sentenced to 10 and 14 years respectively; Longbaugh escaped and since has been a fugitive. June 28, 1897, under the name of Frank Jones, Longbaugh participated with Harvey Logan, alias Curry, Tom Day and Walter Putney, in the Belle Fourche, South Dakota, bank robbery. All were arrested, but Longbaugh and Harvey Logan escaped from jail at Deadwood, October 31, the same year. Longbaugh has not since been arrested.

HARRY LONGBAUGH.
Photograph taken Nov. 21, 1900.

☞ **Officers are warned to have sufficient assistance and be fully armed, when attempting to arrest either of these outlaws, as they are always heavily armed, and will make a determined resistance before submitting to arrest, not hesitating to kill, if necessary.**

☞ **This circular cancels circulars No. 1 and 2, issued by us from Denver, Colo., May 15th, 1901 and February 3rd, 1902, respectively.**

IN CASE OF AN ARREST immediately notify PINKERTON'S NATIONAL DETECTIVE AGENCY at the nearest of the above listed offices.

Or   **Pinkerton's National Detective Agency,**
JOHN C. FRAZER,   Opera House Block, Denver, Colo.
     Resident Sup't., DENVER, COLO.

In the days before the FBI, when the United States had no national police force, the Pinkerton Detective Agency filled the gap.

Although this chapter of their lives was left out of the movie, Butch (far left), Sundance (second from right), and Ethel (right) spent a few years in the foothills of the Argentine Andes as they tried to make a go of it as legitimate ranchers.

Early in the twentieth century, Butch and Sundance made national headlines for their daring exploits. The legend of the Wild West had started even before the actual Wild West had quite ended.

Your author by the purported graves of Butch and Sundance in San Vicente, Bolivia. Experts regard the sign as specious.

16

◆

LAND OF ENCHANTMENT

The robbery they pulled off in Castle Gate, Utah, was never going to be a reputation-making event; rather, just a medium-sized bit of mischief that keeps a gang toned up and ready for bigger things. It probably first surfaced in conversation in the spring of 1897, when Butch and the boys began to bat around the topic of what was next, after Montpelier, over a tin cup of coffee or a game of whist—and someone said, "Why the hell not?" or maybe even, "Geez, haven't we pulled that job already?"

Today it is a ghost town, but Castle Gate—named for the twin rock formations that straddle its main street—had a very obvious raison d'etre in those days: the Pleasant Valley Coal Company. Virtually every one of the five hundred or so people who lived in Castle Gate worked for the PVCC. Coal was king—by far the most common source of energy in the United States at the time—and business was booming. The beauty part from a robber's standpoint was that the payroll of the PVCC consisted of about $8,000 in cash that came to Castle Gate every two weeks via the Denver and Rio Grande Railroad on a day that varied (supposedly for security purposes) but could always be determined in advance. A wagon dependably brought the bags of money from the station to the company headquarters, where two men just as dependably lugged it up an outside stairway to the payroll office on the top floor. None of this was done in secret or with any special precautions. Just in case you missed the arrival of the payroll, in fact, the company blew a loud steam whistle to let PVCC employees know they could start forming a line to pick up their cash. To put it in Utah terms, this job was, for anyone in Butch's orbit, a low-hanging bullberry. The only question was, Who would be going on the raid?

We can see from its various permutations the way the Wild Bunch operated in its glory days of 1897 to 1901: very loosely. Like a pickup basketball team in a neighborhood where the key players are often away on business. Like the writers' warren at *Saturday Night Live*, where people drift into someone's office, spitball about a particular sketch for a while, then move on. As the historian Dan Buck has said in articles and lectures, those boys may have been wild, but they surely weren't much of a bunch. Members, to the extent that we can call them that, came and went depending on whose idea a particular job was and who'd expressed the most interest in the early stages of the planning, often based on their particular skills. Availability was a factor, too, since men such as Harvey Logan, aka Kid Curry, and Ben "the Tall Texan" Kilpatrick sometimes had previous commitments. Even the core group of Butch, Elzy Lay, and (by the mid-1890s) Sundance were seldom all present and accounted for. Whatever their composition, there were never more than about fifteen or twenty of them all told, even when Kilpatrick and Logan brought along their girlfriends, Laura Bullion and Annie Rogers, to hold the horses or just hang around, and probably never more than a half dozen on any one job. That wasn't good enough for the newspapers, though, which sought to titillate and frighten their readers with tales of a highly organized army of some two hundred outlaws always on the verge of sweeping down from the hills and wreaking havoc. To a great extent, the press foisted upon a gullible public a gang that only vaguely resembled the real group that surrounded Butch. "They are lawless men who have long lived in the crags and become like eagles," said the *New York Herald*, on June 25, 1899. Newspaper Butch (as we might call him) was sometimes described as mean and sketched as a fat man with a moustache. He also got killed an awful lot (his death was reported on at least fifty separate occasions, by Dan Buck's count); he ran the Train Robbers Syndicate, the Hole-in-the Wall Gang, and sometimes the Powder River Boys—until reporters settled on the Wild Bunch in 1899.

The Castle Gate heist seems to have been Butch's and Elzy's baby from the start; they were in, and Sundance, despite his budding friendship with the boss, was out—owing, perhaps, to his involvement in an impending bank heist in Belle Fourche, South Dakota, in which he was by default the leader. The one hurdle they had to get over with Castle Gate was that because virtually everyone in town was a miner who could walk to work, or a member of a miner's family, horses and the cowboys who rode them were a rare sight, and two mounted strangers were liable to attract attention. Probably because he always had horse racing on his mind, Butch came up with the idea of posing as trainers, who he knew might pop up at any time in those parts, looking for a race or to make a sale. They fitted their finest horses with small English racing saddles, put on their flashiest "sportsman" clothes, and arrived in Castle Gate on Tuesday, May 20, 1897, at about noon.

Almost exactly twenty-four hours later, as Elzy sat astride his mount in front of the PVCC building, and Butch perused the merchandise in the company store just around the corner, the steam whistle announcing the arrival of the payroll shattered the silence and echoed off the walls of nearby Price Canyon.

Butch calmly left the store, walked to the staircase that PVCC paymaster Edwin Carpenter always used to take the money to his office on the upper floor, and nonchalantly leaned against the outer wall of the building. It took Carpenter and his assistant, T. W. Lewis, a few minutes to make the trip on foot from the train depot, loaded down as they were with money. The former was carrying a leather satchel that contained $7,000 in gold, $860 in silver, and $1,000 in currency, and the latter had a cloth bag holding another $1,000 in cash and checks. As they began to pass by him, Butch stuck a pistol in Carpenter's ribs and told him to drop the satchel. He immediately did, but Lewis, clutching his bag to his chest, darted into the first-floor entrance—nearly colliding, in the process, with another PVCC employee named Frank Caffey, who had seen Butch's gun and was rushing out to alert the sheriff. Caffey got only a few feet, though, before running into Elzy, who stared down at him from his saddle with pistol drawn. "Get back in there, you son of a bitch," he said, "or I'll fill your belly full of hot lead." Caffey did as instructed.

Elzy had untied Butch's horse in preparation for the getaway and was holding the reins. The only thing that went wrong that day was that when Butch tossed him the leather satchel he'd taken from Carpenter, Elzy dropped the lines, and the riderless horse bolted down the street, weaving its way through the crowd of people already gathering to get their pay. Butch, according to several witnesses, remained calm and in command. "Don't anyone make a mistake!" he announced. "Everything is going to be all right." What happened next resembled an equestrian stunt that you might see in Buffalo Bill's Wild West Show: spurring his own mount from a standing start, Elzy ran down the loose horse, and Butch, in an all-out sprint, grabbed the surcingle that held the tiny saddle in place and swung deftly aboard. Then, as four or five riflemen fired at them from the roof of the PVCC building, the two amigos disappeared in a cloud of dust between the twin castle towers.

Posses pursued them, as posses will, but to little avail. Not only did they have a good head start, but Bub Meeks, their compadre on the Montpelier job, and another crew member named Joe Walker, had planted fresh mounts along the way. Whatever you wanted to call this group, it was hitting its stride and doing it in its signature style.

————

If you pull back and look at the arc of Butch's relatively long career (for an outlaw), you'll see that nearly every time he hit a peak, two things happened: he went broke, and he started dreaming of having the relatively quiet, steady life of a rancher. For the former, we can blame the faro tables, which it seems he never could resist. The yearning for the straight life posed a more complicated problem, because peace always looked better from a distance.

In the early 1970s, an eighty-eight-year-old man named Fred Hilman told the outlaw historian Larry Pointer that less than a week after the Castle Gate holdup, a lone rider with "steel-blue eyes" turned up at the ranch owned by his father, Dan, in Wyoming's Little Goose Canyon. He gave his name as LeRoy Parker and said he was hungry and in need of work. Because he had the air of a cowboy about him—Dan Hilman saw him as the slick, haughty sort who "just wanted to sit in the saddle and ride herd"—the master of the ranch was at first reluctant to hire him. In short order, though, LeRoy Parker turned out to be the best ranch hand his father ever had, on most days cheerful, brimming with energy, and up for any fence mending or cow milking that needed to be done. When little Fred admired his .44 carbine, Parker gave him the gun.

But as friendly as he was, the drifter also had an "aloof" and "mysterious" side, Fred said. During the several months he worked at the Hilman place, Parker always kept a saddle horse picketed nearby, presumably in case he needed to make a quick exit. Surely thoughts of pursuers, real or imagined, were never far from his mind. "Relaxing around the table after dinner," Pointer wrote, paraphrasing Fred, "he would set his chair backwards, elbows lightly resting on the chair's back, in a position commanding a view of the door and windows. His actions were quick, almost nervous." Occasionally, Fred said, a friend of Parker's would come by—"tall and dark, with a carefully trimmed moustache, polite but distant." Parker seems never to have introduced the man—who might have been Elzy or Sundance—to the family, but, with Dan Hilman's permission, he would go off with him now and then for a few days on some never-explained mission. One morning in the late summer of 1897, they woke up to discover that the mysterious Parker had gone for good. A note on his bed said, "Sorry to be leaving you. The authorities are getting on to us. Best home I've ever had."

Even today a lot of people in the West will tell you that Butch Cassidy stayed at their granddaddy's house for a spell and helped him milk the cows. Most of these tales can be rejected as false, especially if they supposedly occurred in the 1920s, '30s and '40s, as quite a few do. To me and a good number of the scholars, though, Fred Hilman's story, at the very least, does a bracing job of capturing the nuances of Butch's mood in mid-to-late 1897, when he would have been particularly worried about "the authorities getting on to us." In the months following Castle Gate, his name appeared more frequently in Western newspapers—often coming up speculatively in stories about crimes he was not involved in—and governors of the intermountain West states found themselves under increasing pressure from railroads, express companies, cattle barons, and banks to crack down on the desperado who was a drain on their profits. In early 1898 Colorado governor Alva Adams wrote his Wyoming counterpart, William Alford Richards, that he had hired a professional bounty hunter named James Catron "to go to the land of the rustlers and arrest Cassidy if possible. I am inclined to the belief that he will either get Cassidy or Cassidy will get him, with the chances in favor of him getting Cassidy." A few weeks later, however, Adams became disenchanted with Catron and called off the hunt. "He talked so much that he was more apt to give up his scalp than to get the scalp of the other fellow," he wrote to Richards.

Still, Butch realized that a fundamental shift was under way: that besides being the object of sheriffs and bounty hunters, he'd become a political prize, someone whose demise could lead to someone else's election—and so more than ever, he had to sleep with one eye open and keep moving.

It was that sense of urgency that probably drove him south to New Mexico in early 1898. We don't know how he first met an experienced ranch foreman named Perry Tucker, but when William French, the owner of the WS Ranch in Alma, New Mexico, lured Tucker away from a cattle outfit in Arizona to manage his cows and quell a recent upsurge in rustling, the new hire brought along both Butch and Elzy. In a memoir French would publish in 1928, he said he took to Tucker's two friends instantly. The one who called himself Jim Lowe (Butch) was "stoutly built and of middle height" and "had a habit of grinning and showing you a very even row of small teeth when he spoke to you." As for Elzy, who gave his name as William McGuinness, he was "several years younger, much taller and darker—in fact, a quite good-looking young man, debonair, with a bit of a swagger. He seemed quite above the ordinary cow hand and definitely had more education."

French, who'd been born in Ireland and served as a captain in the British army, appreciated that Jim and Mac, unlike your typical cowpokes, were disciplined in their appearance and demeanor. "When they went on the road, they were the most decorous," he wrote. "There was no such thing as drinking or gambling or shooting up the town. I was frequently complimented by the merchants of [nearby] Magdelena for having such a well-behaved outfit. I was very proud of them."

It was as management-level ranch hands, however, that they impressed him most, helping him turn around the business after a bad stretch. On the trail, said French, "Jim's real genius came under my notice. The way he handled those poor cattle over the long and dusty trail of over two hundred miles was a revelation. Frequently they had to go as much as seventy-five miles without water, but they never dropped a hoof, and there was no tail to his herd when he arrived at the road. Mac usually accompanied him in charge of a bunch of broncos, and when they got through with the trip, they were nice and gentle and furnished new mounts for the hands of the range. Their zeal for everything in connection with the outfit was beyond all praise. Truly, the way these men handled stock was a marvel."

The other thing that struck French was that he was no longer losing animals, like the magnificent saddle horse and a beloved buggy team that had been filched, he was sure, by the notorious Ketchum brothers the previous autumn, as well as many rank-and-file members of the herd that had been disappearing almost daily. He was doubly impressed by the fact that the thieves who'd been preying on his stock did not push back against the crackdown imposed by Jim and Mac. "The rustlers, for the time being, seemed entirely buffaloed," French wrote. In a short time, Jim and Mac were for all practical purposes running the ranch.

Some things about the duo did sort of baffle him, he admitted. When men quit, it never disrupted the operation because Jim and Mac always seemed to have replacements handy; those boys were suspiciously well connected. Strange, too, was how the new hires acted tentative and deferential to each other while he was around, but "in the dusk of the evening, I frequently saw them together, sitting under a fence in close confab like long-lost brothers." French at least once discussed these matters with his second in command but ultimately shrugged and figured that "as long as things were going so well, it was no affair of ours to inquire into it."

Things were going so well, and life was so smooth and predictable, in fact, that Butch and Elzy just had to get the hell out of there.

17

◆

WILCOX

If you can see beauty in the smoking, mangled wreck of a nineteenth-century railroad car sitting in the misty rain on a dark Wyoming morning—well, then, you may have a future as a Wild West outlaw. Butch and his boys certainly derived a full measure of joy from such an apparition, especially since the only one injured in the blast was E. H. Harriman, the owner of the Union Pacific Railroad, and his pain was purely financial.

It was the possibility of a moment like this, in fact, that got Butch, if not Elzy, off the ranch in New Mexico and back into the ball game.

The date was June 2, 1899. The place, Wilcox Station, a spot along the Union Pacific tracks about 110 miles west of Cheyenne. The car destined to get mangled belonged to the No. 1 Overland Limited, a name given to what was actually two trains traveling fairly close together on UP's Wyoming spur. At precisely 2:18 a.m., the engineer of the first train, W. R. "Grindstone" Jones, saw a large man—probably Sundance—waving a red lantern, the universal railroad worker's signal meaning "Stop here, trouble ahead." As Jones pulled up and squinted warily (the lantern business was also a standard train robbers' trick), another man he referred to later as "the leader" (Butch, of course) approached him from behind, crawling, with pistol drawn, over the coal tender. By coming at him at this odd angle, Butch hoped to startle Jones and intimidate him into following orders.

"Now, you son of a bitch," Butch said. "Do what I say, or I will put light through you!" At that point, four other robbers—Harvey Logan, aka Kid Curry; Logan's brother Loney; their cousin Bob Lee; and Harvey's mentor Flatnose George Currie, a Canadian known as Bignose George Currie until a horse kicked him—stepped out of the darkness. All wore "long masks reaching below their necks" (cloth napkins stolen from an early chain restaurant known as the Harvey House), and each one carried "a brace of fine Colt revolvers and a Winchester repeating rifle."

Although the Wild Bunch behaved more humanely than most criminal gangs, they were often not particularly gentle or gracious during a robbery, in keeping with their theory that intimidation is more effective than gunplay. Jones and his fireman were dragged from the engine and frog-marched back to one of two mail cars, locked from the inside, which the robbers loudly demanded to get into. If they were being used as hostages, though, the ploy didn't work. The men inside wouldn't open up and come out until after the robbers had riddled one end of the car with bullets and set off a small explosion at the other. By that time, though, the second "section" of the Overland Limited was bearing down on them, and Butch had to hurry everyone back into the train and tell Grindstone Jones to proceed another mile or so to a spot just beyond a newly constructed bridge that spanned a small gully. When they got there a few minutes later, Butch jumped out and placed what one mail clerk described later as "ten pounds of giant powder" beside the track. Then he lit the fuse and hopped back in the engineer's cab. The night sky turned yellow, and railroad ties flew around like, as the cowboys would say, messkeeters.

The question "why" haunts every corner of outlaw history. Why would a man choose to live a life on the lam with a diet of cold bacon and a rock for his pillow? Money is the most obvious answer, but instant wealth was something only amateur thieves believed in. The veterans knew that sometimes very little was realized from robbing a bank or a train, or from the sale of stolen cattle and horses, and that even a paltry haul usually had to be shared by many. Beyond that stood the inviolable section of the machismo code that required outlaws to spend a small fortune celebrating their success. This may be why so many of them aspired to be saloon keepers. Whiskey, the smart ones often came to realize, was where the real money was. You could go broke in the Wild West being a bandit.

But what about fame? Fame no doubt felt good in the abstract to men who lived in a landscape and an economy that always seemed to be stressing their insignificance. For a lot of outlaws, the pursuit of celebrity—an exciting new concept in the late nineteenth century—was an insistent siren's song. Jesse James, a murderer and thief from the Civil War years until his death in 1882, contrived to become a household name by wrapping himself in the Confederate flag and claiming, via a personal publicist, that his depredations were really just his way of striking a blow for old Dixie. But the more ink you got in the newspapers, the more ink you got on the wanted posters and the larger the dollar amount that vibrated above your photograph. Jesse James's body was still warm when his killer, Robert Ford, wired the governor of Missouri to claim his $500 reward. So it was the year before with Billy the Kid, when General Lew Wallace, the governor of New Mexico, had to interrupt his writing of the future best seller *Ben-Hur: A Tale of the Christ* to cut a check for Pat Garrett. Such were the perils of transforming yourself into a trophy.

As for women, they, too, fail to fully explain the allure of outlawry, which as an aphrodisiac had its limits. Some women were attracted to crooks for their tendency to appear bold and onery, while others saw them as tempting projects, broken versions of proper husbands they thought they might be able to fix. If nothing else, outlaws, in their witless and self-destructive masculinity, provided a chance to exercise one's feminine powers. But most women, even most whores, had the good sense to avoid outlaws because in the end being with one meant being alone. And not *merely* alone, mind you, but stuck quite often in a dark and damp dugout or a wind-ravaged tent while your man was out there in that mind-numbing scenery, running from the sheriff or searching, even though he already had you, for something truly satisfying. Something like Wilcox.

For Butch, Wilcox was as good as it got.

Which is not to say that Wilcox was by any means the perfect crime, or even Butch's best work. It was his first train robbery, and it played out like a rough first draft of what you see in the movies. After that spectacular explosion, the bridge, much to the gang's dismay, remained in place, though, as he turned to look back at it, it seemed pretty unpassable. When Butch again gave the order to move out, Jones had trouble because the train was entering an upgrade. As he struggled with the controls, the engineer said, "one of the smaller men among the robbers" lost patience, "and saying, 'I'll fix you, you ___!' he struck me over the head with his revolver. The blow dazed me. He pulled back to hit me again, and the blow caught me against the hand." At that point, Jones noted, "the leader" intervened and told the smaller man to calm down or he'd likely wind up killing someone. The hothead in that scenario was most likely Harvey Logan, whom Butch always needed to keep on a short leash.

They finally got the engine going, but Butch told Jones to stop again after just a few miles. Because the robbers were running behind schedule, they would need to streamline their plan, which meant forgetting about the mail and focusing on the express car and its two safes, all under the care of the train's cranky thirty-nine-year-old "messenger," Ernest C. Woodcock. When Woodcock refused to let them in with his key, they brushed him aside and blew a hole in the car door with dynamite, then blasted open both safes. "The explosion was so terrific," said one trainman, "that the messenger was stunned and had to be taken from the car." When Woodcock came to, he was pleased to realize that the crimson splotches all over his clothing came from a shipment of raspberries that the blast had turned into flying jam. The red stuff now coated everything in sight—and would later make the stolen bank notes and coins easier to identify.

At last, at about three thirty in the morning, Butch and the boys literally walked away—climbing over the top of a hill and into the featureless landscape, where six fine horses stood pawing the ground and champing their bits, like a vision from a fairy tale—with approximately $55,000 in cash, coin, and jewelry lifted from the train's twin safes. They had come and gone and, with the exception of Jones, hurt no living soul—unless you are the sort who considers corporations to be people. "The passengers were badly scared," said the next day's *New York Times*, "but the robbers made no effort to molest them." Thanks to the magic of the telegraph, E. H. Harriman, the imperious millionaire who ran the Union Pacific and who two years earlier had vowed to eliminate train robbers from the face of the earth, was able to read the first news reports a few hours later over breakfast in his Fifth Avenue mansion.

It is funny how stories sprout and spread. The Wilcox robbery put Butch on the map as a national figure even as it gave rise to a rumor that he wasn't ever there but instead had masterminded the heist from a nearby hideout. Some scholars still insist Butch never went to Wilcox. Really, for a master of misdirection like Butch, there could be no finer compliment.

———

In the immediate aftermath of the Wilcox robbery, with the ruined car smoldering and both sections of the Union Pacific No. 1

Overland Limited unable to proceed, some of the passengers got out to walk around in the light rain, inspect the damage, and shake their heads. One of them, Findley P. Gridley, was the manager of a coal company in Rock Springs that was owned by the railroad, so he took the assault on the rolling stock as a personal affront and was more than a little angry with the robbers. But another passenger he bumped into out there in the middle of nowhere, in the middle of the night, a man he was acquainted with back in Rock Springs—the famous attorney Douglas A. Preston—appeared to be in a much lighter mood. "Don't shoot, Grid! Don't shoot!" Preston said, throwing up his hands theatrically, when he saw himself being recognized. "I can prove an alibi!" Gridley thought it was in poor taste for someone who had gained a measure of fame as Butch Cassidy's lawyer to be joking this way, as if outlaws were just a harmless bunch of bad boys having a hoot at no one's expense but the railroad's. And he didn't like it.

Neither did his ultimate boss, Harriman. Within hours, several hundred men and horses would be dedicated to tracking down the desperados who had dared to rob a Union Pacific train. The telegraph and even the telephone would help coordinate the police effort as well as the pursuit of the story about that effort and the robbery itself. Besides many regular posses, Harriman would also employ his newfangled (and destined to be short lived) "mobile posse"—basically a boxcar full of deputies and horses that would ride the rails to a designated spot, disembark, and go crook hunting. (Screenwriter Goldman rechristened it the "super-posse" and exaggerated its importance for cinematic effect.) Harriman would also sic the Pinkerton National Detective Agency (motto: "We Never Sleep") on the suspects—who would do something very smart and then something else very stupid over the course of the next few days.

The smart thing was that they split into two groups of three. This was a simple maneuver that couldn't be neglected because, in an instant, it made life twice as hard for their pursuers. The group that consisted of Butch, Sundance, and Logan's cousin Bob Lee immediately headed south for William French's WS Ranch in New Mexico. The other group, the ones who would make a serious error, the trio of Harvey and Loney Logan and Flatnose George Currie, lit off for Montana, the Logans' old stomping ground. But for some reason, they got waylaid and two days later were still huddled in an abandoned cabin on a creek six miles northwest of Casper, Wyoming. We know this because one of their neighbors went to call on them to say howdy. When they told him, "Hit the road and hit it quick!" that same neighbor then rode into Casper to report their hostile and suspicious behavior to Converse County sheriff Josiah Hazen.

Because he suspected they were the Wilcox robbers, Hazen rode immediately to the creek with a posse of ten. Butch and his friends had not yet been identified as the perpetrators, so the sheriff had to assume he might be dealing with the kind of typical Western desperados who wouldn't think twice before killing a lawman. In a sense, he was. While the posse approached the cabin on foot, a shot rang out, and Hazen fell, mortally wounded. The Logans had killed before, but the Wild Bunch as a group—despite a good number of shoot-outs with lawmen—hadn't. They had a reputation as a special breed of robber who bothered the big shots but protected the little man. Now, despite Butch's absence from this particular unit, the gang's record was tarnished, as least technically. One thing it surely meant was that the efforts to catch them would be redoubled.

Yet even though the Pinkertons assigned their stealthiest stalker, Charlie Siringo, the Texas-born "original cowboy detective," to follow the thieves and their trail of raspberry-stained money, both groups somehow made it safely to where they were going. The Logan-led ganglet (now joined by Lee) got all the way back to Montana, while Butch and Sundance slipped unseen into William French's bunkhouse. The gang's escape amounted to "the most remarkable flight in the criminal history of the West," a "professional manhunter" named Fred M. Hans told the *New York Times.* Indeed, the only person who caught even a glimpse of them was, by some wild coincidence, a relative of Kerry Ross Boren, the outlaw historian who specializes in wild coincidences. In a 1966 article in *Frontier Times* magazine, Boren wrote that while his granddaddy was tending bar in the whistle-stop of Linwood, Utah, one day in June 1899, Butch and Sundance burst through the swinging doors and proceeded to celebrate their successful escape from Wilcox.

The pardners, however, were definitely in contrasting states of mind by the time they made it back to New Mexico. Sundance, eager to keep moving, took off soon afterward for Galveston, Texas, a trip of more than a thousand miles that may have been motivated by the presence there of his sweetheart Ethel Place. Butch, meanwhile, sank gratefully back into his life as trail boss at the WS Ranch, happy to see all the hands and even happier that his boss didn't ask too many questions, even though by now he realized he'd hired an outlaw. One day a couple of months later, when French mentioned that a Pinkerton agent from Colorado had just shown up in his office and wanted to confirm that he employed a man named Jim Lowe, Butch took the news in stride, grinning his Paul Newman–ish grin and telling French he, in fact, had met the investigator the previous evening and even spotted him a drink in an Alma saloon. Based on their conversation, he said, he wasn't immediately concerned. He knew that a detective with no backup would never try to arrest him. Still, he told French, he couldn't completely discount the Pinkerton's presence; it was a harbinger of something. The day would no doubt come when he'd need to be moseying along.

Many aspects of Butch's life were changing around this time, and not for the good, starting with what happened to Elzy. Less than a month after Butch's return to the ranch, Elzy had up and quit, for reasons, Butch told French, having to do with there being no more broncos to bust. Elzy, Butch said, was something of an *artiste*, or at least a specialist, who had no interest in agriculture beyond the training of green horses.

Of course, that was bull. The truth was that Elzy and some other fellows—the Ketchum Brothers and Will Carver, among them—had hatched a scheme to knock off a Colorado & Southern Railroad train at a spot called Twin Mountains, near Folsom, New Mexico, five hundred miles to the northeast, on the Colorado border. The job initially went much better than anyone had expected; they got about $70,000—a haul so stupendous that the robbers felt compelled to bury most of it, so they could get away faster and then come back for it later when things quieted down. The spot they picked, a remote place called Turkey Creek, not far from Cimarron, New Mexico, was a favorite hideout of theirs; they knew the trails and could get in and out quickly. While they were sneaking away, though, they got cornered by a posse, and a fierce gun battle erupted. Elzy and Sam Ketchum were seriously wounded, but the sheriff of Huerfano County, Ed Farr, and one of his deputies, Henry Love, were killed. Ketchum would also die—in custody, four days later. Elzy, though bleeding and delirious, managed to escape on horseback and remained at large for a month before being arrested 350 miles to the south, in Eddy County, a few miles from the Texas border. He was charged with second-degree murder. When Butch finally told French what had happened, the boss said he was shocked; he had come to think of "Mac," as he knew him, as a man of impeccable character, "the paladin of cowpunchers." Still, he declined Butch's request to contribute to Elzy's legal defense, saying that he "didn't want the outfit to get mixed up in that business."

Outlawry did have a very steep downside. Not only would Elzy soon be sentenced to life in a New Mexican prison, but Bub Meeks, their dependable coconspirator on several fondly remembered jobs past, was doing a thirty-five-year stretch in the Idaho State Penitentiary after being belatedly arrested for his role in the Montpelier heist. Meanwhile, two of Sundance's accomplices at the botched

Malta train robbery currently resided in the Montana State Prison. On top of that, Loney Logan, after trying to pass a reddish, burnt-around-the-edges $1,000 bill in Dodson, Missouri, was shot dead by a Pinkerton who'd trailed him there in connection with the Wilcox heist. And a posse in Utah that was hunting an entirely different crook accidentally shot and killed Flatnose George Currie.

Was somebody trying to tell him something? As the page turned on a new century, Butch seemed to think so, and in the first months of 1900, he headed to Salt Lake City, the capital of his birth state, with a plan for a truly fresh start.

18

ON A ROLL

Butch had intended to quit the WS Ranch sooner or later in any case, but the precipitating cause of his departure had nothing to do with his constant fidgetiness or his yearning for the thing he did not have at the moment: excitement or peace. Rather, it concerned a suggestion made by his boss French that he perhaps take on a more low-profile job than trail boss—in other words, that he accept a demotion—in light of the fact that he was turning out to be the leader of a fairly active outlaw gang. French framed this as the best move for all concerned, a step toward his inevitable amicable departure. But as soon as it became clear that he'd be taking orders from someone else, Butch left for Utah. As cheerful as he usually was, he was also ultrasensitive to the scent of disrespect. "With Jim, it was *Aut Caesar, aut nullus*" (either a Caesar or a nobody), French wrote.

Even when ticked off, though, Butch would always be Butch. As he headed out of New Mexico Territory, he took a detour onto the ranch of a small-time operator whose name we have only as Ayers. Butch believed that Ayers had long been pilfering horses from the WS while at the same time exhibiting a holier-than-thou attitude toward rustlers. Everything about Ayers annoyed the hell out of Butch, and now he took revenge by rounding up all thirty or so of the man's horses and driving them ahead of him down the trail. Poor Ayers "had to walk several miles to his nearest neighbor to borrow a mount" just so he could report the crime, French wrote. A few days later, French got a telegram from a sheriff in Arizona Territory asking if he knew a man named Jim Lowe, who was passing through with a lot of horses, some bearing the WS brand. French wrote back saying yes indeed he knew him, and a fine man he was, too.

By 1900, though, Butch was not considered a fine *young* man any longer. He would turn thirty-four years old that April, and so, by the standards of the day, was decidedly middle-aged. That he hadn't yet settled into a respectable profession seemed to be weighing on his mind when he went to see Orlando Woodworth Powers in his Salt Lake City office, trail-dusty hat in hand. Powers, you will remember, was the prominent Utah attorney who had represented Matt Warner in his manslaughter trial four years earlier. In a 1924 book called *Tales of the Old-Timers*, the veteran Salt Lake City newspaperman Frederick Bechdolt gave an account of their conversation that was taken (Butch biographer Richard Patterson suspects) from Powers's own office notes:

> **BUTCH:** Is what I say to you to go as a client consulting his
>   lawyer from now on?
> **POWERS:** You mean, a privileged communication?
> **BUTCH:** That's it.
> **POWERS:** All right, then.
> **BUTCH:** I'm Butch Cassidy.
> **POWERS:** Well, what can I do for you?
> **BUTCH:** I'll tell you. There's heap of charges out against me
>   and considerable money offered for me in rewards. I'm
>   getting sick of hiding out, always on the run, and never

able to stay long in one place. Now, when it comes to facts, I've kept close track of things, and I know there ain't a man left in the country who can go on the stand and identify me for any crime. All of 'em have either died or gone away. I've been thinking. Why can't I go and just give myself up and stand trial on one of those old charges?

POWERS: No use. You've robbed too many big corporations in your time. I do not doubt what you say, but if you were ever to go on trial, you can depend on it, one of those companies would bring someone to the stand who'd swear against you. No, you'll have to keep on the run, I'm afraid.

Despite the lawyer's discouraging words, the matter did not end there. Somehow the governor of Utah, Heber Wells, became aware of Butch's desire to strike a deal—that is, to accept some predetermined punishment in exchange for a fresh start—and thought the subject worth pursuing. But how all this came about, and what happened once the idea occurred to the governor, has always been hard for the scholars to establish. The problem is that we have too many versions of the so-called amnesty story, and almost all of them are in some way ridiculous. Matt Warner alone supplied two. In the first, which can be found in his memoir, Warner says that upon his release from prison in 1900, Governor Wells asked him to serve as an intermediary, letting Butch know that under the right circumstances, the state would grant him a full pardon "for crimes and offenses he has committed in the past." Of course, since, as the governor well knew, one of the crimes hovering above Butch's head just then was the still-unresolved murder of Sheriff Hazen, an unpardonable offense, that would have been impossible.

In Warner's second, very different story, which came up in the course of a mid-1930s interview with author Charles Kelly, he said that Butch "wanted to get out of the racket" and so proposed that he work for the Union Pacific Railroad as a kind of executive security guard in exchange for absolution. The problem with that story is that E. H. Harriman, that famously cranky capitalist, would never provide employment to someone who had assaulted one of his trains. Still another version of the story has Douglas Preston brokering the deal with the UP for Butch to become a railroad cop. Butch supposedly suggested that they meet to discuss the details at a place in Wyoming called Lost Soldier Pass. Preston arrived late, though, and Butch had already left. In frustration, the lawyer kicked a rock and uncovered a note that said, "Damn you, Preston. You have double-crossed me. I waited all day, but you didn't show up. Tell the UP to go to hell. And you can go with them."

For a while in 1900, the Butch amnesty story was topic A in the Utah newspapers. Seeing an opportunity, a well-known prankster named Angus M. Cannon Jr. started "leaking" fictitious information on the matter to a gullible deputy sheriff named Ben R. Harries, who liked to blab to the press. The result was a series of stories about Butch being (a) eager to talk about turning himself in, (b) hotly contemptuous of Governor Wells, or (c) dead. At one point, Cannon conjured up an imaginary wife for Butch, whose existence he disclosed to Deputy sheriff Harries, knowing full well what would happen next. In June of that year, Harris told the *Deseret Evening News* that Butch's wife was living with the couple's two small children in a "neat cottage" on the outskirts of Salt Lake City while he plotted a way to reenter proper society. Harries had even conducted an interview with the unnamed woman. "There are those who say my husband is a murderer," she said while the kids cavorted. "But he is not, and it was only Wednesday of this week that he congratulated himself on that fact. 'Thank God,' he said, 'my hands are clean of blood stains!'" After a couple of months of crazy stories, Governor Wells was probably happy to announce that Butch had simplified matters for all concerned by returning to his life of crime. "All agreements off," he wrote in a telegram to Warner. "Cassidy just held up a train at Tipton."

The first thing you notice when you study the Tipton train robbery of Wednesday, August 29, 1900, is how similar it was to the Wilcox heist, an homage, almost, with a few almost-eerie coincidences thrown in for good measure. Tipton, like Wilcox, began on a darkened stretch of the Union Pacific Railroad's Wyoming line, with one masked robber, later identified as the leader, climbing into the engineer's cabin from over the coal tender. Harvey Logan was once again present, as was Ben Kilpatrick, along with a fellow Texan named Bill Cruzan and two or three other outlaws whose identities we can only guess at. The engineer—shown a gun, but also given kind assurances that he would not be hurt if he cooperated—was told to proceed slowly to a designated spot just up the tracks (in this case marked by a small campfire), where several other masked men clambered on board. In the Wilcox robbery, the reader will recall, one of the gang felt obliged to whack the engineer in the head with his gun for being uncooperative; at Tipton, it was a pushy passenger who got struck on the sternum by the barrel of a Colt .45. Even the muffled voice of the man refusing to open the express car door had a familiar ring—and with good reason: it belonged to Ernest C. Woodcock, the same messenger who had worked the train at Wilcox. (This was the second of three robberies Woodcock would be involved in during his long career.) Once again, it took an annoyingly long time to deal with Woodcock, but, perhaps remembering how he'd been knocked unconscious by an explosion in the previous robbery, he backed down once the boys starting waving around the dynamite.

Another parallel with Wilcox is that some scholars maintain that Butch was not present at the Tipton affair. They base this conclusion on a cryptic note in the Pinkerton file that says that Sundance skipped Tipton so he could go directly to Winnemucca, Nevada, "to be with Cassidy" at the site of the gang's next job. But that doesn't necessarily mean that Butch was in Winnemucca already. Nor does it outweigh the large amount of evidence that he was at Tipton: the physical descriptions provided by witnesses, the signature techniques he employed, and the cordial way he engaged with his supposed victims. The head conductor, a man named Ed Kerrigan, told a reporter that at one point during the hourlong operation, he had checked the time, and the leader of robbers had admired his pocket watch. "I suppose you will want that pretty soon," Kerrigan said. To his surprise, the robber replied, "No, we don't want anything from laboring men or the passengers. We only want what the company has got—they have plenty." Say what you want about Sundance's whereabouts at that moment; in the entire West, there was only one outlaw who might have calmed the conductor with that slightly Communist manifesto.

This was an unusual gang. "The fellow who guarded us was quite talkative," Woodcock told a reporter. "He said they did not want to kill anyone if they could avoid it—in fact, he said they had an agreement that if anyone killed a man unnecessarily, he himself would be killed by his companions. He further said that there was one man in the crowd who would just as soon kill a man."

That was no doubt a reference to Harvey Logan. A man who fit Logan's description chatted up "Pruitt the mail clerk," as the papers called him, as they both waited for other gang members to ignite the dynamite. "We don't know how we'll fare here," he said, "but we did pretty well at Wilcox. We got a little short of money and came down here to get some more. . . . This ain't the train we wanted, [but] we're pretty sure she got money in the safe. We don't want to kill anybody, but we might do it just the same. . . . There's no use in anybody acting smart with us. . . . We ain't skeered much because we know roads in this country that they don't."

The gang made a clean getaway despite the presence in the main posse of Joe LeFors, a deputy US marshal out of Rawlins, Wyoming, who in the movie is made out to be a lawman of world-class cunning and almost supernatural persistence. He is the head "guy" in the protagonists' memorable mantra "Who *are* those guys?" But in the real story, LeFors played a very minor role. The biggest mystery about Tipton has always been the size of the take. A relatively recent article on the robbery in the *Wild West History Association Journal* that bears the subtitle "Huge Haul or Bust?" fails utterly to answer its own question; but if you read enough accounts of nineteenth-century railroad and bank raids, you get a sense of how the spin around these things worked. The corporate entities who'd suffered the losses always said nothing for as long as possible, then, under pressure to say *something*, lowballed the press—no doubt figuring that a smaller number made them look less foolish and like they'd been better prepared for the hazards of their particular trade. Eventually the newspapers would come up with their own estimate of the take—swollen somewhat, perhaps, by their addiction to sensationalism but in the end likely closer to the truth. In the case of the Tipton robbery, the Union Pacific set its losses in cash and jewelry at $50.40; the press reports, on the other hand, said that the robbers had blasted $50,000 from the express car safe.

And so on to Winnemucca. The boys were on a roll now, finally able to harness and exploit the momentum, the feeling of being warm and loose, which they usually frittered away between jobs while Butch tried to figure out whether or not he really wanted to stay in the outlaw game. Winnemucca, Nevada, may have been nearly six hundred miles west of Tipton, Wyoming, but the gang—Butch, Sundance, and Carver—hit the bank there only twenty-one days later, covering the distance by train and then scrambling to acquire horses and set up their relay system so they could make their signature exit. What was the rush? Why was Butch suddenly trying to steal as much money as quickly as he could?

The answer—of course and alas—was so that he would have enough to once and for all go straight. They were, Butch and (maybe) Sundance seemed to realize, no longer merely in the business of outrunning posses, but in a race with the end of the outlaw era; there was no future in riding around on horses like medieval highwaymen, robbing enterprises made vulnerable by their remoteness, not in an age when remoteness itself was under assault. Yet if they hurried, they might squeeze in another score or two before retiring. Given their growing reputations, their next chapter wasn't going to unfold in the intermountain West; they were far too well known now in those parts. They needed a major change of venue, and South America beckoned.

We don't know how they got the idea, but Argentina, Bolivia, and Brazil were places where North Americans and (to a greater extent) Europeans who thought they'd maxed out their chances or wanted to take a high-stakes gamble at success had lately started to drift. *National Geographic* and a few other magazines featured articles about the friendly (or at least familiar) climate, the stirring scenery, and the booming economies that made the continent seem like the Next Big Thing. It wasn't an easy place to live, though. The rapidity of its development, combined with the tensions that came with the colonial atmosphere, made it dangerous for immigrants. "A man takes his life in his hands when he goes to South America," wrote the Cincinnati businessman Frank Wiborg in a 1905 book about his commercial travels. Butch and Sundance, being outlaws, thought that they could handle South America. If they didn't already have their steamship tickets as they prepared for Winnemucca, at least they had their travel schedule roughed out.

The three robbers convened in the Winnemucca area about ten days after the Tipton holdup, on September 9, 1900, and they appeared to be in an especially good mood. Seventy years later, Vic Button, the son of the man on whose ranch they camped, fourteen miles east of town, said that Butch paid him a lot of attention, gave him candy, and, flashing his famous grin, asked him questions "about the bank and about the country." Butch rode a wonderful white horse, unlike anything young Button had ever seen. "He could jump over high sagebrush, willow fences, or anything. I was about ten years old, and I rode a different horse down [to their camp] every day to race with Butch, but I could never beat the white horse." One day Butch said to him, "You like that horse? Someday he will be yours."

Oddly, much of what we know about the robbery of the First National Bank of Winnemucca, Nevada, in 1900 comes from an article in an English-language Argentine newspaper, the *Buenos Aires Standard*, published in 1912—a time when the authorities in that country were getting serious about clearing the provinces of North American bandits. To show how such nefarious types operated back in the States, the *Standard* presented Sundance's happily and perhaps semidrunkenly remembered version of events taken from an interview that had been done at least four years earlier. The prose in places is more than a little purple—Sundance calls Butch "Our Napoléon, the brainiest member of the bunch"—and the account is studded with obvious errors, such as a reference to Will Carver as George "Flat Nose" Carver. For such lapses, we can perhaps blame his *Standard* ghostwriter or the whiskey.

Sundance says in the piece that he got to Winnemucca ahead of the others, cased the bank, and mapped out their escape route, then went to meet Butch and Carver in Twin Falls, Idaho, where they bought horses to use at the robbery and in the escape relays. On the way back to Winnemucca, short of cash (perhaps because they had buried most of the Tipton haul), they felt it necessary to hold up a general store in Three Creek, Idaho, owned by an old man and his wife. "We called on them after they had gone to bed," said Sundance. "The old man said he wouldn't trust us for a bill of goods, so we showed him our guns; after looking at the forty-fives a half minute, he said, 'Yes, I'll fill your order.' We loaded two packhorses with grub and were about to leave when the old man said, 'Boys, I've got some good hats on the top shelf; perhaps you would like one apiece.' Sure we would. Butch and I got one each, but there was none large enough for the Colonel"—the other nick-name they had for Will Carver. The outlaws would not forget the man's kindness.

On Wednesday the nineteenth, the three came to town just after daybreak and had a casual breakfast, then took a stroll around town—during which Butch noticed a posse was being organized down by the livery barn. Someone had apparently recognized them from their wanted posters, and the sheriff intended to arrest them on suspicion. "So," said Butch to his companions, "it's a chase for us now whether we take in the bank or not." Carver felt they should abandon their plan and get the hell out, but Butch disagreed. Said Sundance: "It was a case of run anyway, and he was going to do something to run for."

They entered the bank just after noon. Butch and Sundance walked to the teller windows while Carver, who had a rifle under his long coat, watched the door. "Butch carried the wad bag to put the money in," Sundance said. "My part was to do the scare act. A nice, pale-looking man with his hair parted in the middle asked, 'What can I do for you, sir?' 'Hand over the money,' I answered, at the same time pulling a pair of forty-five Colts on him. 'Up with your hands,' I said. 'Stick 'em up, everybody!' There was a tall, slim, sallow-faced kid working at a typewriter over in the corner. He didn't hear me at first, then I yelled at him, 'Stick 'em up, Slim, or I'll make you look like a naval target!' When the poor fellow saw what was going on, he collapsed."

At this point, the head bank's cashier, who happened to be

future US Senator George S. Nixon, emerged from the back office. Butch greeted him with a smile and said, "Friend, my associate would like to speak to you at the teller's window."

"What is going on here?" Nixon asked.

"It grieves me to inform you," Butch replied, "that your bank will be losing out."

Sundance then told Nixon, "To feel just how soft and fine the atmosphere is above your head, feel it with both hands at once"—in other words, stick 'em up. While he did that, "Butch went into the vault and filled the wad bag with gold coin."

The posse had positioned itself across the street from the bank and braced for a battle. "They were lined up," Sundance said, "in a brave array behind boxes, barrels, and brick piles." Butch and his companions were not intimidated; they calmly locked the door from the inside and went out through the back, in accordance with their plan. "Their breastworks were of no use," said Sundance, "and we had the open road ahead." But trouble also awaited them. As he spurred his horse into a full gallop, Butch dropped the wad bag, which burst open as it hit the ground. For the next few moments, chaos reigned. "Butch's mare seemed to go straight up when she lost the weight," said Sundance, as the three men then jumped out of their saddles and "scraped up the yellow boys and put them in a new sack." He estimated that besides losing time, they left $5,000 or $6,000 in gold coins on the street.

More trouble lay ahead. As they raced eastward on a trail that paralleled the tracks of the Southern Pacific, a train pulled alongside them, and a rifleman started firing from the engineer's cab. "At the first volley, my old roan was shot in the belly," Sundance said. He tumbled to the ground, then stripped the saddle from his dying horse and carried it to the next relay station, fortunately only a hundred yards distant. Their next stop was the store they had robbed earlier. "We sat down and figured up the old man's bill for groceries and hats," Sundance said. "Then we doubled the amount and put it in a sack, which we left at the store as we passed that night." From there it was on to the farm of a man named Frank Silve, where another batch of fresh horses was waiting. As he dismounted, Butch told Silve to make sure his horse—it was the white one—went to the kid at the Button Ranch. Ten years later, Vic Button still had it. In a letter written to outlaw historian Pearl Baker in 1970, Button said, "For a man, when he was crowded by a posse, to remember his promise to a kid—makes you think he could not have been all bad."

Outlawry had its moments, but even Sundance was starting to be troubled by the limitations of the trade. "If you ask if the pay is worth the work, I would say, 'No'," he told the reporter from the *Buenos Aires Standard.* "But it is a game that once you button into, the law won't let you break away from, unless you go to jail."

No one went to jail for Winnemucca; the gang got away more or less clean once its great innovation—fresh horses every few miles—started playing out. For the record, the bank said it lost $6,500 in the robbery; the newspapers put the take at $32,500. Butch himself verified the number a few years later in a veiled reference he made in a letter to a friend: "Another of my uncles died and left $30,000 . . . so I took my $10,000 and started to see a little more of the world."

———

The world didn't get much worldlier than the forty square blocks of Fort Worth, Texas, known as Hell's Half Acre, where the boys—Butch, Sundance, Harvey Logan, Ben Kilpatrick, and Bill Carver—went next. The occasion that November was Carver's marriage to Callie May Hunt, a well-known Western whore. The wedding likely happened in either Josie Belmont's, Fannie Porter's, or Jessie Reeve's sporting house, the anchor stores, so to speak, of the infamous Half Acre. While it was perhaps an unorthodox place to salute the sacrament of marriage, Logan, Kilpatrick, and Sundance all squired their steadies—Annie Rogers, Laura Bullion, and Ethel Place, respectively; only Butch was stag. It was a happy time, their last happy time together. In less than a year, Carver would be dead, and Kilpatrick and Logan would be in prison. At some point in the proceedings—probably very early on, because they appear fresh and sober—the boys wandered away from their ladies and into the Swartz photo studio, just down the block in that same raucous district, to sit for a portrait. Today the scholars call it "the Fort Worth Five"—which is a lot easier to say than "Four Men Looking off to the Left, No Doubt at the Suggestion of John Swartz, While One Stares Directly and Enigmatically at the Camera"—though it could have been called that, too. By that time, Butch had the alone-in-the-crowd thing down pat.

3

19

◆

IN THE CONE

I am standing in about six inches of llama poop. So, too, I can assume was the man born Robert LeRoy Parker when he committed his last robbery in this same rugged patch of the Bolivian Andes on November 4, 1908, accompanied by the man born Harry Alonzo Longabaugh, aka the Sundance Kid. A lot has happened in the world since then, but not here, in the place the local people call Huaca Huañusca, or Dead Cow, for the shape of the mountain that slumps just above and beyond it. For the sake of history, I tried to plant my boots exactly where Butch's were that long-ago spring morning when a midlevel mining company manager named Carlos Peró, his young son Mariano, and their porter, Gil González, came around the bend to my left carrying several big bags of green and red bolivianos: the weekly payroll. I have even arranged to be here at the exact same time of day that the robbery occurred—nine fifteen in the morning—to see just how the light might have played upon the dramatically broken boulders, the blooming *yareta*, and the Bolivian begonia as Butch and Sundance peered in the direction from which they knew the trio would be approaching: the boy and the servant on mules, and Carlos Peró, in deference to his saddle sores, walking.

Overall, though, I proved to be a poor Butch and Sundance robbery reenactor. First of all, I was there in the wrong month—March, when not just the light but also the very attitude of nature was palpably different from November, South America's late spring. Then there was my gear. While we know from Carlos Peró's testimony that Butch and Sundance both packed brand-new "carbines which appeared to be of the Mauser type, small caliber and thick barrel" in addition to "very small Browning revolvers outside their cartridge belts," I had only a wooden replica of what appeared to be Daniel Boone's Kentucky long rifle—a prop left over from the salad days of Butch Cassidy and the Sundance Kid tourism. My trusty guides, Janet and Freddy, had cheerfully thrust it upon me, along with a corny-looking cowboy hat, as soon as we'd stepped out of the car to start the hourlong trudge to the scene of the crime. A couple of greybeards at the travel agency where they worked in Tupiza had told them about people like me who'd once come from all over the world to see the places in Bolivia that had figured in the movie's dramatic final scenes—scenes that for budgetary reasons had actually been shot in Mexico.

Over the last few decades, the stream of pilgrims had dwindled to an unsteady drip, partly because *Butch Cassidy* was fading from memory but also because the enthusiasts had aged out of the terrain. You won't find any handrails or ramps at Huaca Huañusca, or "themed" Butch Cassidy cafes to provide refreshment; just a big pile of rocks built over the decades by Bolivians who, until the late twentieth century, blended worship of the fearsome condor god into their staunch Christianity. (Hauling a big rock there told the condor god you were sorry for a big sin, while a medium rock covered a medium sin, and so on.) In any case, sartorially speaking, I was highly inauthentic and no match for what Peró, called "the two Yankees who wore new, dark-red, thin-wale corduroy suits with narrow, soft-brimmed hats, the brims turned down in such a way that, with the bandannas tied behind their ears, only their eyes could be seen."

———————

The robbery itself could have gone better: they'd unfortunately caught Peró on an off week when he was carrying just 18,000 bolivianos (the equivalent of about $200,000 today) instead of the 80,000 they'd been expecting. Yet if rust had accumulated during their several years of going straight, they had worked it off in the course of a tune-up caper or two, and at Huaca Huañusca, they acted with panache and authority, two virtuosi deep into their mature prime. Peró ultimately seemed to appreciate their performance even though, when Butch first stepped out from behind a bush with rifle cocked and pointed, he naturally felt scared. In reporting the crime to his bosses, he marveled at how considerate the thieves were, especially when it came to not killing him, his son, or his servant, whose deaths would have helped ensure a successful escape. After first flashing his weapon, "the shorter of the two men," he said, greeted him with a smile and said in English, which Peró understood. "I'd appreciate it if you would get down off those mules and back away, please." As Peró must have known, there'd been a rash of similar robberies that year in Bolivia, including two pulled by a pair of thuggish North Americans—but these guys in red suits were clearly not them, or common criminals of any sort. As he went through their saddlebags (with one hand, while keeping them covered with the other), the same shortish fellow, said Peró, "specified that they were not interested in our personal money nor in any articles that belonged to us, but only in the money that we were carrying for the company."

The pair was never positively identified. In all the many reports, inquiries, depositions, and hearings generated by the robbery and subsequent events, they appeared only as "the gringos" or "the Yankees." Yet can there be any doubt about who robbed Carlos Peró?

The big question, rather, is why, after seeming at last to find a true measure of peace, Butch and Sundance returned to a game that they knew wasn't worth the candle.

———

This final chapter of their lives had begun in the fall of 1900, the gang members toasting one another's futures as they left Fort Worth. Logan, Kilpatrick, and Carver split up and disappeared back into the demimonde. Butch, Sundance, and Ethel headed for New York City, but the latter two took a roundabout route, going first to New Orleans, where they celebrated New Year's Eve, then to Pennsylvania, where they paid a brief visit to relatives in Mont Clare. (Even outlaws have in-laws, it seems.) Sundance, limping noticeably, told his family that he was recovering from a slow-healing gunshot wound to his left leg but offered no further details. (It was probably a souvenir of Winnemucca.) He introduced Ethel as his wife, and she said she was from Texas, but neither she nor Harry, as he was known back home, volunteered much beyond the fact that they were heading to South America to start afresh. First, though, they had a few things to attend to.

In mid-January they took a train to Buffalo, New York, where both checked into Dr. Pierce's Invalids Hotel, a widely advertised combination spa/clinic that specialized in the treatment of "chronic diseases, specifically those of a delicate, obscure, complicated, or obstinate character." Sundance may have sought relief from his chronic sinusitis, or as it was known in those days, catarrh—or the visit may have involved his leg, or something else entirely. He seems to have been a bit of a hypochondriac or maybe a medical buff. We don't know what, if anything, was troubling Ethel, but they were fit enough to make a trip to Niagara Falls, the most popular honeymoon destination of the day, on the way to reconnecting with Butch in New York City.

New York was where the steamships were, and the open water

they pointed toward meant freedom from the lawmen and the private investigators who lately had been violating their privacy in a whole new way. If riding over flat rock or using special "outlaw horseshoes," which slipped easily on and off, confused pursuers out west, imagine what the Atlantic Ocean could do to obscure your tracks. And it was surely time to go. Charlie Siringo, the cowboy detective, had recently showed up at Butch's boyhood home in Circleville, Utah, cadged a meal or two from Maxi and Ann Parker, and even charmed his way into the bed of one of Butch's sisters (though he never said which)—all without finding out very much. In Mont Clare, meanwhile, the Pinkertons, in service to the Union Pacific, were bribing postal workers to monitor Samanna Longabaugh's mail and pass along to them anything that might possibly have been sent by Sundance. The agency's intrusive, illegal tactics were a bracing reminder that "the Pinks," though often described as the precursors of the FBI, cared not a whit about enforcing the law or prosecuting the guilty but only about satisfying their clients so they could keep collecting their monthly fees. Its operatives, charged with eliminating nuisances to the capitalist system by any means necessary, were more like exterminators than police.

The crowds of Manhattan provided good cover for the trio, who, unbeknownst to their pursuers, spent several happy weeks in the city of 4.2 million starting in late January 1901. They booked comfortable but modest accommodations at a boardinghouse run by an Irish widow named Catherine Taylor at 234 East Twelfth Street and did nothing to call attention to themselves. Butch signed the register as James Ryan, perhaps borrowing the name of a saloon keeper he'd known out West; the allegedly married couple he was traveling with registered as H. A. and Ethel Place, Place being, of course, the maiden name of Sundance's mother. Sundance told Mrs. Taylor he was a cattle broker from Wyoming; Butch said he was Ethel's brother.

New York in early 1901, while on the brink of many cultural changes and political reforms that would transform it into the modern city we know today, was still a dirty, smelly, Dickensian metropolis brimming with brothels and gambling dens, managed by an openly corrupt Tammany Hall mayor, and dominated by horses, though here and there one saw an expensive handmade "motorcycle," which is what people called cars then. A strike by the recently organized vaudeville performers association kept many theaters dark for the duration of the outlaws' stay, but they probably caught a few of the primitive (and very short) movies in release, which were shown in storefronts or blacked-out tents. New York was the center of the film industry in those days. One of the more ambitious outfits, the Edison Manufacturing Company, opened for business at 41 East Twenty-First Street on or about the same day in early February 1901 that Sundance and Ethel posed for a now-famous photo in the busy studio of Joseph DeYoung, in Union Square. Two years later, Edison Manufacturing would produce *The Great Train Robbery*, an immensely popular twelve-minute silent feature that might have been inspired by the exploits of the Wild Bunch— but among the even more primitive movies the outlaws might have seen on their visit were *Sherlock Holmes Baffled* and the riveting *Sea Lions Being Fed*.

About their activities in New York, we know precious little. Sundance may have gone to the doctor again, but Butch spent at least one day shopping. The records of Tiffany & Co., established in 1837 and then located in a five-story cast-iron building on Fifteenth Street and Union Square dominated by a huge clock, show that James Ryan of the rooming house address paid $40.10 for what seems to have been a gold watch in a deluxe "hunter case" on February 4. Some scholars believe this is likely the double-eagle-size timepiece that Ethel has pinned, in the then-current style, to the smart dark dress she wore in the DeYoung photograph that has set many an outlaw historian's heart aflutter. Was it a wedding present?

A gesture of affection from a resigned but still-smitten ex-beau? Despite the efforts of the scholars, we still can only wonder.

————

Their idyll in Manhattan lasted less than a month. On February 20 at the Atlantic Dock in Red Hook, Brooklyn, they boarded a 310-foot Scottish freighter called the *Bellarden*—then sat in port for at least two nights due to ice floes in the harbor. The Bellarden, with limited passenger service, was not a terribly comfortable ship for what would be a thirty-three-day voyage, but though they carried plenty of cash, their choices were limited; just one other ship sailed from New York to Buenos Aires in the latter half of February that year, and it was hardly any more posh. The thin schedule reflected a weak demand. While the economies of most South American countries appeared to be on the upswing, and a good number of Europeans were starting to see the continent as their next step or a fresh start, North Americans were then migrating to the so-called Southern Cone at the rate of only two hundred or so per year. Perhaps that's not so surprising. If a US resident was eager to get involved in mining or ranching or simply liked the idea of trying to tame a wild land, the western states still offered more convenient opportunities for such adventures. For Butch and Sundance, though, the time when they could holster their six-shooters, put away their bandanna masks, and blend seamlessly into the American cattle business had long since passed.

While we don't know how they spent their time at sea, the written accounts of others who traveled by freighter to Buenos Aires in those days suggest that the trip—which cost about $90, or about $2,600 in today's money—did not, despite the steep price, usually result in a sack of happy postcards. No bands or other shipboard entertainment broke the monotony, nor were there champagne toasts at sunset with a dinner-jacketed captain. Passengers were largely an afterthought, if not an inconvenience on such steamers. Usually they spent the voyage staring at the whitecaps, strolling the deck, or dozing over a book while the crew swabbed and swore on the outskirts of their personal space. "Those accustomed only to an Atlantic liner might wonder if they were not by chance aboard a cattle ship," wrote the peripatetic businessman Frank Wiborg, referring to the smell of farm animals that frequently wafted from below. Such woeful travel conditions weeded out everyone, Wiborg said, except "the inevitable party of English globe-trotters who went *everywhere*," a few men going to work on the Panama Canal or in the mines of Peru, and "a group not so easily identified—embarking on the risky ventures that a new country always affords."

While, as noted above, not many North Americans fell into the latter category, there was by then a certain right way of going about things if you came from the States and were looking to stay in Argentina for the long term—and Butch, Sundance, and Ethel knew what to do. How three rural Westerners obtained such information can't be said with certainly, but the Argentinian historian Marcelo Gavirati told me over coffee in Puerto Madryn that he believes the many Welsh and English settlers in Patagonia had family connections in Mormon Utah who may have known the Parkers of Circleville and thus created a pipeline of helpful advice. In any case, soon after they came down the gangplank in Buenos Aires, a burgeoning city of more than one million, in late March 1901, they visited the office of a dentist named George Harkness Newbery near the past-its-prime Hotel Europa. Newbery was a native New Yorker who'd been in Argentina for nearly twenty-five years and held the honorary title of United States vice consul. He had friends in high places, and, because he was also a real estate speculator, he knew the characteristics of the Argentine countryside as well as the sometimes sketchy and abstruse homesteading laws that governed its apportionment to settlers. As soon as he learned that the newcomers were interested in raising cows, sheep, and horses, Newbery pointed them in the direction of southern Argentina—specifically to Chubut, a province bordered on the east by the Atlantic Ocean and on the west by a range of the Andes Mountains that separates Argentina from Chile. The climate and topography would be familiar to people from the western United States, he knew, and very few claims had been filed there as yet, meaning that large amounts of prime land were still up for grabs at very good prices.

The trio didn't waste any time. After leaving Newbery's office, they proceeded through the crowded streets to the Banco de Londres y Rio de la Plata a few blocks away, where they deposited $12,000 in Bank of England pound notes, the equivalent of about $250,000 today. Then, after a night or two at the Hotel Europa, they hopped aboard a southbound train to scout out the area that the dentist had recommended. Chubut was sparsely populated but vast, roughly the size of Utah, so they focused, at Newbery's recommendation, on Cholila, a region in the western part of the province distinguished by fertile valleys and situated just over the mountains from prosperous Pacific Ocean ports in Chile. The outlaws were immediately impressed. Writing to Elzy Lay's mother-in-law, Mathilda Davis, a year later, Butch said that Cholila "can't be beat for the purpose of stock raising. I have never seen a finer grass country, and lots of it hundreds and hundreds of miles that is unsettled and comparatively unknown, and . . . good agricultural country . . . with good cold mountain water."

He also noted, "I am a long way from Civilization, 16 hundred miles to Buenos Aires . . . and over 400 miles to the nearest Rail Road or Sea Port." The remoteness might have been a negative for some—the region was still also several hundred miles from the nearest telegraph line—but for fugitives who had the Pinkertons on their trail and wanted nothing more than to live peacefully, it added to the paradisiacal quality of the place. Within a few months, they had filed a claim on more than 1,500 acres of land along the eastern shore of the Rio Blanco River and paid 885 pesos (or about $360) for 16 colts who would form the foundation of their horse breeding stock. They soon added 20 more horses, 1,300 sheep, and 500 head of cattle, purchasing the livestock from reputable, established breeders with checks drawn on the bank in Buenos Aires.

It is touching to see how the outlaws, trying hard to be perfectly good boys for once in their lives, went out of their way to do things by the book during their first years in Argentina. There was a lot of paperwork to be completed when establishing a cattle operation there, and they did it all quite properly, signing themselves now as James Santiago Ryan and Harry Enrique Place. Besides filling out the homesteading claims (something that not everyone bothered to do; quite a few others simply moved onto their property and became squatters), they traveled to Rawson, the territorial capital of Chubut, and applied for ownership of three cattle brands; an *R* for Ryan, a *P* for Place, and a combination of *P* and *R*, so all of their options remained open. They intended to keep their stock clearly marked and well herded, the better to avoid disputes that could get them caught up in the legal system and exposed as outlaws on the lam. Because their Spanish was weak, they also hired an *escribano*, or notary, to help them trademark the name of their joint venture, Place y Ryan, a de facto partnership involved in the commercial production of cattle and other animals.

Although it appeared that only one signature was necessary, both Butch and Sundance, as well as the *escribano*, signed the document just to be certain. By October, they were living in a canvas tent on what was conditionally their property and, with the help of hired hands, building with rough-split cypress logs the first in what would be a small complex of cabins and barns on a flat, grassy stretch of land with a river running through it and an inspiring view of the Andes.

20

FAMILY OF THREE

I**t was a good life** from the start in many ways, settled in among Welsh, Italian, English, Chilean, and even a few American immigrants who, for the most part, remained at a comfortable distance, pursuing their own South American adventures. While those first months in their new land featured some arduous frontier living—June, July, and August are the dead of the Argentine winter, a tough time to sleep in a tent with only a campfire and blankets to keep them from freezing—the three were working toward a common goal of having a more civilized life than Butch and Sundance had known as cowboys up north. By the time they built their houses, they had a well-groomed springer spaniel who slept inside, they dressed up like gentlemen and lady "growers," took afternoon tea, and often spent their evenings reading by the light of burnished brass oil lamps imported from the United States. A man whose father had known the trio told the historian Anne Meadows in the early 1990s, "The Places and Señor Ryan were people accustomed to living well, very cultured. They had a washstand with a fine pitcher and basin, and she put drops of perfume in the water. They set the table with a certain etiquette—napkins, china plates.

Their windows went up and down [in the supposedly more refined North American style].” An Italian immigrant named Primo
Capraro, who would spend a night with them in 1904, wrote later:

> The house was simply furnished and exhibited a certain
> painstaking tidiness, a geometric arrangement of things,
> pictures with cane frames, wallpaper made from clippings
> from American magazines, and many beautiful weapons
> and lassos braided from horsehair. The men were tall,
> slender, laconic, and nervous with intense gazes. The
> lady, who was reading, was well dressed. I had a friendly
> dinner with them, and as I couldn't offer them any gratu-
> ity, I made them a detailed sketch of a bungalow [that they
> might build]. I figured the necessary quantity of bricks,
> windowpanes, ironwork, nails, bolts, metal sheets, and
> even the projected number of windows doors and tables,
> beds, wardrobes, chairs, etc. We agreed that in the event
> they undertook the project, I would come down to Cho-
> lila with workers I would recruit in Bariloche.

One wonders if Capraro noticed while sketching the dream house
that they were a family with special needs, including the need to
get away quickly. When I visited there in 2017, I noticed that every
room in their cabins had a door leading to the outside. Back in the
day, no matter what the time or the weather, three horses always
stood in or just outside the barn, saddled and ready to go. They
even had a primitive walkie-talkie that they used to communicate
with a sentry in a brick building two hundred meters down the road
toward the town of Cholila. Nervous with intense gazes indeed.

Generally speaking, though, they felt comfortable with their
neighbors in Chubut. “The bandits were well liked,” a descendant
of one of their friends told Anne Meadows, “amiable, generous, cordial, polite to the ladies, friendly with children.” The impressions

they made in Patagonia were consistent with the way they had long been perceived up north. Many commented on their devotion to books, as well as their facility with guns, ropes, and horses. "Those who knew them well," said Capraro, "said that they were expert shooters capable of hitting a coin in the air." The local gauchos had at first "chortled at the prospect" of watching the overly refined gringos try to organize the cattle at roundup time, another longtime Cholila resident told Meadows, "but they proved to be very good cowboys, handy with lassos, and the gauchos came away with a new opinion."

Butch, who inevitably charmed almost everyone he met, was seen as gregarious and dependable, someone who "joined in the festivities of the settlement." Sundance struck the locals as highly competent, but often terse and aloof: "Not so much a bad character," a Welsh-born policeman named Milton Roberts wrote later, "as a cold-blooded one—but a genuine cowboy, very capable with animals." Once when the governor of the province, Julio Lezana, came through Cholila and asked if he could stay a night with them, they welcomed him and uncorked the wine. "Place played the samba on his guitar, and Ryan danced with [the daughter of local rancher] Don Ventura Solis." Ethel danced with the governor.

Lezana must have been as dazzled by Ethel as everyone else. She was "good-looking, a good rider, and an expert with a rifle," Roberts wrote. A neighbor named Richard Perkins described her as "very agile and bold . . . she rode with the skill of an equestrian and hunted birds with a revolver." An Argentine researcher who spoke to many who knew her called her "a goddess." Her style of dress, which often tended toward the masculine, was the subject of much local comment. "She wore corduroy *bombachas* [gaucho pants] that fell over men's boots, which she wore when doing ranch work." Another policeman, Julio O. de Antueno, said that "she never wore dresses, just pants and boots" but managed to always project elegance nevertheless. The *comisario*, or police commissioner, of the district, Eduardo Humphreys, was said to have had a crush on her, as did a local teenage boy named John Gardiner, who'd recently immigrated from Scotland. Gardiner, a sickly, bookish lad, felt that as two "educated people" who had managed to find each other "in the wilderness," he and Ethel were fated to be together—a notion which, if sadly misguided, supports the idea that she might have been a teacher, and not a dance hall girl, back in the States. "Ethel was his first love and his only love," said a friend of Gardiner's, who noted that John nursed a corresponding hatred of the man he knew as Enrique Place, considering him "a mean, low cur" for, in his opinion, not appreciating Ethel sufficiently. Señor Ryan, on the other hand, he liked quite a bit.

Over the years, the domestic life of Butch, Sundance, and Ethel, has raised many an Argentinian eyebrow. When I introduced the topic to the testy old proprietor of the El Globo Hotel in Trelew (where legend has it the trio once shared a single room), he said *"Una mujer, dos hombres"*—then shrugged theatrically. The arrangement does not appear to have been an active ménage à trois: Sundance and Ethel slept in one cabin, Butch in another. They also maintained separate relationships with their native land which may have reflected their contrasting views of the future: Butch was becoming rooted in South America while Sundance was clearly not. A little less than a year after arriving, in February 1902, the three traveled back to Buenos Aires, where Sundance and Ethel boarded the British steamship *Soldier Prince*, bound for New York City with its hold full of fruits and vegetables. We know from later Pinkerton reports that their trip to the United States, like previous ones, combined pleasure (they went to Coney Island and Atlantic City, where Sundance's brother Harvey lived, as well as to Mont Clare) with at least one doctor's appointment (possibly at New York's Bellevue Hospital, where they may have both received treatment for an unspecified illness). They returned in August on another clanking British steamer called the *Honorious*, traveling this time as crew—Sundance was the chief purser; Ethel, the stewardess—in exchange for free fare.

Butch spent the first part of his alone time in the Office of Land Management in Buenos Aires, filing more forms aimed at increasing their real estate holdings and trying to secure the title on what they already had. Argentinian land laws were complicated and the procedures unclear, even to some government officials. After a few such dull days, he made the three-week journey by steamship and horseback to Cholila, where, for a stretch of time, he had not much to do except oversee others, play poker with the hired hands, and attend cockfights. "I have a good 4-room house, wearhouse [sic], stable, chicken house, and some chickens," he said in a letter to Mathilda Davis. "The only thing I lack is a cook, for I am still living in Single Cussedness and I sometimes feel very lonely." His poor Spanish, he said, was part of his problem: "I don't speak it well enough to converse on the latest scandals so dear to the hearts of all nations, and without which conversations are very stale." But it wasn't just a lack of language that left him isolated. Something else, something more essential, kept a man who craved society and whom everyone fell in love with from ever having a lover—at least one he could show to the world. But then that, too, was really no different from the way things had been back in the States.

The watershed moment of their South American venture came in mid-March 1903, when a Pinkerton detective showed up in George Newbery's dental office with photographs and questions. The agency was not at that point officially involved in the pursuit of Butch and Sundance, but its president, Robert Pinkerton, the son of the founder, thought he could convince a client or two to support a mission to track down the pair (and their mysterious lady friend, whom the agency mistakenly called Etta). One of his more experienced operatives, Frank Dimaio, out of the Philadelphia office, had just completed an assignment in Brazil, and so Robert Pinkerton directed him to go to Buenos Aires to see what he could learn about the fugitives. He already knew one big thing, thanks to the illegal monitoring of Samanna Longabaugh's mail: that the three were living in cabins in the remote area of Cholila. After Dimaio produced photographs of the suspects, including the group portrait taken in Fort Worth, Newbery confirmed their location but said he thought they were fine, honest folks who since their arrival two years earlier had worked hard and doubled their livestock. If the agent did have a mind to arrest them, Newbery said, the oncoming rainy season was a poor time to make the long journey on his own by steamer and saddle. Dimaio agreed the timing wasn't right and headed back to the United States—where he created a Spanish-language circular describing the outlaws that he would soon begin sending to police chiefs throughout Argentina.

It was standard business practice for the Pinkertons to exaggerate the threat posed to companies and associations by people they wanted to be paid to pursue. From his office in New York, Robert Pinkerton mailed out memoranda linking Butch and Sundance to all sorts of crimes throughout South America that they couldn't possibly have committed. He also wrote and publicly released a letter to the Buenos Aires police chief about the Wild Bunch "hold-up robbers," saying, "It is a firm belief that it is only a question of time until these men commit some desperate robbery in the Argentine Republic. They are all thorough plainsmen and horsemen riding from 600 to 1,000 miles after committing a robbery. If there are reported to you any bank or train hold up robberies or any other similar crimes, you will find that they were undoubtedly committed by these men." The cost of "running down and apprehending Harry Longbaugh, [sic] alias Harry Alonzo, and George Parker, alias Butch Cassidy," he told the Union Pacific Railroad, the American Bankers Association, and a few other entities for which the agency had worked, would be $5,000—and, as an added bonus, Charlie Siringo, the cowboy detective himself, would take part. His pitch seems to have elicited no response, though. Mounted train bandits and bank robbers like Butch and Sundance already seemed quaint to twentieth-century business executives—but beyond that, hadn't the outlaws already solved the problem they posed to corporate America by running away? As far as E. H. Harriman and other leading American capitalists were concerned, as long as those troublemakers stayed in the exotic locales to which Pinkerton claimed he had tracked them, they could do whatever the hell they pleased. At this point, the Pinkertons backed off.

Down in Cholila, meanwhile, the outlaws had no idea they were being featured in a marketing campaign—or even that the Pinkertons knew where they were. Their lives went on as usual. Sundance and Ethel made what was becoming their semiregular trip to North America in March 1904, this time visiting the Louisiana Purchase Exposition in Saint Louis, where they had the opportunity to attend the Airship Contest, marvel at the wireless telephone demonstration, and experience the breakout hit of the midway: ice cream cones. Butch stayed in Cholila and opened a country store on their property, to both amuse himself and make a little side income. He also shopped for himself at similar places. An undated receipt shows that he bought socks, slippers, a sweater, two handkerchiefs, and a dozen *bombillas*—metal tubes for drinking maté tea, like a true Argentinian rancher. In a February 1904 letter to his good friend Daniel Gibbon, a Welsh immigrant who lived nearby, he noted that his pal "Place" was off buying bulls, and that he himself wanted to purchase some rams but was temporarily unable to sit in the saddle due to "a bad dose of the Town Disease." Outlaw scholars have always assumed he was talking, if not almost boasting (since the mention seemed so gratuitous), about gonorrhea. Besides maintaining a few widely scattered whorehouses, Chubut Province also featured horse-drawn, pimp-driven whore wagons, which found no shortage of patrons. Perhaps because of rumors about his sexuality,

Butch seemed eager for Gibbon to understand that he partook of such earthy pleasures.

————

A sharp knock on Butch's cabin door in April 1904 shattered whatever peace the three were finding in the wilds of Patagonia. His visitors were a contingent of provincial policemen who wanted to talk to him and probably Sundance, too, about a robbery that had taken place several days earlier some six hundred miles to the east. Two ranch hands involved in a sheep-shearing operation were suspected of stealing five thousand pesos that their employer, the giant Southern Land Company, had been transporting to a bank in Trelew. The pair, one of whom may have been an American named Robert Evans, had promptly escaped from custody, but the police had reason to believe they were friends of Señors Ryan y Place and had made their way to Cholila to hide out. Butch, they also thought, was likely the owner of the big, shiny Colt revolver that officers took from Evans at the time of his arrest. Was the gun, in fact, his, the stern-faced callers wanted to know? Had they seen Evans and the other fellow recently?

If Butch had one fatal flaw, it was that he couldn't stay away from bad company—and the trouble it ultimately brought him. He judged no one, it seemed; or if he did, he found everyone to his liking somehow, even the amoral sorts like Harvey Logan, the odd ducks like Al Hainer—and the often surly men like Sundance. Thus it had always been. As far as the Chubut police were concerned, the answer to both their questions was yes—it was Butch's gun and the two suspects had stayed in his cabin before and since the robbery— though Butch wasn't about to say any of that. Evans was an ordinary career criminal whom he and Sundance had known to some small degree back in the States as a member of the Ketchum gang, which had hung out in Brown's Park, a gang that at times included their colleagues Ben Kilpatrick and Will Carver. How they connected in

South America we don't know, but once they did, their bond grew stronger, and before long, Evans was sleeping for weeks or months at a time in Butch's cabin.

This was not at all a good idea because his presence could draw the police and their absence usually meant they were somewhere over the mountains once again getting themselves into the kind of trouble that would cause the police to follow them back to Cholila. The officers who came to Butch's door in April 1904 took him to Rawson, 460 miles to the east, to make a statement before a judge. He denied knowing anything about the gringos or the gun and was quickly released. But the world he came back to was different from the one he'd left just a few days earlier. He was a Likely Suspect now, a permanent Person of Interest whose real identity would in time become known.

Butch and Sundance should have hightailed it out of Cholila right then, but instead they hesitated. Winter was setting in, making travel and the business of selling off their livestock more difficult. It is always hard to make a living as a small-time rancher, and there were signs that they were running low on funds, such as Butch's opening a store and Sundance and Ethel's working for their steamer passage. They were still living in their cabins ten months later when Evans and a newly arrived fellow American named William Wilson held up the Banco de Tarapaca y Argentino in Rio Gallegos, the capital of Santa Cruz Province, seven hundred miles south of Cholila, and got away with the equivalent of about $100,000. No arrests were made, but the Santa Cruz police issued a warrant for Santiago Ryan and Enrique Place, whom they thought might lead them to Evans and Wilson—that is, if they weren't the robbers themselves.

It is pretty certain that they weren't. A good number of people saw them in Cholila on the day of the Rio Gallegos robbery. Many weeks went by, and the Chubut police didn't come to even question them, never mind put them in custody. The warrant, in fact, still lay on the desk of their friendly local police commissioner,

Eduardo Humphreys, who was fond of the three (especially Ethel) and wasn't inclined to undertake what he saw as an unpleasant task of arresting them. Instead, Humphreys let them know they were being sought in connection with the robbery, then dithered for several months while they sold off whatever property they could (they never did get title to the land), settled their debts, and prepared to leave. When his behavior came to light, Humphreys was fired, but by the time his replacement arrived in Cholila in early April 1905, the outlaws' cabins were empty, and they were hiding in the nearby hills. On the day they finally left the valley—May 1—Butch posted a brief letter to a neighbor, a former Texas sheriff named John Commodore Perry. He asked Perry to pay his friend Daniel Gibbon the sum of $285.44 to settle a debt, then closed with these words:

"We are starting today."

21

---◆---

BACK IN BUSINESS

They went westward into Chile.

On the twenty-eighth of June in 1905—almost two months after they'd left their ranch in Argentina— Sundance posted a letter from Valparaiso, a thriving Pacific seaport and the second largest city in Chile, to the same Daniel Gibbon.

Dear Friend:

We are writing to you to let you know that our business went well and that we received our money. We arrived here today, and the day after tomorrow my wife and I leave for San Francisco. I'm very sorry, Dan, that we could not bring the brand R with us, but I hope that you will be able to fetch enough to pay you for the inconveniences.

We want you to take care of [their ranch hand] Davy and his wife and see that they don't suffer in any way. And be kind to the old spaniel and give him pieces of meat once in a while and get rid of the black mutt.

I don't want to see Cholila ever again, but I will think of you and of all our friends often, and we want to assure you of our good wishes.

Attached you will find the song "Sam Bass" [about a legendary outlaw killed by Texas Rangers in 1878], which I promised to write down for you. As I have no more news, I will end by begging that you remember us to all our friends without forgetting [other ranch hands] Juan [Vidal] and Wenceslao [Solis], giving them our regards and good wishes, keeping a large portion for yourself and family.

Remaining as always your true friend.
H. A. Place

Although they were homeless now and on the run, they had business to take care of in Chile. A land company there called the Cochamo Company had bought their chattel—that is, their cabin and corrals as well as their homesteading rights—but its representatives, sensing that Butch and Sundance were selling under duress, had subsequently tried to change the terms of the deal and knock down the agreed-upon price of 20,000 pesos to 18,000. Even the lower figure was a considerable amount of money—almost $180,000 today—but given the debts they had to settle in Cholila, it's not clear how much they would ultimately realize. With their futures uncertain and their finances in a turmoil, the extra 2,000 pesos, they felt, were worth fighting for. And they were right about that. After they showed up at Cochamo's Valparaiso office, the company restored the original deal.

The outlaws stayed in Chile for about six months—or at least Butch did, calling himself William Thompson and haunting the bars in Antofagasta, another busy port in the North. For a large chunk of that time, Sundance and Ethel were away in San Francisco, staying with his brother Elwood Longabaugh, a bachelor and day laborer who had a small apartment on the edge of the Tenderloin district. It was probably not an appealing arrangement for Ethel, for whom all the sneaking in and out under various aliases—they were Mr. and Mrs. Matthews now—was, we can see in hindsight, starting to wear thin. Sundance, given to long bouts of silence, had never been easy to live with, and lately his drinking had been getting worse. Alcohol was probably a factor when, shortly after their return to Chile, he got in a tussle with several Antofagasta police officers—who apparently had kidded him about his resemblance to a fellow identified as Enrique Place on a Pinkerton circular that was hanging nearby; a joke he didn't appreciate. To resolve the matter, "Frank Boyd," as he was now calling himself, had to enlist the help of the American vice consul and pay a fine of 1,500 pesos.

But as soon as he got out of trouble, he got back into it in a major way: in the last days of 1905, the three of them dropped any pretense of being law-abiding citizens, returned to Argentina, and, with the help of their incorrigible friend Robert Evans, robbed a bank.

Villa Mercedes, located smack in the middle of the country, was an Argentine cow town—a railway hub rife with livestock fairs, cattle brokers, and fun-hungry gauchos, all of whom helped the Banco de la Nacion thrive. On the balmy, late-spring morning, Tuesday, December 19, the four bandits sat drinking whiskey at a bar two blocks away. Just before the noon hour, when business would be particularly slow, they finished their drinks and rode to the Banco. While Ethel stayed outside with the horses, the three men entered, "knife in hand," said the English-language *Buenos Aires Herald*. They "jumped with such speed and agility over the counter and grating that separates the public area from the offices," said another Buenos Aires paper, *La Prensa*, that the manager and treasurer were caught completely off guard. The *Herald* suggested that the robbers must have been either English or American, "because only people of these nationalities could possibly carry so much whiskey under their belts and at the same time move with incomparable celerity."

The robbers, according to the *Herald*, were remarkably efficient. "The safes were open, and two of the brigands emptied them whilst the other two covered the employees. The manager offered resistance and was wounded [by a blow from a fist or a gun butt]. Before any policemen arrived, the four robbers had remounted and disappeared in a cloud of dust." *La Prensa* noted that the woman, "whom it is supposed was in charge of cooking the meals . . . is a fine rider, to the extent that she is widely admired by the Argentines for her skill and natural ability." The posses never came close to catching the outlaws, but after a few days, the papers were starting to get a bead on their identities, saying that they were the Sundance Kid, Ethel Place, and Harvey Logan, while the fourth man remained unknown. (Although reported sightings of Logan in South America were common, he'd been dead for a year at this point, having killed himself to avoid being captured after a heist in Parachute, Colorado.) The amount stolen was said to be 12,000 pesos, the equivalent of about $120,000 today.

After the Villa Mercedes robbery, Butch and Sundance split up for nearly a year. Sundance, Ethel, and Evans headed south, back to Cholila, to try to collect whatever money had been produced by the sale of their livestock. Butch went east to Buenos Aires, where he reconnected with old cowboy friends who were touring in a Wild West show that featured the famous African American rodeo champ Bill Pickett. The next time Butch and Sundance would see each other, Ethel would be gone for good. It seems that she and Sundance returned to San Francisco in 1906, just in time for the earthquake, then moved on to Denver, one of the places she was said to be from, and, while there, she needed an appendectomy. Sundance took her to the hospital, then went out and got blind drunk. Waking in his boardinghouse the next morning and finding that he couldn't get room service, he fired shots into the ceiling, which prompted the proprietor to call the police. He took off before they could arrive and made it all the way back to Bolivia, which, if you've seen the movie, you know was their final stop.

22

THE END OF THE ROAD

Butch and Sundance reunited—*mysteriously and* possibly accidentally—at the Concordia mine, more than sixteen thousand feet up in the Central Andes of Bolivia.

A few weeks before, probably in August or September 1906, Sundance had found work in northern Argentina with an American named Roy Letson, who was buying mules for contractors building railroads in Bolivia. Letson saw Sundance (who gave his name as Enrique Brown) as a down-on-his luck fellow ex-pat who seemed more than capable of the task at hand, which was to break the animals he'd bought to harness and saddle. "Longabaugh was well dressed, without funds, and had a crust of bread in his pocket for his next meal," Letson told author Charles Kelly more than thirty years later. "He did have a fine Tiffany gold watch." At first, Sundance kept to himself and shunned conversation, Letson said, yet when the opportunity arose to help drive a herd of mules to La Paz, Bolivia—an arduous trip of several weeks—he said yes "gladly." Besides being a crack muleteer, he proved to be an excellent guide. "We would frequently come to a point where trails branched out in several directions," said Letson. "Longabaugh would suggest a trail, and each time he was correct."

The Concordia tin mine, which lay along the route to La Paz, was one of the places they were scheduled to drop off mules. When Sundance and Letson pulled in, Butch, had already been working there for several months as a stockman and payroll messenger, sometimes overseeing the transportation of $100,000 or more through the mountains. Santiago Maxwell, as he called himself, was a rising star at the mine, making $150 a month plus room and board—far above the average Concordia daily salary of 80 cents. Letson, who had no more work for Sundance but wanted to help him catch on someplace else, asked the Concordia manager, Clement Rolla Glass, if he could use another hand. Though Glass, like so many others, found Sundance "sullen," he said yes and told him he could go help out Santiago Maxwell.

We don't know how Butch and Sundance reacted to the sight of each other, but their secret didn't last long. A week or two later, a coworker overheard them reminiscing about a holdup and, thinking they were planning to knock off Concordia, reported them to Glass, who called them in to discuss the matter. Butch convinced him that he needn't worry. "We don't rob the people we work for," he said.

By the time Glass left the mine in 1908, his assistant and eventual successor, a Marylander named Percy Seibert, had already forged a personal relationship with Butch and Sundance. Not surprisingly, he liked Butch especially, calling him "an exceptionally pleasant and even cultured and charming man. He used good language and was never vulgar. He took well to the ladies, and as soon as he arrived in a village, he made friends with the little urchins and usually had some candy to give them. When he visited me, he enjoyed hearing the gramophone records, as I had a large selection of choice music."

Seibert lived with his wife on the mine property, and he often had Butch and Sundance over for Sunday dinner. Sometimes in his back yard he would toss beer bottles into the air, and one of the outlaws would draw his pistol and blow them to smithereens.

Sundance felt safe enough around the couple to open up about himself, saying that he left home "after reading some thrilling novels on the West" to become a cowboy—and that he had sometimes taken part in holdups "just for the excitement." Butch, while invariably charming, seemed also to be, just as invariably, obsessed with the possible need to escape. "He always sat on a small sofa which was placed between two windows," said Seibert. "This seat gave him a survey of three doors and one window. He always seemed to be cool and calculating and protected his back very well."

Both of the outlaws confessed that they had given up on the idea of becoming legitimate ranchers, striking a familiar theme. "There's no use trying to hide out and go straight," Butch said. "There's always an informer around to bring the law on you. After you've started, you have to keep going, that's all. The safest way is to keep moving all the time and spring a holdup in some new place. That way you keep the other fellows guessing." Seibert later told an interviewer that he had a curious relationship with the bandits, based on the unspoken understanding that he would never turn them in, but that if the police came to ask questions about them, he and his wife would cooperate with the law. "It was accepted," he said, "that we were on one side, they were on the other."

On November 12, 1907, during one of the periodic trips they made from the mine, Butch posted what follows from Santa Cruz, Bolivia. It is the longest letter we have from Butch and there is a lot between the lines:

To the Boys at Concordia:

We arrived here about 3 weeks ago after a very pleasant journey, and found just the place I have been looking for for 20 years, and Ingersoll [his playful code name for Sundance] likes it better than I do, he says he won't try to live anywhere else. This is a Town of 18,000, and 14,000 are females and some of them are birds [good lookers]. This is the only place for old fellows like myself. One never gets too old if he has blue eyes and a red face and looks capable of making a blue eyed Baby Boy.

Oh god if I could call back 20 years and have red hair with this complection of mine I would be happy. I have got into the 400 set as deep as I can go. The lady feeds me on fine wines, and she is the prettiest little thing I have ever seen, but I am afraid Papa is going to tear my playhouse down, for he is getting nasty, but there is plenty more. This place isn't what we expected at all. There isn't any cattle here. All the beef that is killed here comes from Mojo, a distance of 80 leagues, and are worth from 10 to 100 Bs [bolivianos]. But cattle do very well here. The grass is good, but water is scarce, there isn't any water in this town when there is a dry spell for a week. The people here in town have to buy water at 1.80 a barrel. They can get good water at 40 feet but are too lazy to sink wells.

Land is cheap here and everything grows good that is planted, but there is damned little planted. Everything is very high. It costs us Bs 100 per head to feed our mules, 250 each for ourselves. We rented a house, hired a good cook, and are living like gentlemen.

Land is worth 10 cts. Per hectare 10 leagues from here and there is some good Estancias for sale, one 12 leagues from here of 4 leagues with plenty of water and good grass and some sugar cane for Bs 5,000, and others just as cheap, and if I don't fall down I will be living here before long.

It is pretty warm and some fever but the fever is caused by the food they eat. At least I am willing to chance it.

They are doing some work now building a [railroad] from Port Suarez here, and they claim it will be pushed right through, so now is the time to get started for land will go up before long.

It is 350 miles from here to Cochabamba and a hell of a road, just up one mountain and down another all the way, not a level spot on it big enough to whip a dog on, and most of the way thick brush on both sides. But there is people all along and lots of little towns. In *fact it is thickly settled. There is plenty of game on the road but it is safe for it is impossible to get it for brush. I killed 1 turkey, 1 Sandhill Crain and 1 Buzzard. We could hear the turkeys every day and seen some several times but I only got one shot. It won't do for Reece [a Concordia employee] to come over that road for he will kill himself getting through the brush after birds. We would of left here long ago, but we had a little trouble with the old mule. Ingersoll hobbled her and tied her to a tree and wore out a nice green pole on her, but I didn't think he had done a good job so I worked a little while with rocks. Between us we broke her jaw and we have been feeding her on mush ever since, but she can eat a little now and we will leave in a few days for a little trip south to see that country. I am looking for the place Hutch [their friend Santiago Hutcheon] owns, 8 leagues long, ½ league wide with a big river running through it from end to end.*

We expect to be back in Concordia in about 1 month. Good luck to all you fellows.

J. P. Maxwell

At the age of forty-one, it seems, Butch remained an adolescent in ways both enchanting and gross. Never forgetting that he was addressing the *boys* at Concordia, he boasted of being a troublemaker who left angry husbands and half-dead mules in his wake. But the predictable macho nonsense comes mixed with nostalgia as well as an abundance of domestic details—about the real estate market, the depth of water, the price of sugar, the availability of game—that all speak of a middle-aged man looking for a nice place to settle. Despite what he'd told Seibert about never being able to quit, maybe Bolivia was a place where he could finally get lost and stay lost. All he needed was the means, one big payday. Not for the first time, he was just one more score away.

They had to quit Concordia in a hurry after Sundance got drunk in a bar and boasted to someone about their Argentine bank

heist. Seeking employment, they headed south toward the burgeoning town of Tupiza, outside of which a Scottish friend of theirs
named James Hutcheon (the Santiago Hutcheon mentioned in the
letter) had a company that hauled freight and passengers by mule.
Their main reason for being there, though, was to do research on
the Banco Nacional, which they intended to rob. While working
for Hutcheon on and off for a month, they crossed paths with a
man who managed gold-mining dredges and who a few years later
would write about his experiences with them for a British magazine
under the pen name of A. G. Francis. Francis guessed that "George
Low" and "Frank Smith" were outlaws, but he admired their swagger ("They were very pleasant and amusing companions"), and they
wound up staying at his place for several weeks. He later found
out that Low was Butch Cassidy but retained the mistaken notion
that Smith was Harvey Logan, and referred to him that way in the
piece. During that time, Butch often spent his days in Tupiza casing
the bank, while Sundance hung around with Francis, talking about
how he had "made several attempts to settle down to a law-abiding
life," and assuring his host that he had "never hurt or killed a man
except in self-defense, and had never stolen from the poor but from
rich corporations."

That bank job wasn't in the cards, though; things just weren't
breaking right. First, Butch was recognized one day in the lobby of
the Hotel Internacional by a Lutheran missionary he had known
around Concordia. "Santiago Maxwell! How are you?" the man
bellowed. Through gritted teeth, Butch said that he was fine but
his name was George Low. Then a few days later, the officers from
a local regiment took up residence in the same hotel, which was
just down the street from the Banco Nacional. That development
convinced Butch and Sundance to consider another project about
which they'd already made some initial inquiries: the payroll of the
Aramayo y Franke mining company. It sounded like a good deal for
bandits: bags of bolivianos still making their way nineteenth-century

style, flung over the backs of mules, in open country, through out-of-the-way places like Huaca Huañusca. They were just the nineteenth-century men for the job.

———

The two were rather merry in their final days, considering that Butch had Bolivia belly and they were both very old in outlaw years and their luck was at last running low. "Don't you know your own horse in the dark, kid?" Butch called out to Francis, who had jumped out of his hammock on the veranda when he heard the two approaching his camp one morning at one o'clock. Butch, being sick, stumbled immediately into bed while Sundance went to the kitchen, where he made himself "a fair meal on whatever I could find" and told Francis the story of how they'd just robbed poor Carlos Peró.

The next morning, Francis tells us, they seemed in no hurry. Not knowing that after Peró and his party had made their way to the nearby town of Salo, a bulletin had gone out to points all over southern Bolivia and even Argentina and Chile calling for two grin-gos of their description to be brought in dead or alive, they woke, stretched, then sat on the veranda. At about ten o'clock "an acquaintance on a spent horse" pulled up in front of Francis's place and said, "You had better get out of this, boys—they are saddling up a hundred men to come after you!" He had seen the soldiers, he said, "mustering on the plaza."

Sundance considered the news a moment, then said to Francis, "You might tell that boy of yours to get breakfast ready quickly, will you, kid? I supposed we had better be moving."

Butch and Sundance told Francis they wanted him to come along with them. He wasn't fond of the idea, but he saddled up, and in a half hour or so, the three of them "started up the river at a gentle trot," with Butch leading the mule stolen from Peró.

"Suppose the soldiers arrive," Francis said. "What are we going to do about it?"

"Well," said Sundance, "we'll just sit down behind a rock and get to work."

It was natural for them to head south into nearby Argentina, but maybe because that was predictable, they asked Francis to guide them north toward Uyuni, a stopping point on the way to Oruro, a relatively cosmopolitan town of 13,500 where they might be able to get lost. That night, "having seen nothing of our pursuers," they shared a room in a lodging place in the Indian pueblo of Estarca, "the two partners occupying a bed in the corner and I a mattress placed on the floor immediately opposite the door," Francis wrote.

"Good night, kid," said Sundance. "I wish we could celebrate tonight, but in the circumstances, it won't do."

The next morning, they told Francis that it was time that he left them and that he should tell any troops he might meet on the way that he had seen them heading south into Argentina. Unbeknownst to them, the police had already arrested two sketchy travelers in connection with the Aramayo robbery: an Englishman named Frank Murray and an American named Ray Walters. Their guilt at first seemed likely. Besides being among the very few gringos in the area, the men had been "armed to the teeth," according to one witness, traveled with a woman's saddle, and, for the most part, balked at answering a magistrate's questions. But by chance, Peró himself had encountered them on the road and engaged in conversation with them the day after the robbery, and he never thought they were the same English speakers who'd held him up, just the kind of drifters one met in the backwaters of Bolivia. The pair would be released a few days later, after authorities were satisfied that they had more obvious suspects, and disappear into the mist of history.

Butch and Sundance were bone tired on November 6 when they pulled into San Vicente, an isolated mining village of 350 souls that sits 14,400 feet up in a dry and relentlessly dreary section of the Andes. They arrived at sundown and, after asking for an inn, were directed to the home of a man named Bonifacio Casasola, who had a room to let—the last one in town, they were told. What they didn't know was that the other rooms, at a nearby boardinghouse run by one Manuel Barran, had been taken a few hours before by three soldiers and a policeman from Uyuni who had spent the last two days combing the countryside for them.

Things went bad rather quickly. When Butch unsaddled the stolen mule, it rolled in the dust to ease its sores, calling attention to itself and the fact that it bore the distinctive Q brand of the Aramayo y Franke company. The mayor of the town, Cleto Bellot, who had come to greet the new arrivals, made the connection, and when Casasola left to get his guests a dinner of beer and sardines, Bellot politely excused himself and went to Barran's house to alert the soldiers.

A few minutes later, two soldiers and a policeman came stealthily, with rifles in hand, through a patio that led to a door to Butch's and Sundance's room. At first, they could see the outlaws inside, eating by the light of a candle near the small beehive oven in which they'd cooked their sardines. The officer in the group, Timoteo Rios, shouted for them to surrender. The outlaws disappeared for a moment, then Butch alone reappeared in the doorway, firing his Colt. One of his shots hit a young soldier named Victor Torres in the neck. Torres returned fire while staggering into a nearby house, where he quickly died.

The other two soldiers retreated briefly to Barran's house for more ammunition, then came back to the patio and fired many rounds into the house. Their commander, Captain Justo P. Concha, appeared belatedly and asked Bellot to gather townspeople to surround the house so the outlaws couldn't escape. The mayor had just started on that task, he said later, when he heard "three screams of desperation" from inside the room and a brief burst of gunfire. After that, everything went quiet.

EPILOGUE

At seven o'clock the next morning, after a cold, windy night during which the townsfolk had kept watch over the battle scene, the oh-so-brave Captain Concha ordered Casasola to go into the house and report back. As expected, Casasola said that both men were dead. It turned out that the shorter one was lying on his back near the doorway with a revolver in his hand. He had been shot once in the temple and once in the arm. The tall one was found sitting on a bench behind the door with his arms around a large earthen jug. He had been shot once in the forehead and several times in the arm. It seemed to the investigators that Butch had killed Sundance, then turned the gun on himself.

At least the Big Men didn't get him. He left on his own terms.

So that is how it ended, not with a wimpy freeze-frame but with a couple of bangs. That is what Hollywood did not want the people waiting outside on line to see on our faces as we filed out.

Or in any case, that is how their *lives* ended. Their stories, in a sense, were just getting started.

As word of the shoot-out filtered back to the States, many of their old cronies hunkered down in denial, saying that they couldn't believe it was Butch and Sundance who'd perished in such shabby circumstances, at the hands of foreigners. That's not the way those boys were supposed to die. Butch and Sundance, their supporters thought, were way too smart to sleep in a *town* in the midst of a huge manhunt—and bed down next door to a bunch of soldiers to boot. Maybe Sundance if he'd had a few, but not Butch. It didn't matter that their heroes had confessed to their host, A. G. Francis, that they had committed the Aramayo robbery—and that the gringos who'd been killed in San Vicente on November 6 had the Aramayo payroll (minus a few pesos) tucked in a saddlebag that was being carried by the Aramayo mule: many of the elbow benders back in Wyoming, Montana, and Colorado simply weren't buying it. That was not the Butch Cassidy they wanted to believe in, so they said that it must have been two other fellows who died down there, and they waited for some kind of sign.

When none came after a few years, William Simpson once recalled, a bunch of them chipped in and sent a Big Horn Basin cowboy named Billy Sawtelle to check things out. Sawtelle returned in 1914 with the news that, yup, they were dead. No, the Bolivians never figured out who they were or bothered to record where their graves were. But they'd been dug up after two weeks so that the man they'd robbed could identify them, and he'd said he'd know them anywhere—because of their hats. Instead of accepting that testimony or commenting on how they buried people with their hats on down there, the Westerners waved away Sawtelle and went back to waiting for a sign.

This was not exactly a rare phenomenon. Outlaws are often said to live on after their deaths. When Jesse James and Billy the Kid were killed by Robert Ford and Pat Garrett, respectively, people said it wasn't true, that it was just the newspapers trying to make money, and subsequent sightings of the two were frequent. The advent of a fair number of Jesse James and Billy the Kid imposters helped fuel the myths. And so it was with Butch, who was seen occasionally out west until the 1920s, when a lookalike named William T. Phillips started impersonating him, whereupon the number of sightings dramatically increased. Phillips had an edge because he probably knew Butch and may have served time with him in Laramie, which allowed him to salt his spiel with a few actual facts. What was in it for him or for any of the other imposters is hard to say, but Phillips apparently slept with a couple of women whom Butch had courted back in Wyoming, and he wrote a hard-to-follow, highly inaccurate third-person autobiography called *The Bandit Invincible* that he pitched, in vain, to publishers and movie producers.

Of course, Hollywood eventually came around to the idea thanks to William Goldman, who heard about Butch and Sundance—he forgot how, exactly, but probably from James Horan's book—growing up in Chicago. Butch, I'm sure, would have approved of the movie, which, as we've seen, was dead-on in some ways and far off in others, because he loved to sow confusion. The soldiers who went through Butch's pockets after he died found—in addition to two notebooks, a pencil, some coins, a linen handkerchief, a metal comb, and a pocket mirror—seven business cards inscribed Enrique B. Hutcheon and seven others inscribed Edward Graydon. Meanwhile, he was calling himself George Low to obscure the fact that he was Butch Cassidy, born Robert LeRoy Parker.

I'm not sure how much he'd appreciate the work of the outlaw scholars, who are, after all, in the business of trying to pin him down. Of all the books that have been published about him, he'd probably be partial to *Sometimes Cassidy* by the late Utah miner Art Davidson, who, as noted earlier, believed that there had been several Butches, one of whom sold uranium to Madame Curie. His Oscar for Best Overall Researcher would no doubt go to Kerry Ross Boren, who for more than thirty years has endeavored to insert fanciful tales into books, articles, and even Ancestry.com, which now contains several fictional family trees that Boren, under different names, has planted. It was Boren who seems to have convinced Bruce Chatwin that in 1966 the president of Bolivia, Rene Barrientos Ortuno, "put a team on to solving the mystery [of how they died], grilled the villagers personally, exhumed corpses in the cemetery, checked the army and police files, and concluded that the whole thing was a fabrication." Despite what Chatwin says, Barrientos never initiated such an investigation, and the Bolivian archives brim with proof that the outlaws died in San Vicente.

Chatwin definitely had a soft spot for Boren. In a letter he wrote to Anne Meadows and Dan Buck not long before he died in 1989, he said, "I felt that [Boren's] imagination tended to get the better of him, but I mustn't malign him because he was very kind." Indeed the fictional material Boren traffics in is for many preferable to the truth, because it keeps hope alive—especially for the "*returnistas*," which is what Dan Buck calls those who insist that Butch, at least, survived South America and came back. Buck, for his part, has given up trying to change their minds. "There's a virus that makes otherwise reasonable people want to prove that their heroes didn't die," he has said.

As for what physical monument to his memory—that is, which Butch-themed tourist attraction—the man born Robert LeRoy Parker might be partial to, I will first say I can guess which one he would be least likely to recommend: the cabin in Circleville where he spent his youth. While that fully plaqued-out and meticulously restored official historic site might be worth a trip for any budding outlaw buff who already finds herself in, say, Salt Lake City, its mission is far too earnest and on the nose to appeal to Butch. No, the place he'd endorse, I think, is the strange little museum dedicated to him and Sundance in San Vicente, Bolivia. If you go there—and you shouldn't—you'll need to fly into La Paz, then hire a guide for the nine-hour drive over rough mountain roads to the guardhouse at the town's entrance. (You'll also need to remember that there are at least four San Vicentes in Bolivia.) The sentry on duty there probably won't let you through unless you act like you're never going to stop begging or you slip him some bolivianos.

Once in, you'll find the woman who has the key to the museum only slightly less dismayed by your existence, but in the end morosely cooperative. The room's seldom-seen wonders include rusty old mining tools, a definitely-not-old beer bottle and sardine tin representing the outlaws' last supper—and a selection of human bones that supposedly belonged to Butch and Sundance. Except that they didn't, and the museum surely ought to know that. In 1991 Meadows and Buck attempted to find the outlaws' graves and perform DNA tests that would finally silence the *returnistas*. After obtaining permission, they dug in the jumbled local cemetery, near where there is a sign that says "Butch Cassidy and the Sundance Kid." But the remains they disinterred turned out to belong to a German miner named Gustav Zimmer and a few anonymous indigenous folks. So that's whose bones are behind glass down there in a rarely visited museum in a town that you practically have to break into.

If you know anything about the real Butch Cassidy, you know he'd think that was a hoot.

ACKNOWLEDGMENTS

Getting the thank-yous right is always impossible, but it's safe to say that this book could not have been written without the help of Daniel Buck, the leading authority on Butch Cassidy in the United States; Michael Bell, his immensely knowledgeable counterpart in England; and Anne Meadows, the author of the simply wonderful book *Digging Up Butch and Sundance*. Dan and Mike helped me at every stage of the book's creation, with facts, opinions, photographs, derisive snorts, travel tips, and introductions. Over the course of more than three years, they never lost their patience with a reformed sportswriter, new to the subject of outlaw history, who specialized in rookie mistakes. Dan and Mike also vetted the completed manuscript and corrected several errors.

On my travels through America I met and was aided by Butch's grand-nephew Bill Betenson, Donna Ernst and her husband Paul D. Ernst (great-grandnephew of the Sundance Kid), Harvey Murdock (grandson of Butch's true best friend, Elzy Lay), and Jim Dullenty, as well as by too many librarians to mention. I should also thank the writer and researcher Mark Mszanski for the wisdom he provided, on the telephone and in print. During and after my Argentina trip I was helped generously by the authors Marcelo Gavirati, Carlos Dante Ferrari, Marcelo Bustos, and Oswaldo Aguirre, as well as by the horsewoman and riding instructor Carol Jones, whose grand-father Jarred Jones knew Butch and Sundance. For my subsequent journey to Bolivia, I owe thanks to Fabiola Mitru of Tupiza Tours, Jhanet Maribel Argota Gerrero, José Victor Martinez Vargas, and Limbert Jerez Lopez.

I am grateful to the support and counsel I received from my agent at ICM, Kristine Dahl, and from Bob Bender, my editor at Simon & Schuster, superstars both. Kris's assistant, Tamara Kawar, and Bob's colleagues at S&S—Johanna Li, Phil Bashe, Lewelin Polanco, Kirstin Berndt, and Stephen Bedford—have also enriched my book-writing experiences.

My wife, Sarah Saffian Leerhsen, is the love of my life, a speaker of Spanish, a convivial companion on research trips to some pretty funky places, and a superb editor. What do you tip for that?

NOTES ON SOURCES

Of the previous books about Butch Cassidy, the Sundance Kid, the Old West, and early-twentieth-century South America, the ones I found most useful are listed here alphabetically, by author:

Henry Adams, *The Education of Henry Adams, An Autobiography*.

Mike Bell, *Incidents on Owl Creek: Butch Cassidy's Big Horn Basin Bunch and the Wyoming Horse Thief War*.

Bill Betenson, *Butch Cassidy, My Uncle: A Family Portrait*.

A. W. Bowen (pub.), *Progressive Men of the State of Wyoming*.

Jeffrey Burton, *The Deadliest Outlaws: The Ketchum Gang and the Wild Bunch*.

Bruce Chatwin, *In Patagonia*.

Bernard DeVoto, *Across the Wide Missouri*.

Donna B. Ernst, *The Sundance Kid: The Life of Harry Alonzo Longabaugh*.

Elnora L. Frye, *Atlas of Wyoming Outlaws at the Territorial Penitentiary*.

Marcelo Gavirati, *Buscados en la Patagonia: La Historia No Contada de Butch Cassidy y los Bandoleros Norteamericanos*.

William Goldman, *Butch Cassidy and the Sundance Kid* (the screenplay).

Howard E. Greager, *In the Company of Cowboys*.

Christopher Hitchens, *God Is Not Great*.

Eric Hobsbawm, *Bandits*.

James D. Horan, *Desperate Men: The True Story of Jesse James, Butch Cassidy and the Wild Bunch.*

Charles Kelly, *Outlaw Trail: A History of Butch Cassidy and His Wild Bunch.*

Christopher Knowlton, *Cattle Kingdom: The Hidden History of the Cowboy West.*

Jill Lepore, *These Truths: A History of the United States.*

John Gary Maxwell, *The Civil War Years in Utah: The Kingdom of God and the Territory That Did Not Fight.*

Tom McCarty, *Tom McCarty's Own Story: Autobiography of an Outlaw.*

Larry McMurtry, *Sacagawea's Nickname, Essays on the American West; Lonesome Dove.*

Anne Meadows, *Digging Up Butch and Sundance.*

Lula Parker Betenson as told to Dora Flack, *Butch Cassidy, My Brother.*

Richard Patterson, *Butch Cassidy, A Biography.*

Doris B. Platts, *The Cunningham Ranch Incident of 1892.*

Larry Pointer, *In Search of Butch Cassidy.*

John Wesley Powell, *Lands of the Arid Region of the United States.*

Robert Redford, *The Outlaw Trail: A Journey Through Time.*

Jon M. Skovlin and Donna McDaniel Skovlin, *In Pursuit of the McCartys.*

Wallace Stegner, *Beyond the Hundredth Meridian: John Wesley Powell and the Second Opening of the West; Mormon Country; The Gathering of Zion: The Story of the Mormon Trail; Angle of Repose.*

Matt Warner, *The Last of the Bandit Riders.*

Other books I consulted:

Edward Abbey, *Desert Solitaire*

E. C. "Teddy Blue" Abbott and Helena Huntington Smith, *We Pointed Them North: Recollections of a Cowpuncher.*

Andy Adams, *The Log of a Cowboy.*

Ramon F. Adams, compiler, *Six-Guns and Saddle Leather: A Bibliography of Books and Pamphlets on Western Outlaws and Gunmen.*

Osvaldo Aguirre, *La Pandilla Salvaje: Butch Cassidy en la Patagonia.*

Warren A. Back and Ynez D. Haase, *Historical Atlas of the American West.*

Pearl Baker, *The Wild Bunch at Robbers Roost.*

Frederick R. (Frederick Ritchie) Bechdolt, *When the West Was Young;*
Tales of the Old Timers.*

James H. Beckstead, *Cowboying: A Tough Job in a Hard Land.*

Harold Bloom, *The American Religion: The Emergence of the Post-Christian
Nation.*

Edgar Beecher Bronson, *Reminiscences of a Ranchman.*

Mike Bell, *Who Are These Guys?: Of Myths and Manhunters: The Union
Pacific Bandit Hunters.*

David L. Bigler, *Forgotten Kingdom: The Mormon Theocracy in the American
West.*

Hiram Bingham, *Across South America: An Account of a Journey from Buenos
Aires to Lima.*

Dee Brown, *Bury My Heart at Wounded Knee: An Indian History of the
American West; The American West.*

Larry Brown, *The Hog Ranches of Wyoming: Liquor, Lust, and Lies Under
Sagebrush Skies.*

Jan Harold Brunvand, ed., *American Folklore: An Encyclopedia.*

John Rolfe Burroughs, *Where the Old West Stayed Young: The Remarkable
History of Brown's Park Told for the First Time Together with an Account
of the Rise and Fall of the Range-Cattle Business in Northwestern Colorado
and Southwestern Wyoming, and Much About Cattle Barons, Sheep and
Sheepmen, Forest Rangers, Range Wards, Long Riders, Paid Killers, and
Other Bad Men.*

Frank Calkins, *Jackson Hole.*

Pamela Call Johnson, *Butch Cassidy and the Wild Bunch in Star Valley, Wyoming, 1889–1896.*

Frank G. Carpenter, *The Andes and the Desert.*

Simon Casson and Richard Adamson, *Riding the Outlaw Trail: In the Foot-
steps of Butch Cassidy and the Sundance Kid.*

Ron Chernow, *Grant.*

Eugene Cunningham, *Triggernometry: A Gallery of Gunfighters.*

David Dary, *Red Blood and Black Ink: Journalism in the Old West*; *Cowboy Culture: A Saga of Five Centuries.*

John W. Davis, *The Trial of Tom Horn*; *Goodbye Judge Lynch: The End of a Lawless Era in Wyoming's Big Horn Basin*; *Wyoming Range War.*

Robert K. DeArment, *Man-Hunters of the Old West.*

Dick and Daun DeJournette, *One Hundred Years of Brown's Park and Diamond Mountain.*

Thomas Josiah Dimsdale, *The Vigilantes of Montana.*

Gail Drago, *Etta Place: Her Life and Times with Butch Cassidy and the Sundance Kid.*

Gail Drago and Ann Ruff, *Outlaws in Petticoats and Other Notorious Texas Women.*

Bob Edgar and Jack Turnell, *Brand of a Legend: Ten Thousand Years in the Valley of the Greybull River*; *Archaeology, Plains Indians, Outlaws, Ranchers, and Wildlife.*

Sean Egan, *William Goldman: The Reluctant Storyteller.*

Doug Engebretson, *Empty Saddles, Forgotten Names: Outlaws of the Black Hills and Wyoming.*

Donna B. Ernst, *Sundance, My Uncle (The Early West).*

Richard L. Fetter and Suzanne Fetter, *Telluride, from Pick to Powder.*

Caitlin Fitz, *Our Sister Republics: The United States in an Age of American Revolutions.*

Harry Alverson Franck, *Vagabonding down the Andes: Being the Narrative of a Journey, Chiefly Afoot, from Panama to Buenos Aires.*

Caroline Fraser, *Prairie Fires: The American Dreams of Laura Ingalls Wilder.*

Captain William French, *Recollections of a Western Ranchman.*

Paul Frison, *Calendar of Change.*

Eduardo Galeano, *Open Veins of Latin America: Five Centuries of the Pillage of a Continent.*

Harry Arthur Gant, *I Saw Them Ride Away.*

William Goldman, *Adventures in the Screen Trade: A Personal View of Hollywood and Screenwriting.*

Robert J. Gordon, *The Rise and Fall of American Growth: The U.S. Standard of Living Since the Civil War.*

Herbert Grice, Larry Pointer, and Osvaldo Aguirre, *Grice, Whom Nobody Could Catch.*

Jeff Guinn, *The Last Gunfight: The Real Story of the Shootout at the O.K. Corral—and How It Changed the American West.*

A. V. L. Guise, *Six Years in Bolivia: The Adventures of a Mining Engineer.*

LeRoy R. Hafen and Ann W. Hafen, *Handcarts to Zion: The Story of a Unique Western Migration 1856–1860.*

W. T. Hamilton, *My Sixty Years on the Plains.*

Donald Loren Hardy, *Shooting from the Lip: The Life of Senator Al Simpson.*

Thom Hatch, *The Last Outlaws: The Lives and Legends of Butch Cassidy and the Sundance Kid.*

James D. Horan, *The Outlaws: Accounts by Eyewitnesses and the Outlaws Themselves*; *The WPA Guide to Utah, the Beehive State*; *The Pinkertons: The Detective Dynasty That Made History.*

James D. Horan and Paul Sann, *Pictorial History of the Wild West: A True Account of the Bad Men, Desperadoes, Rustlers and Outlaws of the Old West—and the Men Who Fought Them to Establish Law and Order.*

Tom Horn, *Life of Tom Horn, Government Scout and Interpreter.*

Emerson Hough, *The Story of the Outlaw, a Study of the Western Desperado.*

Michael Jacobs, *Ghost Train Through the Andes: On My Grandfather's Trail in Chile and Bolivia.*

Robert F. Karolevitz, *Newspapering in the Old West: A Pictorial History of Journalism and Printing on the Frontier.*

Doris Karren Burton, *A History of Uintah County: Scratching the Surface.*

Michael R. Kelsey, *Hiking and Exploring Utah's Henry Mountains and Robbers Roost.*

Herbert S. Klein, *Bolivia: The Evolution of a Multi-Ethnic Society.*

Diana Allen Kouris, *The Romantic and Notorious History of Brown's Park.*

Howard R. Lamar, *Charlie Siringo's West: An Interpretive Biography*; *The New Encyclopedia of the American West* (ed.).

David Lavender, *One Man's West*; *The Telluride Story, a Tale of Two Towns*.

Joe LeFors, *Wyoming Peace Officer, an Autobiography*.

Sylvia Lynch, *Harvey Logan in Knoxville*.

Kim MacQuarrie, *Life and Death in the Andes: On the Trail of Bandits, Heroes, and Revolutionaries*.

Grace McClure, *The Bassett Women*.

Robert S. McPherson, *Life in a Corner: Cultural Episodes in Southeastern Utah, 1880–1950*.

Joyce Mendelsohn, *The Lower East Side Remembered and Revisted: A History and Guide to a Legendary New York Neighborhood*.

A. S. Mercer, *The Banditti of the Plains or the Cattlemen's Invasion of Wyoming in 1892*.

Norman David Moore, *Butch Cassidy and Gang—Old West Photographic Finds of the Century*.

Edmund Morris, *The Rise of Theodore Roosevelt*.

Tony Morrison, *Land Above the Clouds*.

Candy Moulton, *Everyday Life in the Wild West from 1840–1900*.

David Hamilton Murdoch, *The American West: The Invention of a Myth*.

Harvey Lay Murdock, *The Educated Outlaw: The Story of Elzy Lay of the Wild Bunch*.

Paul T. Nelson, *Wrecks of Human Ambition: A History of Utah's Canyon Country to 1936*.

Jerry Nickle, as Told to C. J. Del Barto, *Bringing Sundance Home: Butch Cassidy's Partner, My Great Grandfather*.

S. Paul O'Hara, *Inventing the Pinkertons, or Spies, Sleuths, Mercenaries, and Thugs*.

Francis Parkman, *The Oregon Trail, the Conspiracy of Pontiac*.

Richard Patterson, *Historical Atlas of the Outlaw West*; *Train Robbery: The Birth, Flowering, and Decline of a Notorious Western Enterprise*.

John Alton Peterson, *Utah's Black Hawk War*.

W. T. Phillips, *The Bandit Invincible*.

William A. Pinkerton, *Train Robberies, Train Robbers, and the "Hold-Up" Man*.

Geoffrey A. Pocock, *Outrider of Empire: The Life and Adventures of Roger Pocock.*

Roger Pocock, *Following the Frontier: Horseback Adventures on the Infamous Outlaw Trail.*

Frank Richard Prassel, *The Great American Outlaw, A Legacy of Fact and Fiction.*

Annie Proulx, *Close Range, Wyoming Stories.*

Robert B. Rhode, *Booms & Busts on Bitter Creek: A History of Rock Springs, Wyoming.*

Wilson Rockwell, ed., *Doc Shores.*

Philip Ashton Rollins, *The Cowboy: His Characteristics, His Equipment, Etc.*

Theodore Roosevelt, *The Rough Riders.*

W. J. Rorabaugh, *Alcoholic Republic: An American Tradition.*

Joseph G. Rosa, *The Gunfighter, Man or Myth?*

Michael Rutter, *Wild Bunch Women.*

Herman Gastrell Seely, *Sagebrush Dentist* (as told by Dr. Will Frackelton).

Richard F. Selcer, *Hell's Half Acre: The Life and Legend of a Red-Light District.*

Hampton Sides, *Blood and Thunder: The Epic Story of Kit Carson and the Conquest of the American West.*

Charles Siringo, *Riata and Spurs: The Story of a Lifetime Spent in the Saddle as Cowboy and Detective; Two Evil Isms: Pinkertonism and Anarchism; Cowboy Detective.*

Richard W. Slatta, *The Mythical West: An Encyclopedia of Legend, Lore and Popular Culture.*

Richard Slotkin, *Gunfighter Nation: The Myth of the Frontier in Twentieth-Century America.*

Robert Barr Smith, *Tough Towns: True Tales from the Gritty Streets of the Old West.*

Henry Nash Smith, *Virgin Land: The American West as Symbol and Myth.*

Mark T. Smokov, *He Rode with Butch and Sundance: The Story of Harvey "Kid Curry" Logan.*

Arthur Soule, *The Tall Texan: The Story of Ben Kilpatrick.*

Agnes Wright Spring, *Near the Greats: Prominent People Known to Agnes Wright Spring.*

Wallace Stegner, *The Sound of Mountain Water: The Changing American West; Where the Bluebird Sings to the Lemonade Springs: Living and Writing in West.*

Kent Ladd Steckmesser, *The Western Hero in History and Legend.*

Robert Louis Stevenson, *The Silverado Squatters.*

T. J. Stiles, *Jesse James, Last Rebel of the Civil War.*

Karen Holliday Tanner and John D. Tanner Jr., *Last of the Old-Time Outlaws: The George West Musgrave Story.*

Carol Turner, *Notorious Telluride: Tales from San Miguel County.*

Laurel Thatcher Ulrich, *Men of Wyoming: The National Newspaper Reference Book of Wyoming Containing Photographs and Biographies of over Three Hundred Men Residents, 1915; A House Full of Females: Plural Marriage and Women's Rights in Early Mormonism, 1835–1870.*

Paul L. Wellman, *A Dynasty of Western Outlaws.*

G. Edward White, *The Eastern Establishment and the Western Experience: The West of Frederic Remington, Theodore Roosevelt, Owen Wister.*

Richard White, *"It's Your Misfortune and None of My Own": A New History of the American West; The Republic for Which It Stands: The United States During Reconstruction and the Gilded Age, 1865–1896.*

Frank Wiborg, *A Commercial Traveler in South America: Being the Experiences and Impressions of an American Business Man.*

J. Patrick Wilde, *Treasured Tidbits of Time: An Informal History of Mormon Conquest and Settlement of Bear Lake Valley (Idaho, Utah).*

Gary A. Wilson, *The Life and Death of Kid Curry, Tiger of the Wild Bunch.*

Owen Wister, *The Virginian, a Horseman of the Plains.*

Linda Wommack, *Ann Bassett, Colorado's Cattle Queen.*

Lawrence Woods, *The Lives of Otto Chenoweth, Wyoming's Gentleman Horse Thief.*

Ann Zwinger, *Wind in the Rock, the Canyonlands of Southeastern Utah.*

ENDNOTES

Many sources are noted in the text. Those not so identified are listed below.

1 *The Thorny Rose*

Most of the details and quotes about Laura Bullion were drawn from "The Thorny Rose Behind Bars," an article written by Carolyn Bullion McBryde, the widow of a distant relative of Bullion's, which appeared in the April 1992 issue of *True West* magazine, pages 21–27. A page 1 article titled "Laura Bullion Relates Her Career Among the Outlaws," which appeared in the *St. Louis Republic* on November 8, 1901, was also helpful, as was the Laura Bullion page on FindAGrave.com (https://www.findagrave.com/memorial/23400786/laura-bullion).

On the matter of Etta versus Ethel Place, virtually all of the serious outlaw scholars believe that, whatever her real name was, she went by the latter and that the much less common "Etta" can be traced to a typo made in a Pinkerton report.

Information about Will Carver comes from *Tough Towns: True Tales from the Gritty Streets of the Old West* by Robert Barr Smith; the *Frontier Times*, September 1928, 41; the *Houston Post*, April 8, 1901,

4; the article "Will Carver Checks Out" by Mark Boardman in the November 2, 2007, issue of *True West*; and Jeffrey Burton's *The Deadliest Outlaws: The Ketchum Gang and the Wild Bunch*, in which he cites an account in the April 6, 1901, *San Angelo (TX) Standard* called "Before He Could Cock His Pistol" (no page given) as his source. Those in search of more information on Carver should consult Burton's book, as well as James D. Horan's *Desperate Men: The True Story of Jesse James, Butch Cassidy and the Wild Bunch*.

2 *Rules of the Game*

As Mike Bell notes in his book *Incidents on Owl Creek: Butch Cassidy's Big Horn Basin Bunch and the Wyoming Horse Thief War*, Christian Heiden told the story of Cassidy roping the mountain lion on a Labor Radio broadcast in December 1937. The original incident is also mentioned in Charles Kelly's book *Outlaw Trail: A History of Butch Cassidy and His Wild Bunch*. The information on Heiden's background comes from the passenger list of the SS *Gothia*, which carried Heiden and his parents from Germany in 1892, from US Census forms from 1900 to 1940, and from his World War I draft registration card. The details about Cassidy's personality, here and elsewhere, are drawn from Matt Warner's memoir *The Last of the Bandit Riders*; Kelly's *The Outlaw Trail*; Richard Patterson's *Butch Cassidy, A Biography*; Bill Betenson's *Butch Cassidy, My Uncle: A Family Portrait*; Lula Parker Betenson and Dora Flack's *Butch Cassidy, My Brother*; Burton's *The Deadliest Outlaws*; Horan's *Desperate Men*; Pearl Baker's *The Wild Bunch at Robbers Roost*; the article "Who Are Those Guys?," by Daniel Buck and Anne Meadows in the November/December 2002 issue of *True West*; Butch Cassidy's own letter addressed "To the Boys at Concordia," which appears in this book; and numerous contemporary newspaper articles that report on his robberies and his pursuit.

The information on Tom Ketchum comes from the *Tucson*

(AZ) Daily Star, March 31, 1901, 1; the *St. John's (AZ) Herald*, May 4, 1901, 1; and *Deadliest Outlaws*.

The writer who describes Harvey Logan as having "dark blow-torch eyes" is Thom Hatch, in his book *The Last Outlaws: The Lives and Legends of Butch Cassidy and the Sundance Kid*. The quote about Logan shooting a man just to watch him quiver comes from Mike Bell's book *Of Myths and Manhunters: The Union Pacific Bandit Hunters*; Bell attributes the quote to an article in the *Indiana Call-Leader* of October 4, 1938, "Ex-Rangers Tells of Days of Ban Men of Old West." The descriptions of Logan, alias Kid Curry, in this chapter and elsewhere are drawn largely from *Harvey Logan in Knoxville* by Sylvia Lynch; *He Rode with Butch and Sundance: The Story of Harvey "Kid Curry" Logan* by Mark T. Smokov; *The Life and Death of Kid Curry, Tiger of the Wild Bunch* by Gary A. Wilson; Kelly's *Outlaw Trail*; and Patterson's *Butch Cassidy*, as well as numerous newspaper articles relating to his crimes and reputation.

The friend who said that Butch was "the wisest of all the outlaws he knew" was Matt Warner in his book *The Last of the Bandit Riders*. The judge who wrote the letter on Cassidy's behalf was Jesse Knight. The story of Cassidy shooting a cow so that he and his friends wouldn't have to eat jackrabbit is an oft-told tale that traces back to Butch's days in the Big Horn Basin. The line about Butch taking care of more people than FDR and with no red tape seems to have been repeated often by Josie Bassett and is quoted in *The Mythical West: An Encyclopedia of Legend, Lore and Popular Culture* by Richard W. Slatta. The quote about Butch being "exceptionally pleasant and even cultured" comes from a letter written by Percy Seibert, Cassidy's and Sundance's boss at a Bolivian mine, to an acquaintance in 1964 and first reported in Anne Meadows's book *Digging Up Butch and Sundance*. "Pardon us, but we know you have a lot of money and we have a great need" is taken from a deposition given by Carlos Peró, a man Cassidy robbed in Bolivia in 1908.

Lula Parker Betenson's quote about Paul Newman having "a certain 'family' look" comes from her book *Butch Cassidy, My Brother*. The information about the movie *Butch Cassidy and the Sundance Kid* comes from William Goldman's book *Adventures in the Screen Trade: A Personal View of Hollywood and Screen Writing*. Bernard DeVoto's line comes from his book *Across the Wide Missouri*. John Wesley Powell's line is from *Beyond the Hundredth Meridian: John Wesley Powell and the Second Opening of the West* by Wallace Stegner. The shoes made from George "Big Nose" Parrott's skin are on display at the Carbon County Museum in Rawlins, Wyoming. The Eric Hobsbawm quote is from his book *Bandits*. The Bill Betenson quote is from an interview I did at his Utah home in 2016. The Paul Newman anecdote was told to me in 2016 by Brent Ashworth, a dealer in rare manuscripts, at his collectibles shop in Provo, Utah. I found the working copy of Goldman's script for *Butch Cassidy and the Sundance Kid* among his papers at Columbia University.

3 Promised Land

The information about Mormon history in this chapter comes largely from Wallace Stegner's two books about the sect: the relatively informal history *Mormon Country* and the more scholarly work *The Gathering of Zion: The Story of the Mormon Trail*, as well as *A House Full of Females: Plural Marriage and Women's Rights in Early Mormonism, 1835–1870* by Laurel Thatcher Ulrich; *Forgotten Kingdom: The Mormon Theocracy in the American West* by David L. Bigler; *Handcarts to Zion: The Story of a Unique Western Migration 1856–1860* by LeRoy R. Hafen and Ann W. Hafen; and *The Civil War Years in Utah: The Kingdom of God and the Territory That Did Not Fight* by John Gary Maxwell. I also consulted Christopher Hitchens's book about organized religion, *God Is Not Great*.

Information about the Circleville Massacre comes mostly

from *Utah's Black Hawk War* by John Alton Peterson; an article in the July 2014 *Utah Historical Review*, by Suzanne Catharine, "How Circleville Remembers," 196–202; the UtahHumanties website (UtahHumanities.org); and an article called "The Circleville Massacre: A Brutal Incident in Utah's Black Hawk War" by Albert Winker in the *Utah Historical Quarterly* 55, no. 1 (December 2009).

Information about the Parker family's early days in the United States comes from US Census records; Ancestry.com; Family Search.org; *Butch Cassidy, My Brother; Butch Cassidy, My Uncle*; as well as interviews with Robert Goodwin, an expert who specializes in Cassidy's Utah years, and Mike Bell.

4 *Boy Interrupted*

The stories of Butch Cassidy's childhood come from Parker family lore and legend as recorded by his sister Lula Betenson and his grandnephew Bill Betenson in their books, though both also consulted Mormon Family Group Sheets archived at the Church of Latter-Day Saints History and Archives Library, in Salt Lake City, as well as other works of Mormon and Utah History. Charles Kelly's book *Outlaw Trail* provided stories that came to him from people who'd been Cassidy's contemporaries and sometimes friends. I also derived facts and anecdotes from an interview with Bill Betenson and an interview and correspondence with researcher Robert Goodwin and much back-and-forth with Mike Bell and Dan Buck.

For a history of New York's Lower East Side, see, for example, *The Lower East Side Remembered and Revisted: A History and Guide to a Legendary New York Neighborhood* by Joyce Mendelsohn.

The story about Bob Parker's time working for Pat Ryan can be found in the *Salt Lake City Tribune* of May 14, 1898, and the *Price (UT) News-Advocate* of May 19, 1898.

Abraham Lincoln made that remark about wageworkers in his 1859 address to the Wisconsin State Agricultural Society.

The quote about having the cows being worn out from stealing them so often comes from an article in the *Annals of Wyoming* 29, no. 2 (Oct. 1957), "The Hole-in-the-Wall, Part IV" by Thelma Gatchell Condit.

It is generally accepted, based on US Census records, that women outnumbered men by at least 30 percent west of the 100th meridian in the nineteenth century; in 1850 the population of California was 90 percent male.

5 *To-Hell-You-Ride*

For an excellent life of the eighteenth president, see Ron Chernow's *Grant*.

The information on Robert Parker's early years in Colorado was obtained largely from Mike Bell's article "Butch Cassidy, Horse Marine" in the *Tombstone Epitaph*, June 2019.

The quote about western migration being "one of the greatest social and environmental miscalculations in American history" comes from Richard White's *The Republic for Which It Stands: The United States During Reconstruction and the Gilded Age*.

The statistics on height come from *The Rise and Fall of American Growth: The U.S. Standard of Living Since the Civil War* by Robert J. Gordon.

The quote comparing Ouray and Telluride, Colorado, comes from Ouray's weekly *Solid Muldoon* of September 2, 1887.

The Colorado rancher who called cattle raising "the grandest investment that can be offered" was David W. Sherwood, as quoted in *Cattle Kingdom: The Hidden History of the Cowboy West* by Christopher Knowlton. I am highly indebted to Knowlton for the information his excellent book provided.

Details about the Coad brothers' operation came largely from an article by Carol Enderlie called "The Bay State Cattle Company," which can be found on the Banner County, Nebraska, website (http://banner.wnfrhc.org/Bay%20State%20Cattle%20Company. htm).

For more information on the Swan Land and Cattle Company, see its website at swanlandandcattle.com.

The Wyoming neighbor who boasted about sleeping with Cassidy was Andrew Manseau; Bill Betenson says in his book that Manseau made the claim several times.

The information about John F. Kelly comes from an interview Horan did with Kelly and published in part in *Desperate Men*.

Accounts of the Big Die-Up and its aftermath come from numerous sources, including *The Rise of Theodore Roosevelt* by Edmund Morris; *We Pointed Them North: Recollection of a Cowpuncher* by E. C. "Teddy Blue" Abbott; and *Cattle Kingdom*.

The stories involving Matt Warner—mostly but probably not entirely reliable—come from Warner's memoir *The Last of the Bandit Riders*.

6 *And They're Off*

A trove of information about Matt Warner can be found in "Matt Warner, A Son of a Bishop," a transcription of a talk given by Stacy Osgood, a Chicago lawyer with an avid interest in the Old West, and published in the *Western Brand Book* 27, no. 5 (July 1970).

The staff at the National Museum of Racing and Hall of Fame in Saratoga Springs, New York, was very helpful in obtaining information about racing in the Old West.

Facts, details, and color also came from Matt Warner's book as well as from an article by Mrs. Helen Sargent called "Incidents in the Life of Norris Griggs" in the *Annals of Wyoming* 25, no. 1 (January 1953); "A Brief History of Social and Domestic Life Among the Military in Wyoming 1849–1890" by Alan Culpin, *Annals of*

Wyoming 45, no. 1 (Spring 1973); "Montana's Horse-racing Industry Runs Deep" by Ellen Baumler, *Helena (MT) Independent Record*, April 15, 2006; "Hunting a Desperate Man," *Sundance (WY) Gazette*, June 10, 1892; "A Challenge," *Sundance Gazette*, August 8, 1892, 1; "The Fourth of July," *Sheridan (WY) Enterprise*, July 7, 1892, 4; "The Fair," *Denver Mirror*, October 5, 1873; "Those Race Horse Men," *Colorado Miner* (Georgetown), July 1, 1876. One can get a good sense of the importance of racing in the West merely by paging through old newspapers.

Quotes from and specifics about the Bassett sisters came from *The Bassett Women* by Grace McClure; *Ann Bassett, Colorado's Cattle Queen* by Linda Wommack; and "The Autobiography of Ann Bassett," *Colorado* 29, no. 2 (April 1952).

Information about Cassidy's time at Brown's Park came from Patterson's *Butch Cassidy*; John Rolfe Burroughs's *Where the Old West Stayed Young*; *One Hundred Years of Brown's Park and Diamond Mountain* by Dick and Daun DeJournette; *The Romantic and Notorious History of Brown's Park* by Diana Allen Kouris; *Last Frontier* by V. S. FitzPatrick; and my own visit to Brown's Park in June 2016.

Bob Parker was called a "horse marine" in the June 27, 1888, edition of the *Solid Muldoon*.

In Pursuit of the McCartys by Jon M. Skovlin and Donna McDaniel Skovlin was a good source of information about Tom McCarty.

7 Getting in Deeper

The robbery of the Denver National Bank was covered in the *New York Times*, March 31, 1889, 1; the *Denver Post*, March 30, 1889; the *Aspen (CO) Daily Times*, March 30, 1889; the *Colorado Daily Chieftain*, March 30, 1889; the *Castle Rock (CO) Journal*, April 3, 1889; and the *Ft. Worth Daily Gazette*, May 27, 1890. The Skovlins' *In Pursuit of the McCartys* and U.S. Marshal Doc Shores's book, *Memoirs of a Lawman* were also helpful.

For background on Telluride, see *The Telluride Story, a Tale of Two Towns* by David Lavender; *Telluride, from Pick to Powder* by Richard L. Fetter and Suzanne Fetter; and *Notorious Telluride: Tales from San Miguel County* by Carol Turner.

For information about the robbery of the San Miguel Bank in Telluride, see Patterson's biography; Betenson's *Butch Cassidy, My Uncle;* Kelly's *Outlaw Trail*; the *Cheyenne (WY) Daily Leader*, June 25, 1889; the *Pueblo (CO) Chieftain*, June 26, 1889; the *Rocky Mountain News* (Denver), June 27, 1889; the *Helena (MT) Weekly Herald*, June 27, 1889; the *Sacramento (CA) Daily Record-Union*, July 28, 1889; the *Colorado Springs Gazette*, June 29, 1889; the *Pueblo (CO) Daily Chieftain*, June 30, 1889; the *Salt Lake Herald*, June 30, 1889; the *Rocky Mountain News* (Denver), July 1, 1889; the *Los Angeles Daily Hearld*, July 1, 1889; the *Daily Boomerang* (Laramie, WY), July 1, 1889; the *Helena (MT) Independent*, July 2, 1889; the *Salt Lake Herald*, July 2, 1889; the *Washington (DC) Star*, July 2, 1889; the *Cheyenne (WY) Weekly Sun*, July 4, 1889; the *Salt Lake Tribune*, July 4, 1889; the *Colorado Springs Gazette*, July 6, 1889; the *Morning Oregonian* (Portland, OR), August 9, 1889; the *Aspen (CO) Weekly Times*, August 17, 1889; the *Salt Lake Tribune*, April 19, 1892; and the *Rocky Mountain News* (Denver), June 27, 1893.

For information about Harry Adsit, see *Field and Farm* (Denver), March 15, 1913; "Telluride Man Recalls Interesting Side Lights on Famous Robbery," *Dolores (CO) Star*, February 11, 1938. Patterson's biography is particularly thorough on the gang's escape from Telluride.

8 *Robbers Roost*

Patterson's and Warner's books provided much of the information in this chapter, as did Pearl Baker's *The Wild Bunch at Robbers Roost* and the newspaper sources cited for chapter 7. Robert Redford's

The Outlaw Trail: A Journey Through Time was also useful. Those interested in Bob Parker's brother Dan, a minor outlaw prior to his long prison sentence, should consult "Alias 'Tom Ricketts,' the True Story of Butch Cassidy's brother, Dan Parker" by William Betenson in the Winter 1997 edition of *Outlaw Trail Journal.*

9 *Friends and Neighbors*

The quotes from William Goldman appear in his *Adventures in the Screen Trade.*

The best single source of information for Cassidy's Wyoming years is Mike Bell's *Incidents on Owl Creek.*

Robert Waln's statements were reported by Paul Frison in his *Calendar of Change.*

The information on Eugene Amoretti Jr. comes mostly from Patterson's book and *Progressive Men of the State of Wyoming* by A. W. Bowen.

The information about Heiden's suicide was obtained from his death certificate, available on Genealogy.com.

John Rawson's quotes come from the article he wrote for the June 8, 1922, *Thermopolis (WY) Record.*

The information about Cassidy attending Margaret Simpson's Christmas party in 1889 came from Frederick Bechdolt's *Tales of the Old-timers.*

10 *The Equality State*

Besides the sources already mentioned, a booklet titled *Butch Cassidy and the Wild Bunch in Star Valley, Wyoming 1889–1896* was also useful in constructing this chapter. Butch Cassidy's public drunkenness was reported in the January 12, 1893, *Sheridan (WY) Post.* The quote about "rouged women" comes from Bechdolt's *Tales of the Old-Timers.* The story about Cassidy running afoul of the hitching rack in front of Coalter's Saloon was told by Fremont County deputy sheriff Harry Logue and was first reported in the *Wyoming State Journal* (Lander), April 6, 1950. For details about Arthur Parker's fatal horse racing accident, see the *Salt Lake Herald*, November 1, 1890; 8. Patterson's biography, Bell's *Incidents on Owl Creek*, and Betenson's *Butch Cassidy, My Uncle* provided information about Cassidy's employment history. Background on Rock Springs came from *Booms & Busts on Bitter Creek: A History of Rock Springs, Wyoming* by Robert B. Rhode. The quote about Butch "walking pretty much on the wild side" during his time in Rock Springs comes from Burroughs's *Where the Old West Stayed Young.* It was Harry Adsit who gave an account of Cassidy being such a fine marksman in *Field and Farm* (Denver), March 15, 1913. The anecdote about him being nervous at a country dance comes from Pamela Call Johnson's *Butch Cassidy and the Wild Bunch in Star Valley, Wyoming, 1889–1896.* Background on the Cheyenne Club and the bursting of the "cattle bubble" came from Knowlton's *Cattle Kingdom.* Doris B. Platts's *The Cunningham Ranch Incident of 1892* contains a wealth of information about the cattle and horse wars, and the tension between the big and small ranchers. John W. Davis's *Wyoming Range War* was also very useful.

11 *Captured*

Information in this chapter comes from the court records of State v. George Cassidy & Albert Hainer, Case no. 144 (District Court, Fremont County, WY). The narrative is otherwise woven from information found in Patterson's book; Bell's *Incidents on Owl Creek*; Kelly's *Outlaw Trail*; Platts's *Cunningham Ranch Incident; Brand of a Legend: Ten Thousand Years in the Village of the Greyko River* by Bob Edgar and Jack Turnell; Larry Pointer's *In Search of Butch Cassidy*; and Baker's *Wild Bunch at Robbers Roost.* Baker made a breakthrough when she found a file labeled "Morals, Colorado Project" at the

Utah State Historical Society that contained information about Cassidy's capture. See also Will Simpson's May 5, 1939, letter to Kelly, reproduced in Western waiter Jim Dullenty's "starter kit" of documents for Cassidy researchers called *The Butch Cassidy Collection*, and quoted in this book.

12 *Order in the Court*

The same court records and books used in chapter 11 were used as sources in this chapter. For a short bio of Douglas Preston, see *Men of Wyoming: The National Newspaper Reference Book of Wyoming Containing Photographs and Biographies of over Three Hundred Men Residents, 1915*. Much can be found about the outlaws Billy Nutcher, Al Hainer, and Jakey Snyder—as well as Sheriff Charlie Stough— in Bell's *Incidents on Owl Creek*. Much interesting information on the raucous life of Will Simpson can be found in Donald Loren Hardy's book *Shooting from the Lip: The Life of Senator Al Simpson*. Excerpts from Otto Franc's diaries can be found in Edgar and Turnell's *Brand of a Legend*.

13 *Inside Story*

I toured the Wyoming State Penitentiary in August 2016. The rules of the prison and information about the day-to-day life of the inmates are available to visitors in the form of handouts and booklets, which quote from official records. Information on the population of Wyoming, in Butch Cassidy's day and now, comes from US Census records. Cassidy's quote about "honor among thieves" was told to Larry Pointer by Hank Boedeker Jr., a son of the town constable who accompanied Cassidy on his trip to the penitentiary. The information on the other prisoners locked up with Cassidy comes largely from *Atlas of Wyoming Outlaws at the Territorial Penitentiary* by Elnora L. Frye. Cassidy's pardon document and Jesse

Knight's letter to Governor Richards can be found on the website of the Wyoming State Archives at https://bit.ly/2ZG9tAe.

14 *Elzy*

Information about the Montpelier bank robbery came from the "The Bank of Montelier Robbery" by Jens Patrick Wilde in his book *Treasured Tidbits of Time*, vol. 1; the *Salt Lake City Tribune* of September 9, 1896, 1, and January 21, 1897, 8; the *Idaho Daily States-man* (Boise), August 14, 1896; the *Montpelier (ID) Examiner*, August 15, 1896; the *San Francisco Call*, August 18, 1896; and the *Ogden (UT) Standard*, September 10, 1896. As usual, Patterson's, Kelly's, and Warner's books were also helpful.

For more on Bub Meeks, see the *Salt Lake Herald-Republican*, August 30, 1897, and an article called "Bub Meeks: The Incidental Outlaw" by W. Gaile Meeks, published on an Ancestry.com message board (https://www.ancestry.com/boards/topics.crime.outlaws/234/mb.ashx).

I interviewed Harvey Murdock on April 27, 2016. His book about his grandfather, *The Educated Outlaw: The Story of Elzy Lay of the Wild Bunch*, is slight and awkward but useful nevertheless. Patterson, Kelly, and Pointer include much information about Lay, and there is a bit more in Kelly's research notes on his interview with Vernal Lee at the University of Utah. A lot can also be found on Ancestry.com by searching under his real name, William Ells-worth Lay, and by searching for "Lay" (only single-word searches are allowed) at the Old West Rogues website.

15 *Sundance*

Much of the information in this chapter was drawn from Donna Ernst's books *The Sundance Kid: The Life of Harry Alonzo Longabaugh* and *Sundance, My Uncle*, as well as Baker's *Wild Bunch at Robbers*

Roost, Warner's *The Last of the Bandit Riders*, and Patterson's *Historical Atlas of the Outlaw West*. I also interviewed Donna and her husband, Paul Ernst, at their home, and they gave me a tour of Mont Clare and Phoenixville, Pennsylvania, where Paul's great-great uncle, Sundance, was born and partly raised. Information on Sundance also came from notes in the Pinkerton files, now at the Library of Congress in Washington, DC; from the contributions made to the Old West Rogues website by the late Jack Stroud, a low-profile but much respected authority within the outlaw-history community; and from Ancestry.com. Anyone interested in Sundance's life should read "Surprising Development: The Sundance Kid's Unusual—and Unknown—Life in Canada" by Daniel Buck, *Western Outlaw-Lawman History Association Journal* 3, no. 3 (Winter 1993).

Newspaper sources included the *Daily Yellowstone Journal* (Miles City, MT), April 12, 1887; the *Big Horn (WY) Sentinel*, June 11, 1887; the *Miles City (MT) Daily Gazette*, June 8, 1887; the *Sundance (WY) Gazette*, April 22, 1887, and May 4, 1888; the *Rocky Mountain News* (Denver), June 27, 1889; the *Saratoga (WY) Sun*, June 8, 1899; the *(Buenos Aires) Standard*, April 17, 1912 (discovered by Mike Bell); and the *Silver State*, September 19 through 22 and 27. For Sundance's letter, see the *Daily Yellowstone Journal*, June 9, 1887. For Vic Button's account of meeting Cassidy as a child, see "Butch Cassidy Gave Getaway Horse to 10-Year-Old" by Victor I. Button, *Newsletter of the National Association for Outlaw and Lawman History*, Spring 1974.

Ann Bassett's account of the Outlaws' Thanksgiving comes from her article "Queen Ann of Brown's Park" in *Colorado* magazine 29, October 1952; the article was one of a four-part series, all with the same title, that ran in the magazine from January 1952 to January 1953. Bassett never got Harry Longabaugh's name right, spelling it either Rhudenbaugh or Roudenbaugh throughout.

16 *Land of Enchantment*

Baker's *Wild Bunch at Robbers Roost*, Burroughs's *Where the West Stayed Young*, Patterson's book, and Kelly's *Outlaw Trail* contain information about the Castle Gate robbery, but I also drew from newspaper coverage of the heist. See the *Anaconda (MT) Standard*, September 17, 1897; the *Salt Lake Herald*, April 22, 1897, and May 28, 1897; the *Eastern Utah Advocate* (Price, UT), April 22, 1897; and the *Davis County Clipper* (Bountiful, UT), April 30, 1897. An article by Arden Stewart, "Dad Nearly Rode with Butch," in the Summer 1991 *Outlaw Trail Journal*, was useful, and I found an interesting reference to Castle Gate in a semifictional article by Edward Geary called "The Girl Who Danced with Butch Cassidy" in *Dialogue: A Journal of Mormon Thought* 11, no. 3 (Autumn 1978).

For a discussion of the many false press reports of Butch Cassidy's death, see "Butch and Sundance: Still Dead," by Daniel Buck and Anne Meadows, *Quarterly of the National Association for Outlaw and Lawman History* 30, no. 2 (April–June 2006). The story about Cassidy working for a while at the Hilman ranch appears in Pointer's *In Search of Butch Cassidy*. The *Wyoming State Tribune* (Cheyenne) of June 16, 1939, said that Alva Adams had hired the bounty hunter James Catron to bring back Cassidy dead or alive, but at the Utah State Archives, I found a letter dated March 26, 1898, from Governor Heber Manning Wells confirming Catron's employment; perhaps they contracted for him jointly. The incidents in New Mexico were drawn largely from *Recollections of a Western Ranchman* by Captain William French.

17 *Wilcox*

I reconstructed the Wilcox robbery based on Kelly's *Outlaw Trail*, as well as newspaper sources. See the *Salt Lake Herald*, June 3, 1899; the *New York Times*, June 2, 1899; the *Denver Times*, June

2, 1899; the *Lawrence (KS) Daily Journal*, June 2, 1899; the *New York Tribune*, June 3, 1899; the *Los Angeles Times*, June 3, 1899; the *Carbon County Journal* (Rawlins, WY), June 2, 1899; the *Anaconda (MT) Standard*, June 3, 1899; and the *Monroeville (IN) Breeze*, September 28, 1899. See also "Butch Cassidy and the Sundance Kid Rob a Train," uncredited, EyeWitness to History.com (eye witnesstohistory.com); and "Wilcox Train Robbery" by Donna B. Ernst, *Wild West* magazine, June 1999. For an account of Sheriff Hazen's death, see the *Natrona County Tribune* (Casper, WY), June 8, 1899.

18 *On a Roll*

Charles Kelly provides an account of the conversation in his *Outlaw Trail* but does not give a source; still, as Patterson says in his endnotes, a good attorney would have kept a memorandum of the meeting to which future authors would have had access. For an example of Angus Cannon's newspaper pranking, see the *Salt Lake Tribune*, July 1, 1900. For more on Cassidy's supposed wife, see the *Salt Lake Tribune*, June 29, 1900. Information on the Tipton train robbery was obtained from Kelly, Patterson, an excellent article in the September 1, 1900, the *Rawlins (WY) Republican*, the *Denver Republican* of September 2, 1900, and "The Tipton Train Robbery," an article by Chip Carlson in the Summer 1995 issue of the *Journal of the Western Outlaw-Lawman History Association*.

Frank Wiborg's book is *A Commercial Traveler in South America: Being the Experiences and Impressions of an American Business Man*. Button's quotes appear in Baker's *Wild Bunch at Robbers Roost*. Information on the Winnemucca bank robbery can be found in the *Silver State*, September 20, 1900; the *Denver Republican*, September 20, 1900; and the *Silver State*, September 22, 1900, and September 27, 1900. Information on the Wild Bunch's Ft. Worth interlude was drawn from *Riata and Spurs: The Story of a Lifetime Spent in the Saddle* as *Cowboy and Detective* by Charles Siringo and *Hell's Half Acre: The Life and Legend of a Red-Light District* by Richard F. Selcer.

19 *In the Cone*

I made two research trips to South America for this book, one to Argentina in 2016 and the other to Bolivia in 2017, to meet with experts and to visit the places where Butch and Sundance had been. I also visited Dan Buck and Anne Meadows at their home in Washington, DC, twice, corresponded frequently with Buck and received from him much good information and advice about Butch and Sundance's South American sojourn, as well as hundreds of pages of documents. Anne Meadows's meticulous and entertaining *Digging Up Butch and Sundance* was essential to the preparation of the chapters in this book's part 3, but the couple's subsequent articles and book bring the research up to date by incorporating their still-ongoing discoveries and the work of others. See especially "Leaving Cholila: Butch and Sundance Arguments Surface in Argentina," *True West*, January 1996; "Neighbors on the Hot Seat: Revelations from the Long-Lost Argentine Police File," *Western Outlaw-Lawman History Association Journal* 5, no. 2 (Spring/Summer 1996); "Needles and Cats: The Hunt for Butch and Sundance," *True West*, December 2008; "We Parkers Always Enjoyed a Good Story: Butch and Sundance's Unlikely Reunion in Mexico City," *Western Outlaw-Lawman Association Journal* 15, no. 4 (Winter 2006); "Butch and Sundance, Legendary Outlaws of the Americas," *True West*, November/December 2002; "The Wild Bunch: Wild, but Not Much of a Bunch," *True West*, November/December 2002; "The Last Ride," *True West*, November/December 2002; "Bogus Butches," *True West*, November/December 2002; "The Hole-in-the-Wall Nickelodeon," *True West*, November/December 2002; "Cloud over Cassidy Letters," *Western Outlaw-Lawman History Association Journal* 11, no. 1 (Spring 2002); "That Bandit Girl," *Quarterly of the National Association for Outlaw and Lawman History* 24, no. 4 (October–December 2000); "Butch and Sundance Slept Here," *True West*, September 1999; "Did Butch Cassidy Return? His Family Can't Decide," *Western Outlaw-Lawman History Association Journal* 6, no. 3 (Spring 1998); "The Last Days of Butch and Sundance," *Wild West*, February 1997; "Skulduggery: Three Men and a Shovel," *True West*, September 1993; "Etta Place: A Most Wanted Woman," *Western Outlaw-Lawman History Association Journal* 3, no. 1 (Spring/Summer 1993); "Grave Doubts," *South American Explorer*, June 1993; and "The Wild Bunch in South America," pts. 1–4, *Western Outlaw-Lawman History Association Journal* 1, nos. 1–3 (Spring–Summer 1991, Fall–Winter 1991, Winter–Spring 1992), and vol. 2, no. 2 (Fall 1992).

Most of these articles, along with much other related material, are available on Buck and Meadows's website, Digging Up Butch and Sundance (diggingupbutchandsundance.wordpress. com), along with a useful article by their friend and fellow Cassidy researcher Marcelo Gavirati, "Back at the Ranch," *True West*, November/December 2002. The information about Peró comes from testimony he gave at a formal inquest by government authorities in 1908. The information about Sundance in this chapter comes largely from Donna Ernst's books about him. Siringo says he "became attached to George Parker's pretty, black-eyed sister" in a letter published in the *Frontier Times* 6, no. 2 (November 1928). Mark A. Mszanski's landmark article "The Wild Bunch Visit Tiffany & Co.," in the December 2015 issue of the *Journal of the Wild West History Association*, was very useful in reconstructing the time that Cassidy, Sundance, and Ethel spent in New York City just before their voyage to Argentina. Frank Wiborg's quotes are from his *Commercial Traveler in South America*. Cassidy's letter to Mathilda Davis can be found in the archives of the Utah State Historical Society; it was donated by Elzy Lay's grandson Harvey Murdock. The account of Butch and Sundance's real estate dealings is based on documents retrieved from the archives by Meadows, Buck, Gavirati, and others over the last thirty years, and referenced in articles cited previously. Meadows's book *Digging Up Butch and Sundance* weaves her quest for such paperwork and other clues of the outlaws' movements and living arrangements into an engaging narrative.

20 *Family of Three*

Information on the trio's years in Argentina was gathered largely from *Buscados en la Patagonia: La Historia No Contada de Butch Cassidy y los Bandoleros Norteamericanos* by Marcelo Gavirati, as translated for me by Dan Buck; from Meadows's *Digging Up Butch and Sundance*; and from the articles mentioned above. I also learned much from interviews I did in Buenos Aires and Patagonia with Carol Jones, whose grandfather was an early settler in the area and knew Butch; with Gavirati; and with the brilliant and generous Cassidy scholars Carlos Dante Ferrari, Marcelo Bustos, and Osvaldo Aguirre.

Information on Sundance and Ethel's travel back and forth between South America and the United States comes from "The Wild Bunch on the High Seas" by Mark Mszanski, *Journal of the Wild West History Association* (September 2017). For more about the Pinkerton Detective Agency, see *Train Robberies, Train Robbers, and the "Hold-Up" Man* by William A. Pinkerton; *Inventing the Pinkertons; or Spies, Sleuths, Mercenaries, and Thugs* by S. Paul O'Hara; and *The Pinkertons: The Detective Dynasty That Made History* by James D. Horan.

22 *The End of the Road*

For the information in this chapter, I am indebted largely to "End of the Road: Butch Cassidy and the Sundance Kid in Bolivia" by Daniel Buck and Anne Meadows, *The Brand Book* 51, no. 1 (Winter 2017). I also learned much from interviewing the outlaw scholar

Limbert Jerez Lopez in La Paz. The quotes from and details about
Letson come mostly from the papers of Charles Kelly at the University of Utah. The material about Percy Seibert comes from
Meadows's *Digging Up Butch and Sundance*; from Horan's *Desperate
Men*; from my interviews and correspondence with Buck; and from
the numerous articles about Butch and Sundance in South America
written by Buck and Meadows. Seibert liked to brag about his association with the outlaws and may have enhanced the facts here and
there for the sake of a better story. The original copy of the "To the
Boys at Concordia" letter is in the possession of Brent Ashworth,
a Provo, Utah, dealer in rare manuscripts mentioned earlier. The
piece by A. G. Francis appeared in the May 1913 issue of *World Wide*
magazine.

Epilogue

The information about Billy Sawtelle going to South America to
learn what happened to Butch and Sundance comes from Will
Simpson's 1939 letter to Charles Kelly. For more on William T.
Phillips, see Pointer's *In Search of Butch Cassidy*.

ILLUSTRATION CREDITS

1. Wyoming State Historical Society
2. Daniel Buck and Anne Meadows
3. Mike Bell
4. Pinkerton Archives
5. American Heritage Center, Laramie, WY
6. Harvey Lay Murdock
7. Courtesy San Miguel County Historical Museum
8. Pinkerton Archives
9. US Bureau of Prisons
10. Library of Congress
11. Library of Congress
12. National Portrait Gallery
13. Mike Bell
14. Photo by Sarah Saffian

INDEX

ALSO BY BESTSELLING AUTHOR

CHARLES LEERHSEN

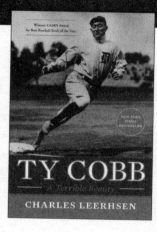

"The best work ever written on
this American sports legend."
—*The Boston Globe*

"Thoroughly
entertaining."
—*The Wall Street Journal*

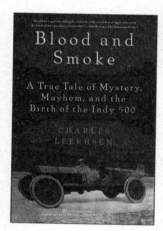

"When you read this gripping account
of the first Indy 500, you'll wonder
why they ever had a second."
—*Greensboro News–Record*

Available wherever books are sold or at SimonandSchuster.com

SIMON &
SCHUSTER
A CBS COMPANY

70494

Willoughby Public Library
30 Public Square
Willoughby, OH 44094

JUL 1 7 2020